What Did You Learn In School Today?

About the Authors

BRUCE BARON earned his Bachelor of Arts at the University of California at Irvine subsequent to studying at UCLA and the University of Nairobi in East Africa. His graduate work was completed at UC Irvine while a member of the National Teacher Corps project. He has taught at both the elementary and secondary level and currently divides his time between teaching and writing.

CHRISTINE BARON earned her Bachelor of Arts at the University of Redlands in Redlands, California, and her Master of Arts at California State University at Fullerton, California. She has taught high school in American Samoa, served as a counselor in Hawaii, and is currently teaching writing in California. She is also a consultant in curriculum development and a free-lance writer.

BONNIE MacDONALD earned her Bachelor of Arts at the University of Redlands and did graduate work at California State University at Long Beach. She has taught junior high, high school, and adult education and was managing editor for an educational product development company. She is currently a communications and public relations consultant to schools and industry, and resides in Laguna Beach, California.

The authors are parents as well as teachers.

What Did You Learn In School Today?

A Comprehensive Guide to Getting the Best Possible Education for Your Children

by
Bruce Baron,
Christine Baron, a
Bonnie MacDonal
with
Bill Beacham
on
*"Working Through
the Rough Spots"*

WARNER BOOKS

A Warner Communications Company

Copyright © 1983 by Bruce Baron, Christine Baron, and Bonnie
MacDonald

All rights reserved.

Warner Books, Inc., 666 Fifth Avenue, New York, N.Y. 10103

W A Warner Communications Company

Printed in the United States of America

First printing: August 1983

10 9 8 7 6 5 4 3 2 1

Library of Congress Cataloging in Publication Data

Baron, Bruce.
  What did you learn in school today?

  Includes bibliographies and index.
  1. Home and school—United States. 2. Parent and child—United
States. 3. Learning. 4. Education—United States. 5. Child development.
I. Baron, Christine. II. MacDonald, Bonnie. III. Title.
LC225.3.B37   370.19'3   82-4729
ISBN 0-446-37210-2 (USA)   AACR2
ISBN 0-446-37285-4 (Canada)

Acknowledgments

In doing the research for this book, we relentlessly pursued educators and parents for whatever advice and insights they had to offer—which were considerable. Our goal was not to formulate new theories of education nor to establish innovative instruction techniques. We simply tried to synthesize the good research that had already been done concerning workable and practical methods of helping children.

To accomplish this goal, we called upon numerous authorities for their advice and, in some cases, their critique of the initial manuscript. We hope these generous people will find their ideas and comments satisfactorily incorporated into the book. We would especially like to thank the following people for affording us the benefit of their expertise: Robert Cummings, M.D., Consulting Psychiatrist, University of California Medical School; Fitzhugh Dodson, Ph.D., psychologist and author; William K. Durr, Ph.D., Michigan State University; Karen Ezaki, President, Gifted Children's Association of the Foothills, Covina, Calif.; I. Lee Gislason, M.D., University of California Medical School; James R. Gray, Ph.D., director of the Bay Area Writing Project; C. D. Johnson, Director of Personnel, Maryland County Schools; June Juntune, National Association for the Gifted and Talented, St. Paul, Minn.; Lauma Lockwood, Chairperson, Citizens for Responsive Education, Grand Rapids, Mich.; Rachael Mitchell, University of California at Irvine; George Nemetz, California State Department of Education; J. William Rioux, Senior Associate, National Committee for Citizens in Education; George D. Spache, Professor Emeritus, University of Florida; Brian Shipton, Ed.D., Private Consultant/Therapist, Quebec City, Canada; Armelle Spain, Ph.D., Laval University, Quebec, Canada; and Dorothy Waggoner, Education Program Officer, United States Department of Education, Office of Bilingual Education.

We would also like to acknowledge the assistance of Lizette Collier, Jean English, Steve Grassbaugh, Alma Hoover, Nancy Noble Hudson, Sharalee Jorgensen, John Keene, Deanna Mason, and Mary Roberts. For research assistance, we especially thank Julie Bolsenga.

*This book is
dedicated to parents
(and teachers) who
care.*

Table Of Contents

Ask Yourself: Can I Answer These Questions?

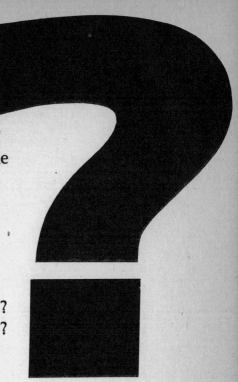

- How do I prepare my child for kindergarten?
- Do I know if my child is reading as well as she should?
- When should my child learn to multiply and divide?
- How can I improve my child's spelling?
- How can my child's learning difficulties go undetected?
- What do I ask at a parent-teacher conference?
- How do I help my teenager schedule his time?
- What are my child's legal rights to a good education?

Think about this: Your child will spend 15,000 hours away from you—at school.

What Did You Learn In School Today?

INTRODUCTION

Education as such has no aims. Only persons, parents, and teachers, etc., have aims, not an abstract idea like education.

—*John Dewey*

Question: What has the greatest effect on a child's success in school?

   a. the money spent on his education

   b. the quality of his teachers

   c. the involvement of his parents

Answer: c. In the last fifteen years, every major study on this topic has concluded that *parents' involvement has more influence* on children's success in school *than the quality of the teachers or the school.*

Parent Power

This is the situation: no amount of change will bring about a school system that will allow parents to turn their children over to the school at age five and then pick them up at age eighteen, with a guarantee of a good education. There are just too many ways for the schooling process to break down.

This may seem like common sense. However, there's still the wish among many parents that the schools will do the job—that they will inspire and teach children and that parents can relax and just watch it happen. In the meantime, while parents hope, too many children flounder. Parents blame the schools; schools blame the problems of our society. And on it goes.

Children are not something to gamble with. They are the greatest emotional investment most people will make in their lives. For many, children are the largest financial investment as well (a recent study now puts the average cost of raising a child at $85,000). And yet, many parents *do* take chances with one of the most important parts of their children's lives—their education.

Why don't parents take the time to insure a good education for their children? Time is spent working to provide a good home—and the home gets insured. Time is spent fixing the car—and the car gets insured. But time is not spent (even fifteen to twenty minutes a day) insuring that children have the support and guidance needed to get the most out of school. *Why?*

Parents don't get involved because they don't know what to do. They don't even know where to begin. They feel frustrated or intimidated or incapable. Parents start their children off in kindergarten anxious to participate. By the third grade, they are no longer sure what their child is supposed to learn; by the fifth, they can't tell what he has learned; and by junior high, many parents have given up hope of ever finding out.

It is hard for parents to participate when they don't know the rules of the game or how to keep score for their child. It finally just becomes easier to let the schools do it all and hope it will work out okay. That's gambling with children—*and it's not necessary.*

We have written this book for parents who want the best education possible for their children.

We know you don't have a lot of time. We know you don't have a lot of energy at the end of the day. So . . .

We took out the jargon and put in the facts.

We took out the university studies, the authoritative references, and put in what they say that you need to know.

We took out the politics, cut through the debates, and tell you how the system works and how you can make it work for your child.

We took out the wishful thinking and show you what can go wrong, how to catch it, and how to correct it.

This is your guidebook for schooling in the United States. It is not an indictment of education in America. We have only one concern—your child's education. We want you to be able to tell if your child is learning what she should. Through all the family moves, the teachers' strikes, the innovations, from the public classroom to the private school, your child needs your help. The schools need your help, *so get involved.*

How to Use This Book

THIS BOOK—

Can give you confidence in your ability to participate in your child's education. If you have a hunch about something, you now have a way to check it out.

Can get the schools to work for you. Identifying a possible problem and notifying the schools gets them to deal with it and will save you time in the long run.

You can—

Read it through once as an overview of your child's educational process, from birth through the twelfth grade.

Use it as a quick reference for what your child should be doing at any given grade level in the major subject areas.

Regard this book as a manual to be used when you need specific information (just before a parent conference, if your child is having difficulty with multiplication problems, to investigate alternative schools).

Frequently consult the chapter on communication, "Working Through the Rough Spots." If you can't talk with your child about school, it's doubtful you can help him with reading or math.

Use this book for all children. You should be staying in touch with each child's education, not just those having problems.

Avoid frustration—

Don't try to work with several children in all subject areas every day. This might be ideal, but it's also totally unrealistic! Besides, most children do not need this much extra help at home. Concentrate on the subject area that is causing difficulty or on the child who needs the most help. It's a matter of priorities.

Don't try to do all the activities described. Pick and choose as you see fit. No parent with two grade-school children and a baby (plus work, Little League, doctors' appointments, and cooking) has a lot of "free" time. Do what you can do when you can. Anything is better than nothing.

Don't be disappointed if your child doesn't take to these ideas. Your fourth grader may participate eagerly in a home reading program, while your eighth grader may flatly refuse. What works one time may fail miserably later on. All you can do is try.

CHAPTER 1

There's nothing in the world more fascinating than watching a child grow and develop. At first you think of it as just a matter of growing bigger . . . but it's really more complicated and full of meaning than that. The development of each child retraces the whole history of the human race, physically and spiritually, step by step.

—Dr. Benjamin Spock

The Preschool Years: A Home Gardening Guide

A FOREWORD TO THE HOME GARDENER

From birth to age six occurs the most rapid period of growth in a human being's life. At no other time will you have a greater influence on your child. Almost all of her later experiences in school will depend on what you do now.

There are many things in your child's world you may not be able to control: moving, income, divorce, work schedules, or a lousy teacher now and then. But you can give your child the kind of foundation that will help him endure these storms. The groundwork should not be left to chance—there's a lot you can do to better the odds.

Here are some suggestions for raising a *seedling* into a strong, healthy plant. Since these incredible first years will never come again, let's not waste a minute.

Consider the following facts:

> ● Babies less than one week old imitate adults.

> ● In the areas of vocabulary, reading comprehension, and general school achievement, one third of what a child has attained by age eighteen develops *before age six*.

> ● If you take away mental stimulation from a child, you will slow down his physical development as well.

> ● Children develop 50 percent of their *general intelligence* before the age of four.

Think about these statements. The implications are staggering! If you ever thought one stage of development is as significant as any other, you can forget it. More and more research shows that the early home environment has a tremendous effect on how children do in school—perhaps more than anyone ever suspected.

PARENTS MAKE IT HAPPEN

No one is better suited to working with a youngster during the first five years than the parents. You are with your child the most during this time, you know your child better than anyone else, and you have a boundless interest in his future. Providing a good start requires no special training or expense. *Any parent can be his child's best teacher.*

Working with a preschooler requires common sense as much as anything else. The point is to *accept your child's natural abilities and rate of development* while providing him with the experiences he needs to reach his full capabilities. After all, this is what parenting is all about. Your involvement is *never more critical* than during these early years. Now's the time to give it all you've got!

A STOOL WITH THREE LEGS

Being ready for school involves many things and it is important that you prepare your child in several areas. We picture parents providing a three-legged stool for the preschooler to sit on. For a balanced and successful school experience, all three legs must be solid. Let's take a look at what each provides:

Leg #1—The mind. It is important for you to expose your child to the many experiences and activities that allow his mind to stretch and grow—to listen, to learn, to compare, to categorize, to perceive, to reason.

Leg #2—The body. Obviously, this is related to the mind. A sound body allows your child to perform at his best. Stimulating the body also stimulates the brain.

Leg #3—The heart. This, too, has much to do with the mind and the body. It involves relations with people—including trust, consideration, and decency. It is how a child comes to feel about himself and his abilities. An open heart usually leads to an open mind.

The legs all need *one another* for the stool to stand up. No matter how smart a six-year-old may be, he's not going to do well in school if he's hitting other kids with his "advanced" reading book. A secure, bright child who is chronically ill may also have trouble keeping up in school. One leg should never be developed at the expense of the others. The results are fine athletes who can't read or geniuses who can't communicate their knowledge to anyone else.

The development of each of these three key areas—the heart, the mind, and the body — *starts at birth*. It's never too soon to begin!

THE ACTIVITY CHARTS

On the following pages you will find lists of activities to do with your preschool child at different ages. They are divided into three key areas: activities for the mind, for the body, and for the heart. Following each section are suggested toys for that age group.

WHY SHOULD YOU DO THESE ACTIVITIES?

1. Studies show that this period in a child's life (birth to age five) is the highest point of *readiness* for these activities: he will learn a skill more easily and quickly now than at any other time.

2. Research has also proven that certain skills must come before later skills can be acquired. Learning that will come later on—in school—must be based on previous knowledge. (You can look at it as a pyramid, with you providing that solid base.)

3. Skills learned early, and at the right time, tend to be learned better and last longer. It is much harder to erase that learning later. (An example of this can be seen in foreign language development: have you noticed how much easier it is for a young child to pick up a second language than it is for someone older?)

4. Current evidence also indicates that attitudes toward learning and discovery —the whole idea of *learning to learn*—are formed very early. The wider variety of experiences a child is exposed to early in life, the better his chances for later success in school.

WHEN SHOULD YOU DO THESE ACTIVITIES?

Most of these activities can be done at any time over the course of a normal day. You'll probably find that you do many of them without even thinking about it. Parents do tend to be natural-born teachers!

You can also schedule an activity period each day to be sure you're allowing enough time with your child. Any family member or friend can do these activities with the preschooler.

HOW SHOULD YOU DO THESE ACTIVITIES?

These activity charts are intended to show you the many kinds of things you can do with your preschooler that are beneficial to his development. Each activity has been researched and is designed to develop a certain skill or behavior that your child will eventually need in school.

For instance, having a three-year-old put a puzzle together teaches her to distinguish shapes—a skill she'll later need to distinguish letters for reading.

Remember: frequent, brief activity sessions (one to five minutes) are more productive than longer ones. If a child gets stuck on an activity, help him and then allow him to proceed.

The suggested activities and toys are just that—suggestions, not gospel. They have proven to be fun and educational for many children and are practical for parents. They may also give you many ideas for creating your own activities.

Remember: these activities are supposed to be *fun* for your child. Learning is *play* for a preschooler.

- If your child is not interested in an activity *forget it.*
- If your child gets frustrated by an activity *drop it.*
- If your child resists an activity *don't push it.*
- If you don't feel comfortable with an activity *skip it.*

> As with all developmental charts, the age guidelines are *only approximate.* Many three-year-olds may take awhile to master an activity in the "Toddler" section, while some one-year-olds may be doing something on the "Young Child" checklist.

The Infant (birth–age 1)

To develop the mind—

____ *Change* the environment by taking the baby to different locations: the living room, kitchen, outside the house.

____ Surround the baby with *sound:* music, talking, singing, noises of a busy household.

____ Provide objects for the baby to *see and touch*—first one object, then two or three (use different sizes, colors, and textures).

____ Make your own *mobiles* by attaching a variety of safe objects to large pieces of ribbon or elastic; change them often.

____ Provide *water* to play in and water toys that float.

____ Play *"peek-a-boo"* and hiding games ("Where's Cary's foot?").

____ Around one year, begin *naming* objects for baby ("water," "spoon," etc.).

To develop the body—

____ Have baby *sit up* in an infant seat as soon as he's able; the view of the world is much different!

____ *Exercise* baby by moving his arms and legs in imitation of adult exercises.

____ Encourage baby *to crawl* and pull up on things as soon as she's able (place an object just out of her reach to encourage crawling).

____ Provide baby with a crib "gym" over his crib to *play* with (available at many stores).

To develop the heart—

____ Put baby in a *variety* of social settings: small groups, large groups, inside activities, outside activities.

____ Expose baby to people who *look different:* young, old, tall, short, men, women, dark-skinned, light-skinned, bearded, clean-shaven, high-voiced, low-voiced, long-haired, short-haired.

____ Have different people *play* with the baby: grandparents, older brothers and sisters, neighbors, and friends.

____ If a woman is the primary care giver, be sure baby spends time with *a man*—either the father or an important man in the family's life; the reverse is true if a man is the primary care giver.

____ If the baby is not nursing, always have someone hold him while giving the bottle so he connects the positive experience of being fed *with people;* most people enjoy doing this for a child—don't hesitate to ask!

Gardening Tip—PLAYPENS

When babies really start to crawl, it's tempting to put them in playpens; that way they're safe and out of trouble. However, recent evidence suggests there's a lot more to crawling than meets the eye. The alternating, back and forth movement of arms and legs stimulates important parts of the brain. The *more a baby crawls,* the better it is for her.

It may be a nuisance, but a baby needs this exercise—not only for physical growth, but for mental growth as well!

Essential Toys:

• A large, wide-mouthed plastic container with a variety of objects that fit in it (safe household items)

• A sturdy book with large pictures (again, you can make this)

• A toy that makes a noise when shaken

• Crib mobiles or a crib "gym" (remember: you can make these!)

• Colorful crib pads, sheets, room decorations (this also goes for the diaper changing area)

• A soft, cuddly toy

The Toddler (ages 1–2)

To develop the mind—

____ Encourage a speaking vocabulary ("What's this called?" or "Try to say 'bowl.' ").

____ Help child identify his own body parts.

____ Help child be aware of *shapes*—circle, square, triangle; *sizes*—big, small, long, short; *colors*—red, blue, yellow; *sound*—loud, soft, high, low; *touch*—rough, smooth, hot, cold; *density*—floats, sinks.

____ Have child carry out simple instructions ("Bring me your ABC book," or "Find your teddy bear.").

____ Ask child to identify objects around her and those she sees in books.

____ Have child identify an object by touch alone (without being able to see it).

____ Have child imitate sounds, identify an unseen sound, and respond to whispered directions.

____ Encourage recognition of *a few* alphabet letters (but not their sound).

____ Have child help in running the household: —pick up leaves —bring in the paper —dust —polish mirrors —put dirty clothes in hamper —put clean clothes in proper rooms —sweep —vacuum —put a few things on the table.

____ Begin providing experiences beyond home: —grocery store —post office —library —cleaners —gas station —different neighborhood —offices —doctor —older brother's or sister's school —pet store —park.

____ *Read to your child!* Even young children enjoy looking at pictures and hearing words read to them.

To develop the heart—

____ *Gently encourage* child to share things —especially as he approaches age three; before that it is *not normal* for a child to share.

____ Have child begin to take responsibility for cleaning up his own toys and accidental spills

____ Encourage child to provide *care* for a doll or stuffed animal

____ Provide time around animals or have a pet in the household

____ Show child how to comfort someone who is hurt or sad ("Let's give Rita a hug," or "Maybe sister would like to use your blanket.")

____ Encourage child to play by himself now and then

____ Discourage child from using physical violence to get what he wants (hitting, biting, grabbing toys)

To develop the body—

____ Help child to eat by himself—including pouring, buttering, etc.

____ Have child stack things into towers (blocks, boxes, etc.)

____ Have child try to put lids on and off, screw tops on and off

____ Have child begin stringing objects on a string

____ Help child trace around objects (his hand, cookie cutters, toys)

____ Help child put *simple* puzzles together (ones with large wood or fiberboard pieces)

____ Let child try riding a tricycle or pulling a wagon whenever possible

Essential toys:

- Paper and crayons
- Basic building blocks (large, wooden ones)
- Bean bag and beach ball
- Things to thread on a piece of string or shoe lace
- A few noise makers of some kind
- Dirt and sand area to play in
- A few puzzles
- Locking blocks (Legos or Tinkertoys)
- Tricycle or wagon if possible
- Books (begin using the library's children's section)

The Young Child (ages 3–4)

To develop the mind—

____ Encourage spoken sentences; try to direct speech to get child to say more (example: instead of "How was nursery school?" which will probably get a one-word reply, ask "What toys did you use today?"). Use different words for the same thing: "big," "huge," "tremendous."

____ Help child identify more colors (orange, purple, black, brown).

____ Have child match items that are alike (start with identical items like two crows and move to grouping crows and robins with "birds"). Old Maid cards, playing cards, and pictures cut out of magazines are good for this.

____ Have child identify items that are different (put four different-sized cars and trucks and one pencil together—ask child which one doesn't belong).

____ Work on opposites (have child pick out a "big" block and then a "little" one—a "soft" object and then a "hard" one).

____ Have child arrange things by size—biggest to smallest or the opposite way (blocks, trucks, or pencils of different lengths).

____ Start counting and provide a simple understanding of number concepts ("How many kittens are there?" "Give me two cookies," and more advanced: "How many forks will we need?").

____ Encourage child to describe how things work (washing machine, dryer, egg beater, vacuum, blender).

____ Demonstrate and use "direction words" whenever you have a chance ("behind," "in front of," "over," "under," "below," "forward," "backward").

____ Direct drawing on chalkboard or paper: *shapes*—start with circles then move to squares, triangles, and finally diamonds; *lines*—vertical, horizontal, left to right, and finally diagonal; *dots*—connect two and then work up to more.

____ Continue to provide books for your child and to read to your child (see the Reading-Readiness section of The Reading Chapter for more specific suggestions). A story before bedtime is a nice habit to get into.

____ Continue to expose your child to new experiences, moving beyond home and the immediate neighborhood: —zoo —airport —Mom or Dad's work place —ocean or lake —museum —aquarium —a large garden —a different climate —construction site.

It is not enough simply to take your kids to these places. You also need to talk to your child about the experience *before* you go, *during* the trip, and *after* it's over. It is this exchange between you and your child that turns the excursion into a real learning experience. Ask questions, explain things, draw comparisons, point things out, make comments, recall the experience later, and recreate the experience at home (draw on paper a picture of the whale you saw).

Isn't it nice to know that by doing this you are providing the best education your child can get anywhere? (Try to remember this as you're driving home in the heat and your child asks you once again, "But where are the dinosaurs now?")

Gardening Tip—*PARENTS* MAGAZINE

This monthly publication has excellent articles on child rearing—from the tiny infant on up. The style is very readable and the research is current. Every issue has special sections on "The One-Year-Old," "The Three-Year-Old," etc.

To develop the body—

____ Expose child to outdoor play equipment that encourages climbing, jumping, going up and down ladders, swinging, spinning

____ Help child learn to do a somersault

____ Help child learn to feel comfortable in the water; try to make the child *pool safe*—able to swim to the side of a pool and climb out, even if he cannot breathe yet while swimming.

____ Allow child to help with simple cooking that includes pouring, beating, mixing, stirring—even cracking an egg if you're brave!

____ Encourage child to start undressing and then dressing herself (tied shoelaces will have to wait!)

____ Provide a 2-inch by 4-inch board for your child to walk on while it's lying on the ground; encourage child to go backward, forward, sideways, "halfway," hop on, hop off. This is a super coordination exercise!

____ Have child lie on floor and instruct her to move different body parts ("move this leg," "move both arms," "move this arm and that leg," etc.)

____ Start teaching child to catch, first with a soft bean bag and then moving on to a large ball

To develop the heart—

____ Allow child to answer telephone, talk briefly, and call an adult to the phone

____ Help child to increase his attention span (listen to an entire story at one sitting, look at an entire book by himself, listen to a whole record)

____ Start *encouraging* your child to take turns, play fair, and be a good loser

____ Encourage your child to say "please," "thank you," "you're welcome," and "excuse me"

____ Increase the period of separation from your child to encourage both independence and trust in other care givers (you can start with relatives or a good neighbor your child knows; move on to baby sitters or nursery school). Do this gradually.

____ Try to see that your child has a chance to relate positively with people from ethnic groups different from his own

____ Put your child's art work and creations up on a bulletin board, wall, or refrigerator (awfully good for developing a good self-image about himself)

____ Provide other children for your child to play with, either in the neighborhood or at a nursery school (see *next section*)

Essential toys:

• Shelf to put books on
• Chalkboard and chalk (on the wall is ideal, but a little one is fine)
• Small scissors (safe children's kind)
• Clay (or Play Dough)
• Little human figures to "act things out" with
• Pegboard

• A "first" dictionary of some kind—with big pictures
• A magnifying glass and/or a magnet
• More books (from the library, garage sales, trading with others)
• Record player and records (or play children's record on family record player)

NURSERY SCHOOL

The growing preschooler, particularly by age three, is ready to expand his horizons. He needs to become more independent, he needs still more experiences, and he needs to be around other kids his age. A good nursery school is *one way* to meet these needs.

When the term *nursery school* is used throughout this section, it refers to any school-like situation your child is involved in *before kindergarten*. A nursery school involves other children and costs money, with the exception of the Head Start program. Nursery schools are actively involved in child development—as opposed to just baby-sitting.

There is a tremendous variety of nursery schools, with many kinds of programs. Some are held in a family's garage and involve five children; others meet at a large commercial school building with two hundred kids. Some provide special educational toys, some teach reading, and still others teach religious concepts.

We realize fantastic nursery schools are not available for everyone. For many reasons—from economic to geographic — your choices may be very limited. However, if you are able to send your child to nursery school (or are even concerned with finding decent day-care), this section has important information.

Why Nursery School?

What can a nursery school provide that the home cannot?

- A chance to play with other children in a supervised situation
- An opportunity for your child to learn skills that will provide a good foundation for later schooling
- The chance to learn to be independent, away from parents, brothers, and sisters
- A comfortable *first school* experience before kindergarten
- An atmosphere for creative play, exploration, and developing vital social skills (like sharing, playing fair, nonviolence, and cooperation)
- Exposure to a wide variety of children (different races, backgrounds, and personalities)
- An opportunity to learn some important skills and have fun while parents are working and unable to watch the child
- A break for parents, allowing them time to pursue some personal goals or simply renew their energy!

Nursery school is particularly important if—

- There are few children to play with in your neighborhood
- The home situation is fairly small and there's not much room for your child to play
- Your child tends to be shy, dependent, or needs some bringing out
- Your child is having difficulties that could use some help from another adult (such as a tendency to bite!)
- Your family is undergoing a crisis and needs another adult to be involved with your child (due to illness, death, divorce, unusual demands from another child in the family)

16

When Should a Child Start Nursery School?

If you have a choice, most experts agree that age three is about right for starting nursery school on a half-day basis (9:00 to 12:30). You might want to start off with just two or three mornings a week. As the child gets older, you can increase the days (still *half* days) provided both you and your child want that.

How you space the days will be up to you and your child and what he seems to deal with best. Some do well with every other day, others prefer the days together. In any case, most nursery schools will charge you a flat fee per week (or per month). If you miss a day, you will *still* have to pay for it. The people who run nursery schools or day-care need an income they can depend on—not one that fluctuates with your child's health.

You might delay nursery school if—

• Your child is a little behind in some area (toilet training, for example)
• There is a health problem you'd like to get under control
• There's a new baby in the house and your child may view nursery school as a means of getting rid of her

To help your child look forward to nursery school—

___ Go visit the school with your child before he starts on a regular basis
___ Buy some new clothes or a special lunch pail for school
___ Talk about the fun things your child will be able to do at school that aren't available at home
___ Tell other people (so your child can hear) that she's now "old enough" to go to her own little school

How to Choose a Nursery School

If you live in a small town or rural area, there may be few nursery schools and very limited family day-care available. In the larger cities and suburbs, the choice can be overwhelming. In just one California county, for example, there are 2,065 nursery schools and family day-care homes.

The first thing to do in deciding on a nursery school for your child is to draw up a *pre-list* of preschools or family day-care homes you'd like to visit. Here are some things to consider in preparing this list:

1. Include schools that seem to offer the kind of program you want for your child (small groups, a religious emphasis, strong parent participation, etc.). You can get *some idea* of this from a phone call or advertisement.
2. Include schools that another parent has recommended. This time-honored method is hard to beat.
3. Include schools that are a reasonable distance from your home. This should not be a major factor, but realistically a thirty-minute drive for a three-hour morning may turn into an ordeal. It's also too tempting to skip days if the school is too far away. If you can arrange a car pool with another parent, this may open up some options.
4. Include schools that fall within your price range, but try to be open about this. Schools with the most highly trained staff pay their teachers more and thus cost more. Don't ever choose a nursery school because it's the cheapest one. *This is no place to try and save a buck.* Many experts feel it's as important an expenditure as college. A fine nursery school is worth every penny it costs!
5. Plan ahead: don't wait until your child is ready to start. Enroll him *at least* three months ahead to ensure he'll have a spot.

Types of Nursery Schools

The following pages will describe some of the types of nursery school experiences available in the United States. These schools may be called by different names than those given here, so it is important to read the *description* of each.

FAMILY DAY-CARE HOMES

Description: This is a nursery school program that is provided in the family type atmosphere of someone's home. We are dealing here with the type of family day-care that offers a program—not just baby-sitting.

Age: This will be up to the provider. Many family day-care homes take very young infants—but not for nursery school programs—as well as older children who may need care after the regular school day.

Size: The number of children at a family day-care home will depend on: (a) the individual state licensing regulations, and (b) the age of the children involved. A typical license allows a family day-care provider to watch six children (only three of which may be under the age of two); this includes the provider's own children as well.

If the provider wants to qualify for a larger family day-care license (up to twelve children), a helper who is at least fourteen years old must be hired as soon as there are more than six children.

Hours: This will depend on the provider and the part of the country you're in. Most offer both full- and part-time care with a flexible rate schedule. Most also offer child care before and after the nursery school program.

Cost: Obviously this will fluctuate with local economics and inflation. As of 1982, an average half-day schedule (five mornings a week from 3½ to 4 hours) runs about $30 a week. This works out to around $120 a month, $6 a day, or $1.50 an hour—depending on how you want to look at it. In family day-care homes that *do not* offer a nursery school program, the cost will probably be less.

Training of teachers: At the present time, there are no requirements for becoming a family day-care provider as long as you are eighteen years of age and have no police record. Some states, as part of their licensing program, require an orientation session for all persons applying for a family day-care license.

Activities: Along with simple baby-sitting, many family day-care homes are now providing a structured learning program. There is a trend to upgrade the quality of family day-care by organizing providers and offering them special training and conferences.

Gardening Tip—
PARENTS' NEWSLETTER

This is a brand new publication by the Children's Television Workshop (*Sesame Street*). It features up-to-date articles on safety, health, and education. Write to: *Parents' Newsletter*, P.O. Box 2889, Boulder, Col. 80322.

How to find: Family day-care providers are often advertised in the classified section of local newspapers. You can also get in touch with a local child care referral agency (Child and Family Service, Catholic Service Bureau, Children's Home Society, and the like). There may be a Day-Care Association in your area which can help you, or try the county Department of Social Services.

Licensing and inspection: All states issue a license for family day-care except: (a) Massachusetts, Pennsylvania, Michigan, Texas, South Dakota, Iowa, Georgia, and Montana, which have registration requirements only—the provider simply applies for a license and inspections are conducted on a random basis; and (b) Mississippi and Louisiana, which have *neither* licensing nor registration. Ohio inspects only federal or state subsidized children in family day-care homes.

Here is what is *usually* involved in obtaining a family day-care license:

1. Home must be clean and safe with adequate bathroom facilities.
2. People in the home must not have a police record of a serious nature.
3. Homes will be inspected about once a year in states that have inspection and in *all states* if there is a complaint.
4. Providers must renew their license at regular intervals.
5. There are specific restrictions on home safety and the number of children allowed in the home, depending on individual state regulations.

In most states, it is illegal to care for any children in your home for a fee without being registered or licensed. If you are not *sure* if a family day-care home falls in this category, call the Department of Social Services or the agency that handles child care licensing in your area and check. They will have a list of all *legal* family day-care homes.

It is safe to say that the tighter the regulations and the more frequent—and unannounced—the inspections, the better quality family day-care you can expect. (Minnesota and Colorado lead the nation in this respect.)

At the time of writing, there is a trend toward loosening standards and moving toward registration only (not licensing) due to the expense and red tape involved. There is also an attitude that "what's done in one's home is nobody else's business" and that the parents themselves should regulate day-care.

Gardening Tip—BONDING

Recent studies have indicated that the more parents and babies are together right after birth, the stronger the emotional attachment or *bond* becomes. It has also been noted that parents who had a lot of early contact with their infants

1. used more interesting language with their babies.
2. gave fewer commands.
3. asked more questions.
4. gave their children more intellectual stimulation.
5. seemed more aware of their children's needs.

FAMILY DAY-CARE HOMES

Most experts we talked with in the field of family day-care feel that a move away from regulation and licensing could have harmful effects. Even in states that require licensing or registration, there are people who care for children illegally. Negligent care is far more common in unlicensed homes. Take a look at this list of complaints received by one county agency in 1980:

Nature of complaint	against licensed homes	against unlicensed homes
too many children to safely handle	24	123
inadequate supervision	9	67
safety hazards in the home	4	51
child abuse	6	32

With statistics like these, you might wonder why anyone would be against licensing or would try to loosen standards. The answer is quite simple, according to the Children's Foundation in Washington, D.C.: *Parents are not informed about the facts.* Now that you know the importance of licensing and regulation, support them! When it comes to the health and safety of our children, it's hard to "overdo it."

Pros

The *family* type atmosphere of a home may make this type of nursery school particularly suitable for the young child (ages two and three).

There tend to be fewer children involved than in many large private preschools and therefore it is less overwhelming for a child.

There tends to be little turnover, as the day-care provider does not usually change very often.

This type of preschool experience can provide an ideal transition between a child's own home and a larger nursery school.

Cons

As a rule, family day-care cannot offer the range and amount of activities or equipment that a large private nursery school can.

An older child may need stimulation and experiences more similar to kindergarten.

The licensing and regulations governing family day-care are not as strict as for the other types of schools discussed in this section.

The person running day-care from the home still has to run the home as well.

20

COOPERATIVE NURSERY SCHOOLS

Description: These schools are usually owned and run by a group of parents for their own children. As a rule, the parents hire a teacher-director, buy or rent a facility, assist the teacher-director in the classroom on a rotating basis, and keep the school financially afloat.

Age: This will be up to the parents and the teacher. The usual age is 2½ (toilet trained) through five.

Size: The size of the school will depend on the size of the facility in accordance with state licensing regulations. Some co-ops may have as few as fourteen participating children and some as many as seventy-five. The usual number is about twenty-five per day—although more children may be involved on alternate days.

Hours: Many co-ops run a half-day program from 9:00–12:00 or from 1:00–3:00. Some co-ops may offer extended day-care beyond the regular education program.

Activities: The program at a co-op nursery will depend upon the philosophy of the parents and the teacher-director they hire.

Training of teachers: Since co-op schools fall under state licensing in most states, they must have a director who meets legal education requirements. In almost all co-ops, education classes are required for parents who assist in the classroom. These are often given by the co-op's teacher-director.

Licensing and inspection: The same licensing rules apply to co-ops as to regular commercial nursery schools in that state.

How to find: It is often difficult to locate a co-op nursery. They may be listed in the Yellow Pages under "Parent Participation Nursery Schools" or advertised in the classified sections of small local papers. Word of mouth is often their number-one form of advertisement. Many states have a Parent Participation Council that may be able to help you.

Cost: Co-op nurseries are considerably less than either family day-care or commercial nursery schools. Charges vary, of course, but a typical fee would be $25 a month for a three-hour program, three days a week, or $32 for a three-hour program, five days a week. Some co-ops have had to take on children whose parents do not participate in order to make ends meet. Naturally, these parents pay a higher tuition fee.

Pros

Parents have a large amount of control over the kind of preschool experience their child will have.

Parents inevitably learn more about their own child and child development in general by participating in a preschool experience.

In most cases, it is a very comfortable adjustment for a child to have his parent involved in his first preschool experience.

The cost of a cooperative nursery school is considerably less than another type—but equally good—preschool.

Cons

There is a significant time involvement expected in cooperative schools that many parents cannot afford.

As in all such setups, there may be personal disagreements between parents, or a few parents may end up doing most of the work.

Occasionally, it may not be a good idea for a parent to be in the classroom with his own child.

The economy today—and the two-paycheck family—is making it increasingly difficult for co-op schools to make it.

MONTESSORI SCHOOLS

Description: The term *Montessori* comes from the famous preschool educator, Maria Montessori (1870-1952), who founded a method of teaching young children. Ms. Montessori did not patent her idea, however, and now the term Montessori may be used by just about any school.

There are approximately 2,000 schools in the U.S. that claim to be Montessori schools. About 267 are affiliated with the Association Montessori Internationale (AMI), based in Holland. Another group, the American Montessori Society (AMS), broke off from AMI in the early 1950's and claims about 500 affiliates. The rest of the schools using the name Montessori are independently run.

Size: Montessori schools vary in size. A number of them tend to be more like primary schools with about thirty children to a class with a teacher and perhaps one or two aides. Students, as a rule, are not grouped by any age basis but usually work individually. They move on to a different activity or skill when they are ready to, regardless of age.

Age: Again, this varies from school to school. Some Montessori schools take children as young as eighteen months. Some extend their programs through junior high. Most, especially AMI and AMS affiliates, take children from two and a half to twelve (preschool through sixth grade).

Hours: Some Montessori nursery schools run a half-day program from 9:00 until 12:00. Most, however, run a program longer than most nursery schools—9:00 to 2:30 or 3:00. Many Montessori schools offer extended day-care as well.

Cost: Because Montessori educational materials and the training required for their teachers are expensive, these schools cost more than most nursery schools. Prices for the full-day program (9:00—2:30) run all the way from $185 a month to $300 a month, with schools on the East Coast being more expensive.

Training of teachers: Montessori schools affiliated with AMI and AMS require that their teachers have a B.A. degree plus about a year's graduate work in Montessori techniques. They must also student teach in a Montessori school before becoming fully licensed.

The requirements for independent Montessori schools vary tremendously from almost no training to training equal to the AMI and AMS requirements. One school, for example, required prospective teachers to attend weekend classes for eight months.

Gardening Tip—BASIC READING (in addition to Dr. Spock)

ILG, FRANCES L., and AMES, LOUISE B. *Child Behavior*. New York: Harper & Row, 1955. This book covers the basic stages a child goes through from birth to age ten. You will, for instance, be relieved to know that turning the chairs upside down is quite normal for an eighteen-month-old!

DODSON, FITZHUGH. *How to Parent*. New York: New American Library, 1973. A pediatrician we know recommends this book to all new parents. The toy guides in the back are particularly good.

Both titles are available in paperback.

Activities: It is in this area that Montessori schools are different from other nursery schools. Although there is no absolute Montessori method, most schools using the name try to follow the principles set down by Maria Montessori in the early 1900's.

In general, the Montessori method involves a sequence of activities and exercises using specially designed materials. Play activities and toys teach specific educational skills. For example, one involves placing round cylinders of different sizes into a board containing holes of corresponding sizes.

Ideally, a Montessori *director*, which is what their teachers are called, sets up the classroom very carefully. Montessori is *supposed* to be a combination of structure and freedom.

Licensing and inspection: Since Montessori schools fall under the category of private nursery schools, they are therefore licensed and inspected by the state according to the individual state's regulations. In addition, Montessori schools affiliated with AMI or AMS are licensed and inspected by the national organization as well.

How to find: Montessori schools can be found under *Nursery School* in the Yellow Pages and under the word *Montessori* in the white pages. If there is a listing for American Montessori Society or Association Montessori Internationale in your white pages, either of these can direct you to a school in your area.

These schools are particularly difficult to evaluate due to the tremendous variations in schools using the name *Montessori*. Therefore, the statements that follow are of a very general nature. Just because it's a "Montessori" school doesn't mean it's good. Check each school out carefully.

Pros

If you want your child to receive instruction in reading and writing at a fairly early age (before kindergarten), it is available in most Montessori schools.

Children have the opportunity to work independently.

Since Montessori *toys* are self-correcting, children can use them without a teacher present once they have learned how.

The training required for AMI and AMS Montessori teachers is well above that for *most* nursery school teachers.

Montessori schools and teachers have a structured program that has had some results; it's not a hit-or-miss presentation.

Cons

In some Montessori schools, there is less emphasis on creative play (i.e., more push toward realistic tasks).

Some feel the Montessori equipment is too structured and does not encourage creativity. (This would be debated by Montessori teachers.)

Some Montessori curriculums do not provide much in the way of outdoor play, art, and music.

Some children may have a problem switching from the highly independent Montessori type program to a public school program that is more structured.

HEAD START

Description: The Head Start preschool program was started by the federal government in 1965 in an effort to help economically deprived children do better in school. Head Start presently serves about 376,000 children with a paid staff of 70,000 and 400,000 volunteers.

Children eligible for Head Start come from families currently on welfare or at poverty level incomes. (In 1982, a poverty income for a family of four was $10,570 in Alaska, $9,720 in Hawaii, and $8,450 in all other states of the union.)

Age: Eligible youngsters must be from three to five years old, or even six years if they live in a state that does not have a public kindergarten system. It is suggested that parents apply in April if their child will be the right age to begin Head Start the following September.

Size: Head Start centers are encouraged to keep their enrollment at about fifteen. There are guidelines set down as to the number of teachers: one adult for every five children. At a typical center there is one teacher, one aide, and one volunteer.

Hours: The Head Start program is 3½ hours long and is offered in morning or afternoon sessions from September through May. Extended day-care is usually not provided, although some centers are involved in this service.

Cost: The federal government provides 80% of the Head Start budget. Each center must then raise 20% on its own through volunteer services, garage sales, donations, etc. There is no cost to the child or his family.

Training of teachers: A director of a Head Start center must have a B.A. degree in Early Childhood Education and an administrative credential. A Head Start teacher must hold a Child Development Associate degree (12 credits in Childhood Education plus related job experience) and comply with individual state regulations as well.

Activities: Besides regular preschool educational activities, Head Start centers also provide nutritional, medical, dental, and social services. Some centers also have teachers visit the children's homes once a week.

Parents are actively involved in the Head Start program. They help with school planning, budgets, and fund raising. They are encouraged to attend meetings once a month and volunteer in the preschool classroom.

Licensing and inspection: Head Start centers are licensed by the federal government and inspected by them once every three years. In addition, they are also subject to state licensing, when applicable, as with any commercial preschool.

How to find: Head Start is listed in the phone book in various ways. You can always get in touch with Head Start by calling your county government offices or your local school district. You can also try Head Start in the white pages, but many centers do not have the words *Head Start* in their name.

Gardening Tip—KIDS' MAGAZINES

Since preschoolers love to receive mail, why not get them a subscription to their own magazine? Three magazines they might enjoy are:

Highlights for Children
Humpty Dumpty magazine
Sesame Street magazine

Pros

Recent studies by Cornell University have shown Head Start to be a highly effective program which does indeed make a difference. Youngsters who had the Head Start experience did better at *all* levels of school than children who had no such experience.

Since standards for Head Start are set nationally, you can expect a more even quality from state to state.

In doing this study, we found people involved with Head Start to be unusually dedicated and enthusiastic about the program.

Cons

There is a heavy demand in many areas for the Head Start program. Some centers have waiting lists of 100 children.

Head Start is only a half-day program and other arrangements usually must be made for a child whose parents work all day.

As with cooperative nurseries, Head Start requires a good deal of parent involvement to get results. This may not be possible for some parents.

Gardening Tip—
TELEVISION WATCHING

Television is a fact of life—and certainly not *all* bad. However, certain guidelines should be observed with the preschool child:

1. Never leave the TV set on as a "background" for play.

2. Encourage the child to watch a selected program and then *turn the set off* when the show is over.

3. Limit your child to no more than one to two hours of TV per day.

4. If at all possible, try to have someone watch TV with the child and *talk about the program* while it's on; this turns TV watching from a passive to more active experience.

UNIVERSITY/COLLEGE NURSERY SCHOOLS

Description: These schools are located on university, college, or junior college campuses and are primarily for use by the students, faculty, or staff of the educational institution. Occasionally remaining spaces are open to the community outside the college. Many institutions of higher education offer both a nursery school and day-care facilities; they may be held in the same facility, or separately.

Size: The size of these schools varies, but most schools try to maintain a small children-to-staff ratio. This ratio often depends on how the school is funded. The state may set a limit of one adult for every eight children, ages three and four. On the other hand, the county may allow as many as twelve children for every adult. As a rule, the younger the children, the more adults there must be.

Age: This varies depending on what the institution offers. If it is a regular nursery school, the ages are usually 2½ (toilet trained) to five. If day-care is also offered, they may take infants as young as two months and children older than five. Sometimes, as in other types of nursery schools, day-care is offered after the regular nursery school program.

Hours: The hours will also vary, but they tend to operate around the college parents' schedule. Centers are often open as early as 7:30 A.M. and as late as 6:00 P.M. The regular nursery school program, however, usually runs from 3½ to 5 hours.

Cost: Cost will vary tremendously, depending on the funding of the school and the income of the parents being served. If the school receives special funds, such as grants from the state, the tuition may be greatly reduced for low-income families. There also may be separate fees for the nursery school program and for extended day-care hours. Many schools charge more for infant care (under two years of age) than for services to older children.

You would need to check with the school concerning the rate you would be charged. In general, these types of facilities are reasonably priced. This is probably due to the fact that they are geared toward providing a service to students while they are in college.

Gardening Tip—SETTING LIMITS

All children test their parents to see just how firm they are about what they say. If tested too far, parents often resort to spanking. Unfortunately, spanking has little effect—unless it borders on abuse—and it teaches the child it's OK to hit someone smaller.

Many psychologists now feel that a more effective form of discipline is having your child spend some time by himself. The child will then want to do what's right so as not to have to leave the fun and the friends.

Training of teachers: Most of these schools tend to have teachers who are qualified well above the minimum state standards. In addition, many have education students assisting in the classroom as part of their college training.

Activities: Again, this will depend on the type of nursery school program offered. Most schools affiliated with a college or university offer fairly comprehensive child development programs, since the school is often a training ground for future nursery school educators.

Licensing and inspection: Because of the great variety in the way that these schools are operated and funded, licensing and inspection requirements do not fall into any general pattern. Some of these nursery schools may fall under the jurisdiction of the state Department of Education, under the county, or simply under the umbrella of the university itself. Ask the school you are interested in how it is licensed and who inspects it and how often.

How to find: You can find out if a junior college, college, or university offers preschool education by calling the main switchboard and asking for the "child care center" or "preschool."

Most college-related nursery schools tend to be very popular. The UCLA preschool, for example, had a waiting list of 800 for the 1981–1982 school year! Some parents register their children *before* they are born in hopes of securing a spot. This is a bit extreme, but if you are interested in such a school, or if a family member is planning to attend college, it might pay to put your name in *well before* you plan on having your child attend.

Pros

A college-affiliated nursery school may be more in touch with current knowledge in the field of early childhood education.

Since the public tends to expect more from educational institutions, they have a certain image to uphold in providing a quality program.

In some cases, the pay is higher for the staff at these schools because special funds are available.

There is often a higher degree of parent involvement at these schools than at many private nursery schools. (The exception would be, of course, parent participation, or co-op, nurseries.)

If you are attending the college, your child will be in close proximity to you and you'll both be going to the same location.

Cons

Unless you are a student or have some connection with the college, it may be quite difficult to get into one of these schools. The waiting list for outsiders may prove too long and discouraging.

There tends to be a fairly high turnover of children at these schools since the parents may only be at the college for a short period of time. This could be difficult for some children to adjust to.

A variety of college students may be coming and going into the nursery school as part of their educational training. This could be a bonus for some children, while the frequent turnover might bother others.

PRIVATE NURSERY SCHOOLS

Description: Without a doubt, this category is the most difficult to describe since it includes so may different types of nursery schools. These nursery schools are *usually* held in a nursery school center or church, as opposed to a private home. They can be nonprofit (such as a community-sponsored program), but most in this category are run for profit—especially the programs of large corporations, like Kinder-Care, or Gerber Children Centers. They are also called commercial nursery schools, proprietary nursery schools, and related names.

Age: Most private preschools will take children as young as 2½ (if they are toilet trained) and on up to age five. Many such preschools also include a year of kindergarten and sometimes even first grade.

Size: The size of a private nursery school varies tremendously depending on the population of the area served and the size of the school facilities. Schools vary widely in enrollment, from as small as six children to as large as 200. There are guidelines, however, as to the amount of room children must have. Most states require 35 square feet of indoor floor space and 75 square feet of outdoor space per child.

There are also rules pertaining to the number of adults required to supervise the children. A ratio found in many states is 1 to 12; this means there *must* be one adult for every twelve children. However, this *may* be figured on an average—for example, a group of six three-year-olds and their teacher combined with a class of eighteen four-year-olds and their teacher *averages out* to a 1 to 12 ratio. A number of states do not average, but have a set standard for the number of children of a particular age which may be with one adult (the younger the children, the fewer per adult).

Hours: In many private nursery schools, only a half-day program is offered. Still others may offer both a half-day and a full-day program, plus extended day-care.

Cost: There is a huge variation in cost. We found a price range from $90 to $170 a month for five half-days a week (9:00 to 12:30 or 12:00 to 3:30). Church-affiliated schools tend to charge a bit less. Schools with expensive equipment and elaborate programs will cost more. Geographic area may have a lot to do with prices.

Training of teachers: This will vary depending upon the school you choose and the state you reside in. As a rule, most states require very minimum standards to operate a private nursery school. Almost all states now insist teachers have some education classes in the area of early childhood development. A number of states now issue a "Childhood Development Associate" degree which is required for nursery school teachers. What is usually required to obtain this degree is a combination of education classes and experience in the field.

Gardening Tip—
COMPANY-SPONSORED CHILD CARE

Studies have shown that companies which provide day-care for their employees can cut absenteeism, increase company loyalty, and improve staff morale. Despite these findings, very few have picked up the ball (with the glowing exception of Stride-Rite Shoes).

If your company is providing tennis, racquetball courts, and saunas, you can also suggest they consider child care. Speak up!

Activities: Almost all private nursery schools offer some type of program for children, along with supervised indoor and outdoor play. The quality of the educational program and the amount of equipment available will depend upon the resourcefulness of the teachers and the school's budget.

How to find: Private nursery schools advertise in the Yellow Pages under a number of possible headings: "Nursery Schools," "Child Care," "Day Nurseries," "Schools," "Learning Centers," etc. You may also call your local licensing bureau if you want to find out if there have been any complaints or problems. The case records of all private day-care facilities are public information.

Licensing and inspection: This also varies from state to state. The basic health and safety requirements (building code, fire prevention, sanitation, nutrition, amount of room) tend to be fairly standard throughout the nation. Variations occur in the number of children allowed per adult and the necessary qualifications of the staff.

Inspection of nursery school facilities also changes from state to state. Usually there is a pre-licensing inspection with inspections every year or two thereafter. Licenses are usually renewed every year. Nursery schools must always be inspected whenever there is a complaint.

In some parts of the country there is a current move, based on the principle of church and state separation, to exempt church nursery schools from licensing and inspection.

Pros

These facilities may offer more activities and equipment than family day-care.

As a rule, there are higher requirements for private nursery school teachers than for family day-care providers.

The regulations governing private nursery schools are tighter than for family day-care due to higher visibility.

The private nursery school staff's sole responsibility is the school itself. They leave their own homes and chores to come *to* the school.

Cons

The ratio of children to adults can be very high in these schools and may be overwhelming to the young child.

A child may not receive as much individual attention as in a smaller family day-care setting.

The turnover of help due to low salaries can be high at a private nursery school.

The atmosphere may be more like an actual school, which might be OK for the older child but too demanding for a 2½-year-old.

Visiting a Nursery School

After you have made a list of possible nursery schools for your child, the next step is to get out and visit them.

• It is usually acceptable to drop by a fairly large commercial preschool unannounced. This allows you to see the school as is, with no special preparations for your visit. For a small facility or family day-care home it is probably wiser to call first (especially if there's only one person in charge). This ensures that the person in charge will be there to talk with you and that the children will not be on an outing. If you want to leave some element of surprise in the visit, simply indicate you'll be dropping by "sometime in the morning."

• Arrive at least a half hour after the preschool begins so you can see the actual activities in progress; limit your visit to about an hour, or possibly two.

• Be silent and stay in the background. Do not ask questions while the teachers are working with the children. Wait for a logical time to talk, or wait until you are approached.

• Leave your own children at home for the first visit—otherwise your attention will be too wrapped up with your child and what he's up to.

• The following checklists will help you to evaluate the facilities, teachers, and program.

The school or home itself:

____ Is the school or day-care home registered and/or licensed by the state? (Ask to *see* the license of the family day-care home.)

____ Is the place basically clean and pleasant? (A certain amount of disorder is to be expected!)

____ Is there an adequate outdoor play area?

____ Is it *safe* (fences where they should be, swimming pools totally inaccessible, hot water taps out of reach, etc.)?

____ Is there a clean bathroom available? drinking water?

____ Is there enough equipment to play with? different kinds? in good repair? appropriate for different age levels?

____ Is the area set up for small children (little tables and chairs, stepping stools)?

____ Is there a separate area for children who may become sick during school?

The teachers, director, and helpers:

____ Are the people loving individuals who obviously enjoy children?

____ Do they make you feel welcome and encourage questions?

____ How do they handle misbehavior? (calm and firm? listen to child's side of it? avoid screaming, spanking, or name calling?)

____ Do the adults talk to the children on an individual basis? stoop down to the children's level? allow the kids to finish sentences? answer questions patiently?

____ Do the children readily approach the adults in charge? What do they call them? (It should not be "Teacher.")

____ Do the instructors spend about equal time with all children?

____ Do the people seem too bossy or pushy with the kids? Do they give too many directions—or do too much of the activity themselves, rather than letting the children do it?

____ Are they flexible (allow for changes in schedule)?

____ Do the teachers utilize what the kids bring to share or comment on things the children want attention for?

____ Does anyone seem tired, harassed, or impatient? (If so, they're in the wrong business.)

____ How many adults are there for each child? (Look for about one adult to four kids if they are under age one; one adult to six or seven kids if they are two- and three-year-olds.)

The program being offered:

___ Do the activities the children are offered seem interesting and fun (or are kids bored and wandering away)?

___ Are the projects easy enough for the children to do themselves without too much direction or outside help?

___ Are children forced to sit still too long? (30 minutes at a time is too long for kids under age five.)

___ Are there lots of activities and toys to choose from?

___ Do the children have a *supervised* play period outside?

___ Is sharing encouraged? hitting discouraged? taking turns? treating property with respect?

___ Is time provided for quiet play? for playing by oneself?

___ Does the program include music, singing, art, and drama?

___ Are nutritious meals and snacks part of the program?

___ How are the children organized? Are the little ones together or do big kids overwhelm the younger ones?

___ How is bad behavior handled? (Isolating the child from the group is one acceptable approach.)

The children:

___ Do the children seem happy and involved in the nursery school or day-care home?

___ How do the children get along with the adults? with the other children? Are they respectful? Is there too much hitting?

___ Do any children seem lonely, lost, or left out?

___ Are the children of mixed ethnic backgrounds? (The more mixed, the more opportunities for your child to know and get along with all kinds of people.)

___ Do the children obey the rules that have been set up?

___ Do the children have responsibilities? help clean up?

___ Do the children seem too tired or overly active?

After you have visited the nursery school or family day-care home, talk with the person in charge. Here are some key questions to ask:

• What is the basic philosophy of the people in charge? What are their feelings about what children should be learning at this age? Do they teach reading or reading-readiness? Do their ideas match *yours*?

• What are their goals for your child? What kind of growth are they trying to encourage? How will they measure this growth?

• What is a typical day's schedule?

• How are parents involved? Is it OK to drop in any time? (As a rule the best schools are *very open* to parents.)

• What materials or special programs does the school use that you may not have seen during your observation?

• Are field trips provided? Who provides the transportation? Are there seat belts or car seats for *every child?*

• What insurance does the school carry? Is the day-care provider's car insured to carry extra children?

• What if your child should become ill?

• What training do the director, teachers, and aides have? You might also ask what they are paid. If it's a minimum wage — and it often is — the turnover is going to be high.

• What are the costs of attending the school? How are the fees paid? What happens if your child misses a day of school? May you leave your child longer if necessary?

The next step is to bring your child for a visit. Many schools feel the parent should stay for all or part of this visit. This aids in making a smooth transition from the home to the new school environment. It also lets your child know that you think this is OK and enjoy being there too. Most educators feel this will not harm your child in any way, but will make him more confident and secure in the long run. Some children will not need you to stay and that's fine too.

TAKE THESE CHECKLISTS WITH YOU TO YOUR NEXT CONFERENCE.

Keeping Tabs on Your Nursery School

Look back over the reasons on page 16 that you send a child to a preschool and some of the things a nursery school can do for a child. Do you see these things happening? Are you satisfied with your child's behavior and progress? Is your child happy in the preschool situation you've chosen?

If the preschool experience is a positive one, you should see—

• An increased confidence in your child, a growing independence, the ability to be away from family members for longer stretches of time (there may be a few stages, such as at 3½, where your child is a bit more "clingy"), greater willingness to try new things.
• New experiences and activities that come from outside the home (samples of art work or cutout shapes, stories about the visit to the fire station).
• An increasing ability to get along with other children and play with them without major difficulties (more sharing, less hitting, more attempts to please the playmate).
• An excitement about things that are going to happen at the nursery school (the Valentine's Day party, making the piñata, the nature hike).

If the preschool experience is a negative one, you may see—

• Your child continuing to cry or acting depressed *quite awhile* after you've left the school (fussing when you leave is normal at first). Either the child-care director will tell you this or you can observe your child, unseen, if you suspect this is happening.
• Your child becomes very anxious for your return and is almost waiting for you to come back; he may even cry with relief when he sees you. A contented preschooler will not do these things, but will want you to come see what he's doing. (Often he may not want to leave at all!)

• Whiny, tired, and apathetic behavior at home. Your child seems overly tired or overly stimulated.
• A sharp increase in dependent behavior. Your child may seem reluctant to leave you at all, refuse to try new things, or even venture out of your sight.
• *Continual and strong* protests about going to the nursery school or day-care home; some lagging is normal, but it should cease when the child is actually on his way to school. If, after the first couple of weeks, your child begs to stay home, something is wrong.

Monitoring your preschool

Being aware of what's going on at your child's nursery school is even more important than monitoring elementary or high school because the factor of *safety* plays a much bigger role. A family day-care home or private nursery school does not have the visibility of a public school.

There is sometimes more behind the cute advertisements for "Happy Land Nursery School" or the "nice-looking" family day-care home. Horror stories and actual tragedies *do occur* in these places. Unfortunately there are some frighteningly irresponsible people in the nursery school/day-care business. There are also many dedicated and wonderful people. We're not asking you to be paranoid—just careful. May we suggest a few guidelines?

• Do not make a habit of dropping your child off in front of the school or picking him up at the door. Allow time to *go inside* the nursery school or day-care home—perhaps even sit awhile to observe and chat.
• Arrange, now and then, to pick up your child before your usual arrival time. This is often a good way to see the school as it really is.

- If you find out a parent has withdrawn a child from the school for a reason other than moving, contact that parent. This is not being nosy—it's being sensible.
- If you have any doubts about the school, contact some other parents and see how they feel. (This does not exclude, of course, speaking with the people who run the school.)
- If you have a bad experience with a nursery school or family day-care home, *you have a moral responsibility to report it* to your local child welfare authorities. You may even choose to call the police if the infraction seems serious enough.

Remember: *if the situation is bad enough to remove your child, it should be reported. The welfare of other children may be at stake.*

If there's a problem with your nursery school or family day-care home, what should you do?

1. First of all, discuss the problem with the teachers or day-care provider. If they are not already aware of your child's problem, they may be able to start dealing with him in a special way.

2. Try another observation of the preschool. If the school has a one-way viewing window (where you can see your child in the schoolroom, but she can't see you) this is ideal. If not, you can try sitting in on the class while your child is there (and staying in the background) or visiting without her. Some problems may show up that will give you a clue as to what's wrong (too strict, big kids bullying others, boredom, too much confusion).

3. If you think you may know what the problem is, discuss it with the teachers or day-care provider. It may be a criticism of the way they're handling things, but you have nothing to lose. It will not get better if you don't speak up; it may get worse. (Example: "I feel you need to supervise the larger children like Howard a bit closer. He grabs things away from my child and I think Mike may be afraid to come here.")

4. One solution may be to cut down on the number of days your child is attending nursery school, *if* the problem appears to be that she is somewhat overwhelmed by the new experience.

5. If you discover, at any time, something about the nursery school or family day-care home that is dangerous or illegal (even though it may not be bothering your child), bring it up. Chances are the preschool will remedy the situation. If they do not you have a duty to report it to the proper authorities. They will investigate any school or home that has been reported.

What if the problem cannot be solved?

You can try switching to a different school or to a different type of school. If your child is currently in a fairly large private nursery school, you might try a family day-care home. In any case, try to select a school that is not like the first one—either smaller, with a different emphasis, or a new appearance.

You may have to drop nursery school for a while until your child is more prepared for this type of experience. Try it again in six months—a lot can change in this period of time. However, if you must have day-care due to working, try to have someone come into your home or make arrangements to leave your child with a responsible friend or relative for a while.

KINDERGARTEN

Did you know that—

The word *Kindergarten* is German for "children's garden" because Germany is where it started?

85 percent of the children in the United States attend kindergarten?

A large number of nursery schools offer kindergarten for the same price as nursery school?

Legally, you do not have to send your child to school until the first grade?

Kindergarten is designed as a preparation for first grade?

Although some people feel kindergarten is nothing more than an extension of nursery school, they couldn't be more wrong. There are some significant differences:

How does Kindergarten differ from nursery school?

1. Kindergarten follows a more regulated schedule than most nursery schools. The child is not as free to do *what* he wants *when* he wants.

2. Kindergarten teachers cannot spend as much time with each child as a nursery school teacher can due to the larger class size. A nursery school may have twelve children to every adult; a kindergarten may have thirty children to one teacher.

3. Kindergartens may offer activities similar to nursery schools, but with more structured expectations as to how they will be carried out. (Any result will be accepted in nursery school; kindergarten is moving toward some definite goals.)

4. Kindergarten students are expected to conform more to standards of school behavior. A child must be more self-disciplined and can't just do "his own thing."

5. Kindergarten begins, in earnest, the task of preparing children for reading, writing, and arithmetic.

Gardening Tip—STAR CHARTS

This is a great method for encouraging your child to do what you want her to do. Stars are given at the end of each day for what was done right, thereby rewarding good behavior. A sample chart might look like this one:

THINGS I NEED TO DO					
put toys away					
take a bath					
ask permission to turn on the TV					

After your child gets five stars in a row in any column, she gets a reward.

34

When Should Your Child Start Kindergarten?

Here is one time when parents *can really affect* their child's success in school—when he's about to start kindergarten. There is no "right age" to begin kindergarten. Every school district has a different cut-off date as to how old a child must be to enroll. A district in Massachusetts says 4½ by October 1; another in the same state says five by October 1. A child must be five by November 15 in Corvallis, Oregon, and five by December 5 in Irvine, California.

Age cannot guarantee readiness for kindergarten. It is only one of many indicators. If your child just squeezes under the wire for admission, or he "just misses" and you're considering sneaking him in, *first* answer these questions:

1. Can my child be alone in a strange place outside the home without crying or being overly fearful? (Examples: birthday parties, baby-sitter's home, nursery school.)

2. Can my child attend to his personal needs without difficulty? (Example: go to the toilet, ask for a drink, take his clothes on and off.)

3. Can my child follow spoken directions, particularly several given at one time? (Example: "Go to your room, get your Tonka truck, and shut the door after you, please.")

4. Can my child keep his attention on a task long enough to finish? (Example: putting a pile of blocks away, looking through a twelve-page picture book, listening to one side of a children's record.) Aim for a *ten-minute* attention span.

5. Can my child play with other children without being overly fearful or overly aggressive? Can she take turns, share, follow the rules, and play fair?

6. Can my child clearly tell people his needs with a loud enough voice, a clear voice, and using the right words?

7. Does my child *want to go* to kindergarten? (This may not be evident until she's actually started.) Does she continually balk or cry about going after the first few weeks?

If you can clearly answer "yes" to all these questions, your child sounds ready to begin kindergarten. A firm "no" to even one question, however, should give you pause.

Readiness for kindergarten, contrary to most parents' beliefs, does not mean the ability to recognize alphabet letters and numbers. Even a child who can almost read may not be ready emotionally and physically for the demands of a school environment.

Consider these points:

• The younger a child starts school, the more stress he will be under.

• It's *always better* to be at the top of the class than struggling to keep up.

• It's easier to wait a year to start kindergarten than to end up having to repeat first grade. Waiting a year gives your child a twelve-month edge in both physical and mental growth.

• Many parents start their children in kindergarten, perhaps due to pressure from friends and relatives, before they should. Hold firm!

• There are increasing numbers of educational experts who now ignore the usual school starting ages and say flatly: "Unless your child is *five by September 1st*, wait a year to start kindergarten."

How to Prepare Your Child for Kindergarten

Many children are counting the days until they can begin school—especially if older brothers and sisters already attend. Still, there are some things you can do ahead of time to give your child as much confidence as possible:

- Take your child to the school, walking along the actual route she will take every day.
- Visit the school several times before he starts, at least once while school is in session so he can see all the kids.
- Try to meet the teacher ahead of time, or at least know her name.
- Go to the kindergarten playground and let your child use the equipment there.

- As with nursery school, talk it up around others. Brag about your child being old enough to attend kindergarten.
- Buy some special things "just for school" (such as a backpack to carry papers home in, a new box of crayons, or some sharp looking school clothes!).
- Get your child on a school schedule *well before school starts.* (Get up early to allow time for a good breakfast.)

The most important thing to prepare is your own attitude. Be cheerful, confident, and fairly matter-of-fact about this new step.

SURVIVAL SKILLS CHECKLIST—

We asked kindergarten teachers what skills they would like each child to have when coming to school. Their answers are incorporated in the following checklist.

How many can your child do?

____ I can say my first and last name

____ I know my address and phone number

____ I know my parents' first and last names (especially important if the last name is different from the child's name)

____ I can recognize my own printed name

____ I know how to use zippers, shoe laces, and buttons, can take my outer garments on and off

____ I can speak in a voice loud enough so people can hear me

____ I know how to use a handkerchief or tissue and can ask for one

____ I can use the toilet, toilet paper, and the flusher

____ I know what to do (and what not to do) with crayons, paste, and scissors

____ I can take responsibility for my own actions. (If I spill something, I clean it up!)

____ I can listen and sit quietly while others are talking

____ I can share things, take turns, and play by the rules

Making the Switch to First Grade

Just as kindergarten is significantly different from nursery school, first grade is a big switch from kindergarten. Let's examine some of the changes:

1. First grade is much more structured than kindergarten with much less free time.

2. First grade teachers do less "mothering" than do kindergarten teachers.

3. First grade is when all children are expected to begin reading, printing, and doing arithmetic.

4. First grade expects that certain levels will be met by all students at the end of the year; there is less room for individual differences.

It is important that your child is ready for these demands. There are a few warning signs to watch for during the early weeks of first grade:

- Stalling in the morning
- Complaining about "feeling sick"
- Crying
- Begging to stay home
- Disruptive in class
- Constantly acting silly in class
- Cannot do the work
- Will not stay seated

If your child is displaying any of this behavior, he may be in over his head. If you have any doubts, talk it over with the first grade teacher. Your child may be mentally ready for first grade, but that is not enough. His behavior and general maturity must also be ready.

Remember: kindergarten is the easiest grade to repeat. There is little stigma attached and the schools are usually supportive. Repeating fourth grade, however, is rarely done and would be much harder on your child.

Now your child has started first grade, the first step of the twelve-year hike that is mandatory education.

The next chapter will show you how to make that trip the best one possible!

Gardening Tip—CAR SEATS & SEAT BELTS

The best preparation for school is to be sure your child gets there in one piece. This may sound dramatic, but auto accidents are the #1 killer of children. Studies show that over 90% of these deaths could have been prevented by using a proper restraint system.

A FINAL WORD TO THE HOME GARDENER

Current research indicates that a child's first educational experiences—at home, in preschool, kindergarten, and first grade—will have more to do with his performance in the later grades than anything else.

At no other time is your involvement in your child's education so crucial. *Do not leave these early years to chance.* They are far too important. Now is the time to carefully nourish the body, mind, and heart of your young child.

CHAPTER 2

_____

_____

_____

_____

_____

_____

No man is fit to educate unless he feels each
pupil an end in himself, with his own rights and
his own personality, not merely a piece in a jig-
saw puzzle, or a soldier in a regiment, or a citizen
in a state.

—*Bertrand Russell*

Getting Through the School Daze

How do you know what's going on with your kid at school? Well, you get report cards several times a year, plus various school mailings. You see bits of homework now and then, trade gossip with other parents, and listen to your child's stories at dinner. These are all valid sources of information *but* they're all secondhand. If you're going to keep tabs on your child's education, you have to maintain direct communication with teachers at *each level* of schooling.

In the early years of school, parent-teacher contact is at an all-time high. You walk your child right to the kindergarten door. Mrs. Evans becomes an old friend. A little gift is chosen for Mr. Rodriguez at the end of the year. A SRO crowd attends the primary grade's Spring Sing. Both the school and the parents make an extra effort to reach out. But each year your child advances through school, this relationship erodes. By junior high, it can be nonexistent. What happened?

A third grade teacher has thirty-five students in the class; a seventh-grade teacher may have 175 students a day. Meanwhile your junior high–aged child now sees six teachers a day instead of one. Is it any wonder things get less personal? Parents change too; school is no longer a novelty now that little Billy has become Bill. Younger children in the family need more attention. The high school may be clear across town.

Direct contact with teachers is a major way to ensure the best education possible for your child—*all through school*. Not only will you receive vital information on how your child is doing, you can also give important information. You can let the teacher know your expectations and any essential information about your child. It's a two way street and the rewards are worth the effort.

Contacting Teachers

Look what direct contact can do:

1. You meet some of the most important adult influences in your child's life. Teachers serve as role models. In fact, they may spend more hours a day with your child than you do! It's important to see who they are.

2. You see where your child spends most of his day. A visit will give you a feel for the school and what it's like for your child.

3. You can ask direct questions and get direct answers. There's no need to rely on gossip or to "take someone's word for it."

4. You can let the teacher know clearly what you expect of your child. This shows the teacher that you care. Parents who make an effort to stay in touch with their child's teacher get more effort from those teachers.

Open House

The usual contact most parents have with their child's school is through "Open House" or "Back to School Nights." Most schools hold these once or twice a year to give parents an opportunity to see the school and meet the child's teacher and other school officials. Often children prepare special room decorations or folders containing examples of their work for Open House.

These functions are great for getting general information about your child's classes and teachers each year. At the elementary level, this is often the time to sign up for an individual conference at a later date.

Since scheduled conferences are less prevalent at the junior high and high school levels, Open House and Back to School Nights take on a special importance. Despite this fact, such functions in the higher grades are notoriously ignored by parents. Compare the number of parents in any first grade classroom with those found in a high school English class: the evidence speaks for itself. In many classes only three parents will show up. But those parents stand out. If only two parents go to Mr. Yamato's eleventh grade U.S. History class, be sure you're one of those two. Your child will be the winner.

Back to School Nights and Open House are important—for the teacher, for the parents, and for the child. It may be the last thing you want to do after a full day's work, but it's only once or twice a year. Teachers notice which parents attend these functions and which do not. It's obvious: *The parents who come care.*

Parent-Teacher Conferences

Open House and Back to School Night can give you the big picture, but you need a personal conference to get a close-up of your child. The parent-teacher conference is your #1 link with the schools and its importance cannot be stressed enough.

In elementary school. To lay a solid foundation—kindergarten through sixth grade—it is necessary to bring parents and teachers together once or twice a year. This *begins a pattern* of parent involvement in the school. You may be hesitant at first, or worried about the loss of time from work. But the earlier you begin this pattern the better. Remember, involvement is essential—try not to let any excuses keep you away from these conferences.

More and more school districts are requiring parent conferences and setting them up on special "conference days." The teacher is in charge of scheduling and tries to make allowances for working parents. Still, it may be necessary to take off work for an hour. Remember, it's only once or twice a year. If an employer gives you trouble, you might suggest the old "ounce of prevention"—time spent at a conference may mean less time off the job later if trouble should occur.

If your child's elementary school does not have regularly scheduled conferences, *you will have to set up your own* during the school year. A good time for the first one would probably be in late October. This allows the teacher enough time to get to know your child and his abilities. A second conference, if possible, can be scheduled toward the end of the year, perhaps in April.

In junior high and high school. When your child reaches junior high and high school, there will probably be no more arranged conferences. The reasons for this are obvious. If your child has six classes, that would be three hours of conferences for you. For a teacher with as many as 200 kids, the meetings would never end!

Some junior highs and high schools in the nation have a conference system where *one* teacher (perhaps the child's homeroom teacher) meets with the parents and discusses *all* the child's classes with them. However, in most upper grade schools, you will have to be selective about whom you see and how often.

How to Prepare for a Parent-Teacher Conference

Imagine a photograph of your child cut in half. Give one side to the teacher, which will represent the school half. Give the other side to the parent, which will stand for the home half. It is only when you put these two sections together that you have the total picture. Ideally, this is what happens in a parent-teacher conference: you each provide the "half" the other needs.

Since conference time is limited, it is important to decide ahead of time what to include in your half. Furthermore, parent conferences are extra work for the teacher. They may extend beyond the regular school day, with no extra pay. Most teachers put time into parent conferences—you need to put the same time into preparing for it.

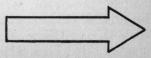

Conference Checklist

You should mention—

1. Any physical or emotional problem your child has (or has had) that could affect school work in any way.

2. Your child's role in the family (youngest, oldest) and the effect other brothers and sisters may have on her.

3. *Any family crisis that may be affecting your child.* These would include a death in the family, serious illness, or a divorce or separation. It may be hard to be up front about such things, but this information can help a teacher in lending important support.

4. Your opinion about your child's reading, math, and writing abilities in order to check it against the teacher's view.

5. YOUR EXPECTATIONS FOR YOUR CHILD IN SCHOOL. Let the teacher know your feelings about your child's education. Be as specific as possible ("We do not want Dan turning in sloppy work," or "We do not want him reading comics during the free reading period").

If you have been staying on top of things you will probably know much about your child's classroom before any direct contact with the teacher. You should already be aware of:

- Subjects covered during the school day
- Approximate daily schedule
- Books being used
- Homework assigned
- Kind of work done in class (work sheets, tests)
- Level of the class (high, average, low, mixed)

You should ask—

___ Your child's strongest subject area.

___ Your child's weakest area, the cause of her problems, and what can be done about it.

___ Your child's grade level in reading and in math, how he stacks up with the rest of the class, and how this matches your own view of his ability.

___ Any discipline problems your child is having, any social adjustment difficulties, or any attendance problems.

___ What the teacher's homework policy is, how often you can expect homework, and how it will be graded.

___ What you can do at home to help your child at school. (Try to seek specifics: flash cards, reading aloud, etc.)

___ The teachers and/or classes your child should take the following year, if you want this information.

___ If the teacher clearly understands your goals for your child.

___ If there are any materials you should have (school handbooks, etc.).

TAKE THIS CHECKLIST WITH YOU TO YOUR NEXT CONFERENCE.

Setting Up Your Own Contact

Although the regular once or twice a year conferences may be adequate, there may be additional times you need to contact your child's teacher. There is a time in most children's lives when, for whatever reason, things may start slipping at school. Even the best students may hit a bump somewhere along that twelve-year roller coaster ride. (Some of these problems are discussed in a later chapter, Working Through the Rough Spots.) It's times like these when you may have to initiate a contact *other* than a scheduled conference. Don't be afraid of being a pest. The teacher may need your help too.

Contact the teacher if—

1. A grade in a specific subject area suddenly takes a dramatic plunge.
2. Your child's attitude toward school changes for the worse.
3. Your child never seems to have any homework in subjects that should have some.
4. Your child has received a grade much lower than he feels he deserved.
5. Your child is having trouble getting along with the teacher or with students in the class.
6. Your child has been kicked out of a class. (This would usually occur only at the junior high or high school level.)
7. You do not feel you are getting the true story from your child about a class or grade.
8. A personal or family problem has developed that you feel the teacher should be aware of.
9. You have a major disagreement or dissatisfaction with something the teacher said in class or with curriculum content.
10. You will be removing your child from school for a period of time long enough so that his grade might be affected.

Ways to Contact the Teacher

To see the teacher in person—

1. Contact the teacher by calling the school and leaving a message or sending a note with your child.
2. Set up a time to go to the school (it will almost always be before or after school). You will have to work around the teacher's schedule.
3. *Let the teacher know* ahead of time what it is you are concerned about.
4. Be sure the problem could not be handled with a phone call or a note.

To call the teacher by phone—

1. Call the school and leave a message for the teacher to call you back.
2. Include the following in your message:
a. the reason you wish to talk to the teacher
b. where you can be reached and when (include both work and home phone numbers).

To write the teacher a note—

This method has been pretty much ignored as an effective way to communicate with a teacher. But we believe it to be very effective. Perhaps a teacher "testimonial" will sell you on the idea.

I teach English at a large suburban high school. This year I sent a letter home to parents describing the course and my expectations. The parents were asked to sign the letter and make a comment if they wished. Hundreds of signed letters came back, but *only one parent* bothered to write anything else. She asked me to pay special attention to her son's spelling because she and his father were concerned about it. I was so impressed by this one comment that I did spend extra time with the boy and even sent spelling lists home to the parents.

So you see, a few scribbled words brought a whole year of extra attention for one fortunate student. Teachers feel that any parent would jump at the chance to fill in a comment section—but most don't, because parents do not realize how meaningful their special interest *is* to a teacher.

Once you get into the note habit, it will be easier to do. You may even get a real dialogue going with the teacher over the course of a school year. One teacher reported to us that she began to look *forward* to notes from her parents.

Here are some sample notes that will give you the general idea. You can take off from here!

• "We were disappointed to see Greg's score on the fractions mastery test. Is there any extra work you could send home that might help?"

• "Sharon does not know how to do her bibliography. Could you explain to her once again how you want it done?"

• "We do not like to see Manuel turning in sloppy work like this. Please make him re-do such papers in the future."

• "We're going to be back East for two weeks visiting Kathy's grandparents. What work can we have her do during this time?"

• "I can't tell you how pleased Mark's mother and I were to see a paper with perfect spelling. Your work with him has really paid off. Thanks!"

It is hard to overstate the effect a comment like the last one would have on a teacher. Most teachers go the entire year *without one word of praise* from anyone, neither the boss nor their "clients." If parents started letting teachers know what they're doing *right*—and there's plenty — there's no telling what it would do for teaching!

A final thought: Don't assume that the school will necessarily contact you if your child is having a problem. The if-anything's-wrong-we'll-hear attitude doesn't always work. You need to keep a hot line going with your child's school every year. Even if things seem fine, *stay in touch. Don't ever think you can let things go for a while.* Direct contact is *essential*—from kindergarten through the twelfth grade.

Checking the 3 R's

Checking the 3 R's

It is very important for you to check your child's ability in reading, writing, and arithmetic yourself. Though the school will usually keep you accurately informed of your child's skills, this is not always the case.

Take a look at the case of Steve, a fifth grader. Each of his report cards in the fourth and fifth grade had been the same: C, "at grade level," "satisfactory." By the end of the fifth grade, however, Steve's mother was convinced that things were far from "satisfactory." Steve balked at homework, refused ever to read aloud, often felt "sick" in the morning, and expressed an increasing dislike of school. Still, Steve's report cards had not indicated a problem. Frustrated, Steve's mother decided to act on her own. She had Steve tested by a friend skilled in the use of reading tests. Her worst suspicions were confirmed: Steve was reading two years below grade level. As a fifth grader, he read only as well as the average third grader.

When you have put your trust in your child's school, this kind of information comes as a great shock. How can it happen? The reasons are as varied as teachers and schools.

What Can Go Wrong?

• The child who is *not* a behavior problem is often ignored and gets lost in the shuffle. (Steve, for example, was quiet and never asked questions.)

• The child is not performing at a level *low enough* to get special attention. (Linda reads one year below grade level, but there are eight kids in the class reading two to three years below. By comparison, Linda is not doing too badly.)

• The child who is very bright in one area may be allowed to coast in other subjects. (Kirk is a gifted artist who works on the mural during the silent reading period.)

• The child may have been placed with an incompetent or burned-out teacher. (Mr. Reynolds, a twenty-year veteran near retirement, does not put the energy into the job he once did.)

• The child has been able to "con" the teacher about her ability. (Mary Lou answers questions about stories by looking at the pictures and asking her friends for help.)

• The teacher may have lower expectations of the child because he is different in some way: handicapped, an ethnic minority, or a student just beginning to speak English. (The teacher is reluctant to correct Keith—the only black student in the class—because she does not want to direct attention to him, the unfortunate result being that Keith does not get the same amount of help and constructive criticism as the other students.)

• The teacher may have as many as forty children in class. Without assistance, it is extremely difficult to know each child's true abilities and potential.

REMEMBER

Even well-meaning educators can make mistakes. If parents are on top of things and do their "homework," they will catch a major problem. *You cannot expect the school to do the job alone.* The more people involved in your child's education, the better—it's that simple.

In the next three chapters we will provide you with the information you need to check your child's progress in the basic skills. Look for this information and use it.

CHAPTER 3

I like books. I was born and bred among them,
and have the easy feeling when I get in their presence, that a stable-boy has among horses.

—*Oliver Wendell Holmes*

The Reading Chapter

The most important skill taught in formal education is reading. It is required in 80–90 percent of all school course work. The child who does not read well not only struggles through school, but many times carries a stigma that may lead to complicated emotional problems. And yet, approximately 20–30 percent of the students in the average school population cannot read well.

The subject of reading problems is one of the most controversial and complex topics in education today. We are not going to enter the debate on whether the schools are doing their jobs in teaching reading, or whether national reading scores have gone up or down. Learning to read is an incredible undertaking. The ability to read well is a magnificent accomplishment. Learning to read is so complex that specialists have cited over 200 reasons why the process might break down.

As a parent, you want to take the gamble out of your child's education. It wouldn't matter if 95 percent of all children learned to read well. What parents would want *their* child to be the *other* 5 percent? *You want your child to reach his full reading potential. That's what this chapter is all about.*

STARTING OFF RIGHT

When Should a Child Begin Reading?

There are a few children who can comfortably start learning to read at five years old or younger. More children are ready to begin the reading process as they develop through their sixth year. By the age of six-and-a-half to seven, most children have acquired the skills that will enable them to read. Because of faster rates of development, girls are usually ready to begin reading sooner than boys.

You can do many things for your child that will help her get ready for reading. However, the actual ability to read depends on a kind of inner time clock. This inner time clock determines the neurological, mental, and emotional growth of your child. Just as you would not expect a two-year-old to follow a series of commands such as "Take your glass to the sink, then go get me your sweater, and then bring me Teddy Bear," you cannot expect most five-year-olds to be able to make words and thoughts out of letters. Just as the time comes when a child is able to follow a sequence of instructions, the time will come when your child will be ready to begin reading.

Readiness to read is *not* an intelligence test. A child's readiness can depend as much on his personality as it does on his mental and neurological growth. Highly energetic and very social children sometimes get off to a slow start. Children who are impatient and who set very high standards for themselves may also find early frustration and problems. Children who have not grown up around books, and are not excitedly awaiting the chance to unlock this source of pleasure for themselves, may also find it hard to get involved in the work needed to learn to read.

There is nothing to gain by *pressing a* child into reading before he is ready. There is a great deal to lose, however, from the feelings of frustration and failure that can be brought on by such attempts. Some countries avoid early reading problems in youngsters by simply waiting until children are past seven years old before starting them off in reading. In the United States, reading-readiness programs start in kindergarten with perhaps some elementary reading skills also being taught that year. However, regular reading programs generally begin in first grade when most children are between six and seven years old.

Whether some children should be taught to read before first grade has been the topic of debate in educational circles for the last twenty years. It used to be considered poor practice to teach reading skills to even desirous children before the first grade. The fear was that since the child was not "really ready" before the first grade, he would acquire bad reading habits during these early years that would later have to be undone.

Many educators are now shifting to the idea that children who show an active eagerness to learn reading before first grade will benefit if parents and kindergarten teachers respond by teaching some of the fundamentals of reading, such as the alphabet and memorizing certain words by sight.

Many parents find their children acquiring some of these reading skills — even phonics — just by continual exposure to the P.B.S. shows *Sesame Street* and *Electric Company.*

Our bottom line of advice is this: if your child asks you to teach some reading skills ("Mommy, what's that word?" or "Daddy, write my name!"), go ahead and help. If your child's interest is there, feel free to encourage it and be of assistance—however, don't push! If your child becomes an early reader, make sure it is because he wants to, not because you want him to. *Remember: the key to reading success is not an early start, but a successful start.*

In general, if your child starts a reading program sometime during the first grade, that will be soon enough. We are not going to tell you how to teach your child to read. If your child is actively trying to become an early reader, the local librarian can show you books that will help you assist your child.

Just because formal reading instruction will probably not start for your child until first grade *does not* mean that you, as a parent, can forget about getting your child ready for reading. You need to take responsibility for helping your child get the best start possible by building a foundation of reading-readiness at home.

Building a Foundation for Reading-Readiness (Ages 3-6)

Have you ever wondered what those kindergarten teachers are up to? What's behind all those little games and activities your child does in the first year of school? The answer in part is *reading-readiness*.

A major responsibility of kindergarten teachers is to build a foundation of skills that will help your child more easily adapt to reading. *The better the foundation, the better the chance of success in reading.* This is where you can play a major role. You can help that kindergarten teacher build a strong reading-readiness foundation for your child. You can do it at home—with love, fun, and without pressure or anxiety.

Reading-Readiness Activities (Ages 3–6)

• If you want your child to enjoy reading, she needs to see *you* enjoying reading. Be excited about reading and share what you read with her.

• Read aloud to your child as much as possible. Children love books and often memorize favorite parts. They soon recognize that the print somehow leads to the story.*

• Ask your child questions about the stories you read to him. Questions like "Why was Momma Cat angry?" work on recall and comprehension. Questions like "*What do you think* would have happened if Pedro found the buried treasure?" work on inferential thinking.

• Show your child that words are everywhere: on cereal boxes, stop signs, grocery stores, etc.

• Teach your child how to listen carefully to the different sounds around her. Teach your child rhymes; this will help her learn phonic sounds and word meanings.

• Ask your children lots of questions. Help them learn to make decisions and answer clearly.

• Play word games with your child that teach him meaning through context by filling in the missing word or phrase in a sentence. For example: "I put ice in my juice and it got _____."
Or "After the little boy fell and hurt his arm, he _____."
This is an important skill for reading comprehension.

• Use complete sentences in speaking to your child. Children who listen to complete sentences will later find it much more natural to read full sentences and thoughts.

• Help your child learn to speak clearly. When it's time to learn phonics, the child who can hear and repeat sounds clearly has a big advantage.

• Help build your child's attention span. Give him projects to work on and see that they are completed. Reading will take concentration.

• Help your child distinguish shapes. Puzzles and other games with different shapes are great for children to play with. The better a child can recognize shapes, the better she will be able to recognize letters and word shapes. As she gets older, help her learn the shapes of the ABC's.

• Help your child learn left-to-right eye movement. Have him follow your finger along as you read; have him look at comic book pictures from left to right; move objects in your hand from the left to the right. Reading is a left-to-right skill.

• Develop your child's fine hand–eye coordination. This will be important for the flip side of reading: writing. Some fun activities that work on this skill are stringing beads, drawing pictures, and tracing.

• Encourage your child to watch *Sesame Street* and other similar learning programs developed for children this age. The repetition of numbers, ABC's, and phonic sounds will give your child a head start in kindergarten.

• Provide lots of books for your child. He can't read yet, but he can look at the pictures and learn that books are fun.

• Most important, help your child feel good about herself; help her feel secure; let her know that she is loved.

---

*There is a strong correlation between children who are frequently read to and children who have good reading and reading comprehension skills. Being read to helps children become accustomed to the special flow of literature.

The Beginning Reader (Grades 1-2)
Learning to Read

A tremendous amount of research and debate has taken place on what is the best method for teaching reading. Most teachers now use a combination of several methods.

Your child should learn to use phonics. Many of the words (or parts of words) we use have phonetic consistency—that is, they can be *sounded out.* Children must learn how to sound out new words. It takes the first three grades of school for a child to learn most of the rules of phonics.

Your child should learn to recognize certain words by sight. This is sometimes called the *look-say* method. Some of the words we use can't be sounded out very easily (words like *school, two, know, could,* etc.). Children need to memorize how these words look. Young children can also learn difficult words like "elephant" and "giraffe" once they are introduced to them because the look and shape of such words makes them easy to remember. Even words that are first learned by sounding out are read by the look-say method once they are mastered. Obviously when we see the word *stop,* we don't sound it out—we just know it means stop.

Your child should learn that the purpose of reading is to help people find out what they want to know. Too often, children concentrate so hard on saying individual words correctly that they forget to make sense out of it all. *Reading without understanding is not reading; it is merely "word calling."* Remind your child that reading must make sense, that what he reads must sound like language and be understood like spoken words.

The most important aspect of the parent's role in the beginning reading years is to be supportive and positive. Some children catch on fast; others seem to muddle through for a while and then blossom. Learning to read will be very exciting for your child. Share in that excitement. With the help of the teacher, librarian, or bookstore salesperson, select some books written at the primer (or beginning) level. Keep these around the home for your child to look over at his pleasure. He'll probably be overjoyed to show off his new reading skills.

DO'S AND DON'T'S FOR HELPING YOUR BEGINNING READER:

DO: Pronounce words for your child that he cannot figure out for himself. Do this in a friendly and positive way. (Give him several seconds to try on his own before saying it for him.)
BECAUSE:
a. It helps your child to learn words by sight;
b. It does not imply criticism because there are obviously tons of words your youngster knows which you don't expect him to; and
c. It keeps the story moving so the activity stays enjoyable.

DON'T: Constantly ask your child to sound words out through phonics.
BECAUSE:
a. It implies that she *should* be able to pronounce the word (and by not doing so, she is failing you);
b. You may be asking her to use a phonics skill that she has *not* been taught to use by her teacher; and
c. It slows down the story and takes the fun and pride out of reading.

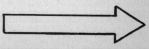

DO: Continue to sit down with your child and read to him for enjoyment. Just because he's learning how to read now doesn't mean you should stop reading to him.

BECAUSE: Children who learn the joy of books want to learn how to read them for themselves.

DO: Encourage your child to read to you. If possible, have her bring home the book she's learning from at school. (In the beginning she will probably be able to read only a few words, but later on she may attempt an entire little story.)

BECAUSE: Children are proud of their new reading skills. The more they show them off, the faster they learn.

DON'T: Pressure your child into reading for you.

BECAUSE: Reading needs to be a pleasurable experience. If all your encouragement and support does not result in your child wanting to read for you, contact his teacher and find out if he's experiencing frustration in the school reading program.

Following Your Child's Progress in Reading (Grades 1–2)

Unless otherwise advised by your child's teacher, we suggest that during the first two grades of reading you concentrate on building your child's sight vocabulary and leave the teaching of phonics to the school.

Obviously personalities are as varied as children. You may have a child who thrives on home instruction and encourages you to teach him more and more. If this is the case, then you must be the judge on how far to go in your teaching of reading skills. On the other hand, some children need to be pressed a little. They may do much better with stated high expectations than they will with subtle encouragement.

Throughout this entire process, there is one very important piece of information to keep in mind. A large number of disabled readers have some sort of emotional problem involved in the reading disability. Overzealous parents, pushing their children too hard to succeed too early, are responsible for some of these problems.

You will become aware of the general progress your child is making in reading by listening to him read and by talking with his teachers. Each child's rate of growth is slightly different from the next. You must also be aware that there are a number of methods or programs used to teach children basic reading skills. Children learning to read by different programs acquire different skills at different times. (Most reading programs include "phonics instruction." If it appears that your child is not learning any phonetic decoding skills at school, find out why.) Because there are various ways by which your child may learn basic reading skills, we cannot give you a cut-and-dried formula for determining how well your first or second grader is learning to read.

If you feel, for any reason, that your child is not making adequate progress or reading as well as he should be, go see the teacher. Ask the teacher for his evaluation, specifically how he has arrived at this opinion and how you can tell for yourself. Your child's teacher should be able to explain the basics of the reading system he uses. He should also be able to give you some ways to monitor your child's progress at home.

Checking Your
Child's Reading Ability

In our section "Staying on Top of the Three R's," we detailed some ways your child might get lost in the school shuffle and have his problems overlooked. It can happen! And while you might be able to tell if your child is having major reading problems, it is much harder to be sure if your child is struggling with the more normal types of reading difficulties. It is very difficult for parents to judge how well a third grader should read as opposed to a second grader or fourth grader.

Certainly there is an accepted range of abilities within each grade level, and parents must never forget this. But if your child is developing reading problems, you need to be aware of them early on. If your child is already into the upper elementary grades or beyond, and if reading difficulties exist, you must become aware of them *now*! You need to ask teachers and perhaps reading specialists for extra help. To do this, however, you must first become aware that there may be a problem.

Reading is not something you take chances with! The best way to eliminate the chance that undetected problems are developing is to verify for yourself how well your child reads. To this end we've provided a set of readings that, when used properly, can indicate the general reading ability level of your child.

How Well Can Parents
Assess Reading Ability?

Can parents, with no special background in reading, administer a reading test and come up with a reasonable measure of their child's ability? We asked a number of reading specialists this same question and they said yes . . . *with some qualifications.*

Before we go further, let's clarify exactly what our home reading assessment can tell you. What we're talking about here should actually be called a *screening device*. Teachers use this term to describe a "test" that provides only the most general information.

One reading specialist put it this way: "Sure there are problems with parents assuming they are experts. Testing reading ability and reading problems is very difficult. However, it would be useful if parents could spot some obvious reading problems. Then they can bring their child to us for a closer look."

If your child had a fever and a sore throat for three days, you wouldn't take him to a doctor and declare, "My child has a strep infection! What are you going to do about it?" The point is you knew enough to take him to a doctor in the first place. That's just what this reading assessment is for. It can tell you if you need to see a professional. It can also give you confidence that all is well with your child's reading.

When Should You Use This Reading Assessment?

WE SUGGEST: Beginning in the third grade, check your child's reading ability a few months into each school year. Check your child's progress once again a couple of months before the year ends. The reading selections are actually written for children in the middle of each grade level.

AN IMPORTANT WORD OF CAUTION:

Wait until your child is in the third grade before using this reading assessment with him. During the first and second grades, children are acquiring different skills at different rates. This is normal. It is not until the third grade that you can expect your child to have learned enough of the basic skills to allow you to assess his ability. Even for teachers, testing first and second graders is very difficult, because children of this age seem to learn in "growth spurts." *The reading assessment we provide is not valid for checking children in the first and second grades.* By "testing" too early, you may become overly concerned about your child's ability when there is really no problem present.

The Reading Selections and Assessment Process

For each grade level, from first through eighth, we have provided two readings. (The first and second grade selections are included only for use with children in the third grade and above who might be reading below grade level.)

Each selection has been written and evaluated for the appropriate grade level by using the same "readability formulas" currently used in preparing the basic reading textbooks used in schools today. The selections have also been "field tested" with numerous children known to be reading "at grade level" to determine approximately how well a child reading "at grade level" should do on each selection.

These selections can be found on pages 66–81. The selections are coded with letters instead of grade level numbers to help ease any tensions your child may develop from reading material that is labeled below the grade level he is in.

The selections are coded to grade level in the following way:

Selections A and B—grade 1
Selections C and D—grade 2
Selections E and F—grade 3
Selections G and H—grade 4
Selections I and J—grade 5
Selections K and L—grade 6
Selections M and N—grade 7
Selections O and P—grade 8

Make photocopies of the selections you may be using. As your child reads each selection aloud, you will be recording the number of errors he makes. Your child will be reading from this book. You need to be following along and recording his mistakes on a separate photocopy of the reading that you have made beforehand.

LISTEN FOR THESE READING ERRORS

When anyone reads aloud, he is bound to make mistakes. The purpose of this reading assessment is only to give you an estimate of how well your child reads. This assessment process is not part of our reading instruction program. Therefore, when doing this assessment we ask you to pay attention to only three major kinds of reading errors. Later, after you find out how well your child reads, we will describe how you can help him improve his reading with our "Home Reading Program," pages 86–97.

The chart below lists the three types of errors you are to listen for during this assessment process. When your child reads aloud, quietly record his mistakes by circling or checking your photocopy at the spot where the error occurs.

Error	Example
Mispronunciation	*Actual reading:* The little boy's heart . . .
	Child says: The little boy's hurt . . .
	or substituting words of similar meaning
	Actual reading: There were a hundred men . . .
	Child says: There were a thousand men . . .
"Nonpronunciation"	*Actual reading:* The scientist made an analysis . . .
	Child says: The scientist made an . . . (after four or five seconds the child still doesn't pronounce the word)
	or
or Omission	Actual reading: There were a dozen birds . . .
	Child says: There were birds . . .
Repetition (of two or more words)	*Actual reading:* The cat sprang on the mouse . . .
	Child says: The cat . . . the cat sprang on the mouse . . .

THE "PASSING" NUMBER

After your child finishes reading a selection, total the number of mistakes you have checked on your photocopy. Count only errors of the type described above.

At the bottom of each reading selection you will find a circled number. This is the "passing number" for that reading selection. If a child makes more than this number of errors, it probably means that the reading selection was frustrating for him. If he had to read a book that difficult by himself, he probably would not enjoy it or understand it. If a child makes fewer or the same number of mistakes as this passing number, it means that he has "passed" that particular reading.

61

SETTING THE PROPER MOOD

• *Be sure your child is in a good mood before testing.* No one performs really well when he is sulky or out-of-sorts.

• *Be straightforward with your child.* By the time most children are in the fourth grade, they know a reading test when they see one. Tell your child that you want to listen to her read so you can see how she's doing. To take the pressure off, tell her she can show you how she's doing any time she wants. In no way should this be a "go for broke" situation for your child.

• *Don't force your child to sit down and read for you.* If Mary Jane refuses to read aloud, you've *already* got some kind of problem on your hands.

• *Try to eliminate as many outside distractions as possible.* This should not be done during normal play or TV time. There should not be friends or siblings hanging around. Radios should be off, lighting should be good, and both of you should be comfortably seated.

• *Give your child a hug and say something nice to him* (even if he's an ungainly junior high schooler trying to be as independent as possible!).

• *If your child's uneasiness, for whatever reason, interferes with reading aloud, then relax and try it again some other time.*

TESTING INSTRUCTIONS

1. *Start assessing your child with the reading selections that are two grade levels below the grade he is currently in.*

It is important that your child does well on the first selections that he reads to you. By starting at these lower level readings, you will let your child begin this assessment process with confidence. (If you have assessed your child before, start at a point where he last passed both selections for a particular grade level.)

2. *Ask your child to read each selection silently before he reads it aloud to you.*

Children usually read better silently than they do aloud. Having your child read the selection silently builds his confidence and helps to eliminate his nervousness. Children who are nervous oral readers may unnecessarily alarm parents.

3. *Tell your child to read at a relaxed pace.*

Remind your child that you don't expect him to know every word; you just want him to do the best he can.

4. *Read the caption of the selection aloud to your child before asking him to read the selection silently and aloud.*

For example, say to your child, "Jimmy, I want you to read this 'to find out how Mary and Dad get ready for their fishing trip.'" By doing this, you have set the stage for meaningful reading.

5. *If your child gets stuck on a word, give him four or five seconds to figure it out and then say it for him.*

Be sure to record this as an error.

6. *If your child mispronounces a word and then corrects himself, do not count this as an error.*

If he mispronounces a word and does not correct himself, count this as an error and let your child continue reading without your correction or interruption.

7. *Progress through both reading selections for each grade level until your child is unable to pass either selection at a particular level.*

If your child does not pass either selection from the original grade level you started with, drop back two more levels and start again. (Example: If you have been working at the fourth grade level, go to the second grade selections.)

8. *After your child reaches a point where he cannot pass either selection at a particular grade level, stop your assessment.*

Compliment your child for his cooperation, effort, and ability. Let him know that you are proud he is your child. You are now at the point where you can begin to interpret your results.

A SPECIAL NOTE: If your child gets too tired or agitated from reading aloud, stop your assessment, and continue it later. This assessment does require a fair amount of reading, and some children may do better if the assessment is done in two sessions rather than all at once.

CHECKING FOR READING COMPREHENSION

You have just screened your child for an estimate of his reading ability. This process is for "assessment" purposes only, so we have tried to keep the procedures as simple as possible. Therefore, we had you concentrate only on some key aspects of your child's oral reading skills.

Obviously, however, it is very important that your child not only read well but that he can also understand what he reads. This is called reading comprehension. Usually in the elementary grades a child's comprehension level is at or above his oral reading level. That is what this assessment and the placement chart on the following page assume.

You should be aware, however, that this is not always the case. Some children may be able to read orally at or above their grade level but are not able to really understand the material. This may be particularly true for students who speak English as their second language. (If you can read this book,

you can certainly read Swahili on the fourth- or fifth-grade level. Unfortunately this will not indicate anything about your comprehension of the material.)

For a rough check of your child's comprehension ability, you may want to ask him a few questions about each selection. The type of questions you should ask should check both understanding of general ideas and ability to pick up details. Ask a variety of questions, then, such as (a) What would be a good title for this story? (b) What did the little girl forget on the table? or (c) After the father chopped the wood, what did he do next?

If you become concerned about your child's comprehension ability, consult with his teacher for a more in-depth look. In our section entitled "The Home Reading Program," we also discuss methods of increasing your child's ability to understand what he reads.

INTERPRETING THE RESULTS

Remember, you are just looking for a general estimate of your child's ability. This assessment cannot provide an exact measure of your child's reading skills. In fact, many reading specialists even question using "grade level" as a measure of reading ability. However, because "grade level" designations are the kind most commonly used in school and are probably the easiest measure for parents to understand, we have presented you with a "grade level" placement chart. You can use this chart to help interpret the results from your reading assessment.

Please remember that most children will not fit neatly into one grade level or another. And once again, *this assessment is not meant to make you experts in reading diagnosis, but to give you some essential information with which to approach the schools.*

Checking Your Child's Reading Ability

Difficulty of Reading	3 Years Below	2 Years Below	1 Year Below	School Grade Level	1 Year Above	2 Years Above	3 Years Above	Placement
SUCCESS ON READING BOTH SELECTIONS PER GRADE LEVEL — PASS = X FAIL = □	—	X X	X X	X X	□ □	—	—	AROUND GRADE LEVEL
	—	X X	X X	X □	X □	□ □	—	AROUND GRADE LEVEL
	—	X X	X X	X X	X □	□ □	—	A LITTLE ABOVE GRADE LEVEL
	—	X X	X X	X X	X □	X □	□ □	ABOVE GRADE LEVEL
	—	X X	X □	X □	□ □	—	—	A LITTLE BELOW GRADE LEVEL
	X X	X □	X □	□ □	—	—	—	BELOW GRADE LEVEL

The Reading Selections

Read to find out how Lisa learns to swim.

Lisa wanted to learn how to swim.
Her mother took her to a nearby pool.

At first Lisa just splashed and played. Next
she tried to float. Then her mother said,
"Try to swim now."

Lisa put her face in the water. Then she
began to kick her feet and move her arms.
"Did you see me?" she cried. "I was moving."

"Good," said her mother. "You are getting better."

Lisa kept trying to swim. "This is fun,"
she thought. "Soon I will be able to swim."

4

B

Read to find out about Jeff's trip to the store.

Jeff was reading a book.
His father came into the room.

"I have to go to the store," said Dad.
"Can I go with you?" asked Jeff.
"Sure," answered Dad. "Let's go."

Dad and Jeff drove to the store.
Jeff looked at the toy shelf while
Dad did the shopping.

Soon, Jeff's father was done shopping.
"Time to go, ' he said.

Jeff looked at his father. "Dad, can I
please get this red truck?" he asked.

"Yes," said Dad. "That truck looks like
lots of fun."

 "Thanks Dad!" cried Jeff. "I can't wait to
get home and see how fast it goes."

Read to find out how Jennie gets a book.

Jennie walked down the street. Suddenly she saw a big sign that said, BOOKS FOR SALE. "Oh good," said Jennie and she rushed into the book store.

"Hi," said Jennie.

"Hello," said a cheerful man. "May I help you?"

"Do you have a book about horses?" asked Jennie.

The man showed Jennie several books about horses. All of them looked interesting. "How much is this book?" asked Jennie.

"It costs four dollars," answered the man.

"Oh," said Jennie, sadly. "I only have two dollars."

"Well, I have a wonderful idea," said the man. "If you come back tomorrow, I will give you a chore to do and you can earn enough money to pay for the book. You will even have some money left over for yourself," he said.

"That's a neat idea!" cried Jennie. "I can't wait to tell my mother how I'm going to earn my new book."

6

D

Read to find out about Matt's visit to the hospital.

One day, Matt went with Mother to visit his grandfather in the hospital. It was a long drive in the car. When they got there, Matt was amazed to see how big the hospital was. It had ten floors and rose way up into the sky.

Matt and Mother walked inside and then went up the elevator. At last they got to the right room. Grandpa was sitting up in bed. He smiled when he saw them.

While Mother talked to Grandfather, Matt had to be very quiet. Then Grandpa showed Matt how to make the bed move up and down. All you had to do was press a button!

Soon it was time to leave. Matt and Mother kissed Grandfather good-bye. On the way home, Matt thought about the hospital. He enjoyed his visit, but he would be glad when Grandpa was back home.

6

Read to find out about kite flying.

Some days are perfect for flying a kite. The sky is blue with big white clouds and a gentle breeze blows through the trees.

All over the world, people fly different kinds of kites. You can probably find several types of kites at a nearby store. You can also make your own special kite out of newspaper, string and some thin sticks.

When you fly a kite, remember to follow some simple safety rules. First, fly your kite in a safe place. Never fly a kite in the street. If your kite gets tangled in a high tree or an electrical wire, ask for help. Remember to fly your kite in good weather, not in the rain.

Kite flying is the most fun when it is done safely. So, go fly a kite.

5

F

Read to find out what science books can tell you.

Why is the sky blue, and what makes the moon glow at night? Where does snow come from, and why does the wind blow? How far away are the planets and stars in outer space?

There are so many things we want to know. You may have some special questions of your own. Where can you find the answers?

You might start by looking in a science book. Ask your teacher where you can find a good science book that will answer some of your questions. The library should have many interesting science books.

Continue asking questions and perhaps some day you will be a scientist yourself. Maybe you will discover the answer to a very important question!

5

Read to find out what happened to Charlie's cat.

Charlie frowned at his vegetable soup. "Try not to be so upset, Charlie," said Mother. "You haven't touched a bite of your supper." But Charlie didn't even hear his mother because his mind was far away, thinking about his little cat, Whiskers.

Yesterday, Whiskers went outside after breakfast and no one had seen her since. It was like she just disappeared. Sometimes Whiskers would roam around all day, but she was usually back before dark. But Whiskers didn't come home and now another day had gone by without a trace of the little cat.

Charlie began to cry. "Whiskers is gone forever," he moaned. "I'm certain I'll never see her again."

"Try not to be so gloomy," Mother comforted, "because cats have a way of appearing when you least expect them."

Just then, there was a scratching on the screen door. "Whiskers!" screamed Charlie, and he raced to the door to find his little cat.

7

Read to find out how Mary and Dad get ready for their fishing trip.

The alarm clock rang before the sun came up. Slowly, Dad climbed out of bed and stumbled over to Mary's room. "Wake up, Mary," he said. "It's time to go fishing."

Mary rubbed her eyes, got out of bed, and with one big yawn and stretch was wide awake. She loved going fishing with Dad on early summer mornings.

Quickly, Mary got dressed and went into the kitchen to make breakfast. Dad and Mary had their jobs memorized. Dad would get the fishing equipment ready and pack the car while Mary fixed eggs and toast. Dad always had some coffee and Mary always fixed herself a cup of hot chocolate.

Only a half an hour after the alarm clock went off, Mary and Dad were out the door. The sky was beginning to show the first light of dawn as Dad backed the car out of the driveway and headed toward the mountain road. Mary smiled as they left town and drove up into the foothills. She could already feel the fish tugging on her line.

7

Read to find out about Sam and the talent show.

Sam saw the notice on the school bulletin board about the talent show and decided he would enter. Since he could now play a number of songs on his trumpet, it would be fun to perform.

Every day after school, Sam and the other students had to practice for the show. At first everyone made mistakes, but gradually they improved. Other children, who were not in the show, sold tickets and decorated the auditorium.

Finally the night of the show arrived and Sam was very nervous. Many children did their acts before it was Sam's turn. There were three singers, a piano player, and a boy who did magic tricks.

When Sam's turn came, he played a song called "Star Dust." When it was over, everyone cheered loudly. The lights were so bright that Sam could not see the audience, but he could sure hear them! He smiled and bowed as the clapping continued. All that work had sure been worth it.

6

Read to find out about overnight trips on railroad cars.

If you had been a train passenger on the world's first sleeping car in the 1830s, you might have found that an overnight trip was anything but comfortable. The first sleeping car was just a small wood railroad coach. It was heated by a stove and lighted by candles. The berths where people slept were very narrow shelves of wood lining the walls of the car.

People traveling by train today find that an overnight trip can be almost as pleasant as sleeping at home. Many different kinds of sleeping arrangements are available. You can choose from large shared rooms to private ones. There are also rooms just for families.

Just because sleeping cars are now so comfortable doesn't mean everyone sleeps while on the train. Some travelers would rather spend their time looking out the window, watching the world go by.

Read to find out about a city that floats.

If you can imagine a city floating on the ocean, then you know what an aircraft carrier resembles. These huge ships go on long journeys around the world and act as floating airports for the world's most modern airplanes.

It is very tricky landing a jet airplane on one of these ships. The problem is that the plane needs help coming to a quick stop. When a pilot comes in for a landing, a strong metal hook comes down from underneath the plane. This hook then catches on a cable stretched across the deck of the ship, which brings the plane in safely. The giant deck can park about 80 airplanes at one time.

Since these ships are often at sea for a long time, and because they have as many as 5,000 crew members, they must be self-sufficient. There are stores, a laundry, radio station, post office, and hospital on board. Ladders connect the many decks, and each deck is divided into different sections.

A special language is used on board ship. The left side is called "port," the right side is called "starboard," and the walls are "bulkheads."

If you ever have a chance to visit one of these large ships, you will find it a fascinating experience.

8

L

Read to find out about a backpacking adventure.

Neil Kaufman and his dad were going on a backpacking trip in the wilderness for three days. Since they would carry in all the supplies they needed in packs strapped to their backs, such an adventure required a lot of planning.

First they spread everything they needed for the trip out on the living room rug. Next, each item had to be fitted into the backpacks. Mr. Kaufman took the heaviest articles, like the tent, the ax, and the camp stove, while Neil had the cooking utensils and most of the food. Each pack also contained a fishing rod and a tin cup especially designed for camping.

Finally, the packs were ready and Neil couldn't wait to try his on. At first the pack felt awkward and heavy, but Neil figured he would get used to it after several hours on the trail.

At last everything was ready. Mr. Kaufman placed the packs carefully in the rear of the station wagon and then he and Neil got in the automobile. "Okay, mountains, here we come!" shouted Neil. His dad grinned at him and started the engine.

7

Read to find out what's happening at summer camp.

Judging from the number of advertisements in magazines, more and more young people are heading for summer camp each year. Many of today's campers, however, are going to camps that are much different from those their parents attended. If you are planning to go to camp this year, you have many kinds of camping experiences to consider.

Camp directories list wilderness camps, backpacking camps and every kind of sports camp from basketball to karate. There are camps where you can lose weight or build muscle. At other camps you can learn rodeo or scuba diving skills.

There are also camps that are like super fun summer schools. Some camps can improve your reading or math skills. You can find a camp that offers advanced science courses with lots of experiments. Then again, you might be interested in one where campers learn how to work computers.

While most summer camps are located in beautiful outdoor settings, the fun at camp is no longer just campfires, blue skies and new friends, although you'll find those too. It shouldn't be too hard to pick a camp that just suits you and offers almost anything you would like to do. Summer camps like these cost money, but some also offer scholarships. So don't sit around this summer—try camp!

9

N

Read to find out about something you take to school every day.

It seems that everybody has a pencil, or has just lost or misplaced one. In the United States alone, billions of lead pencils are made and used each year. But as widely used as these writing tools are, very few people know how pencils are made. In fact, when is the last time you ever thought about what a marvelous invention the lead pencil is?

Interestingly enough, lead pencils contain no lead at all. What is referred to as "lead" is actually a thin stick of material composed of graphite mixed with clay. This mixture can be varied to make a very soft or hard substance. Soft lead pencils make wide, heavy-looking lines, while hard pencil lead results in sharp, thin lines.

To prepare pencil lead, clay, powdered graphite and water are combined to make a dough-like substance. This mixture is then pushed through tiny holes in a metal plate, and out come thin ribbons of lead that are then cut into pieces. The leads are placed into narrow slabs of wood, topped then with another piece of wood to complete the pencil. Next comes a coat of paint or varnish, and the addition of the all-important eraser. Now the pencil is ready to help you write a note, compose a poem or take a test.

9

Read to find out about a famous race.

In 490 B.C., a Greek soldier ran over twenty miles to announce to his city that they had been victorious at the Battle of Marathon. The legend says that after gasping out the good news, the soldier supposedly dropped dead from exhaustion.

Today, people throughout the world compete in races equal to the distance that the Greek soldier ran over two thousand years ago. Named after the famous battle, these races of exactly 26 miles, 385 yards, are called marathons. The marathon is one of the longest running races in the world today.

It may seem incredible, but some people can complete this race in less than two and one half hours, although most people take considerably longer. Because this race is so demanding, some competitors never finish it at all.

Preparing for such a long distance race takes a tremendous amount of practice. Anyone who even hopes to finish this race in less than four hours must train by running ten or more miles a day, month after month. It is only after this lengthy preparation that a runner is ready to enter serious competition.

Each year, the men and women who participate in this race get swifter and their speed reaches new heights. Someday soon, someone will most certainly complete the marathon in less than two hours. What an unbelievable time!

There is no doubt that the Greek soldier of long ago would be amazed if he knew what he had begun.

10

P

When asked what you would like for lunch, are you one of millions of Americans who frequently answers, "A peanut butter sandwich, please"?

The peanut traveled a considerable distance before arriving in the U.S. to become the popular food treat it is today. Many scientists believe the peanut originated in South America. Archeologists have discovered that the peanut was part of the Inca Indian's diet in Peru, as far back as the 14th century. Later, in the early 1600s, Spanish explorers in South America discovered the peanut, took some plants home with them, and soon peanut crops flourished in Spain.

Next the tasty, nutritional peanut journeyed to Africa when Spanish traders found them valuable in exchange for spices. Eventually, peanut plants were transported to the U.S. from Africa during the time of the slave trade. Peanut plants became a popular crop in the southern states in the late 1800s, and today the primary growers of peanuts are still located in the south.

Throughout history people have been fascinated by the way the peanut plant produces its peanuts. The plant, a small bush with yellow blossoms, does not appear unusual at first glance. But when the flowers die, they form a stem which begins to grow down into the soil where the peanuts then begin to grow and mature underground. A healthy peanut plant, carefully tended, usually produces about 40 peanuts in about 5 months. How long do you think it would take you to consume those 40 peanuts?

10

Working with the Results

We've provided you with this screening device *not* because we feel the school is usually wrong, but because it is important to eliminate the risk of incorrect information. Parent must be able to confirm for themselves their child's progress in this essential skill.

Now that you have gone through the necessary steps to evaluate your child's reading ability, you will have come to one of two conclusions:

1. *Your* evaluation has reinforced the evaluation provided by the school. Confident of your child's reading ability, you are now ready to learn what you can do to assist his progress.

2. You feel there is a significant differenc between your own evaluation and th evaluation that your child's teacher ha given to you. *If you find yourself in thi position, then this next section is for you.*

If your evaluation of your child's reading ability is considerably different from the one pro vided by the school, the first thing to do is contact your child's teacher. (In our chapter o parent-teacher contact we detail how to set up a parent-teacher conference.)

____ *Set a good tone for the meeting.* Remember to thank the teacher for taking the time to see you. *Do not* come on as a reading expert who has positive proof of your youngster's ability. Try to avoid making the teacher feel defensive.

____ *Tell the teacher that you are concerned with your child's reading ability.* Perhaps the difference of opinion is simply one of interpretation. (You evaluated your child as being a "little below grade level" and the teacher's report card said "at grade level." The teacher agrees that your child might be up to a half year behind; however, close to 50 percent of the students in his class are more than a full year behind. Considering this, the teacher did not feel that your youngster was far enough back to merit a "below grade level" marking.

____ *Explain to the teacher how your concern has come about.* Show the teacher this book and the screening device that you used. Describe any other factors that you feel support your opinion.

____ *Ask the teacher how he has determine the reading level ability of your chila* Has the teacher used an individualize reading test? Is he relying on informa tion given to him by your child's previ ous teacher? Perhaps he is dependin upon the results of a standardized test (Standardized tests are given to the en tire class at the same time; children d not get a chance to read aloud in dividually.)

____ *Insist on an individualized reading test* In the final analysis, a teacher can b certain of your child's reading skil only through the use of an individual oral reading test. Other methods c evaluating a child's ability can man times give an accurate measuremen However, these other methods (such a standardized tests, word recognitio tests, silent exams, other teacher's in formation, etc.) need to be used alon with an oral reading test. Almost an teacher can cite examples of how usin just a single method of evaluation ca sometimes prove very inaccurate. Un fortunately, class size and the lack of trained aides sometimes keep teachers from taking the time necessary to test all their students individually, and so they turn to quicker, more general, but less accurate forms of assessment.

___ *If your child wasn't individually tested, ask the teacher if he might not take the time to conduct such a test. If he has* *already done so, ask him if he could repeat a similar test again in your presence.* If the teacher is willing to go through this process for you, you should be able to reach a common understanding of your child's reading ability.

___ BE SURE TO THANK THE TEACHER FOR HIS TIME.

If the meeting with your child's teacher is unsatisfactory, contact the principal.

___ *Make an appointment with the school principal and carefully explain your concerns.* Focus attention on your concern for your child, *not* on what you feel is the uncooperative attitude of his teacher.

___ *Request that the principal have a qualified person on his staff do a careful diagnosis of your child's reading ability.* If the principal is going to refer your child to a specialist, be aware that you will most likely be asked to sign several forms of consent to special testing.

___ *Allow at least several weeks before you expect to be called in for an evaluation of the test results.* Principals are usually very cooperative in these matters. If you have gone this far, your child will almost certainly receive individual attention and you will end up feeling confident that you have an accurate total assessment of your child's reading ability.

If you are still not convinced, go outside the school system.

___ *Contact someone in private practice if you still feel that you are getting the run-around.* Reading specialists and reading clinics are listed in the Yellow Pages of most phone books.

___ *Testing and an analysis of the results will probably cost somewhere between $30 and $50.* This charge will cover the use of four to five different reading tests to ensure an accurate picture of your child's ability. The reading specialist will then tell you at what level your child is reading, what skills he has, what skills he lacks, and what can be done to improve the situation.

___ *Some reading clinics may offer to meet with your child's teacher to discuss the results.* At least, most will send the teacher a formal evaluation of your child's skills.

HELPING CHILDREN WITH READING DIFFICULTIES

Most children who read below grade level have the potential to succeed at reading and become literate members of our society. National surveys show that nearly two-thirds of all children with reading problems have normal or above average intelligence.

Reading problems are usually caused by several different factors. Only rarely can you isolate one specific reason for a child having reading difficulties. Reading specialists have cited over 200 different technical reasons for reading problems. If a cause for a reading disability can be determined, it will certainly help in correcting the problem. The truth is however, that you may never be able to determine exactly why your child developed reading problems. This need not be a major concern, though, because it's always best to help your child using methods that allow for a number of possible causes.

Some Reasons Why Reading Problems Occur:

1. *The home environment* has an effect on a child's aptitude and motivation for reading. Children who see their parents enjoy reading and children who have their own books and a quiet time available to enjoy their books are more inclined to be better readers than children who come from homes without these things. So important is this home environment that university studies consistently show that reading difficulties are more often directly linked to emotional and motivational problems that stem from the home than they are to vision, hearing, or speech problems.

2. *Visual problems* can also cause reading problems. If your child squints, holds the book too close or too far away, closes one eye when he reads, complains of headaches or eyes that tear, burn, or itch, it would be wise to have him checked by an eye specialist. Be sure to tell the optometrist or the ophthalmologist that you are concerned that a vision disorder might be interfering with your child's reading. (Incidentally, the letter chart used to test vision in many schools measures only long-distance vision. Used alone, this common test provides no measure of the type of vision used in reading.)

3. *Hearing and speech problems* are rarely the sole cause of a child's reading difficulties, but problems of this nature can contribute to reading difficulties. For example, hearing loss in the high tone range causes certain consonant sounds to blur together and the child may have problems learning the use of phonics. If you suspect a problem, request that your child's hearing be tested by the school or district nurse. Speech problems, on the other hand, may be a symptom of some other neurological or emotional problem that is also causing a reading disability. Speech problems can also create emotional problems that could interfere with reading progress, though certainly there are many children with speech problems who are excellent silent readers.

4. *Early educational experiences* with reading may also contribute to long-range reading problems. A child's self-concept and attitude toward reading are formed very early. If, for some reason, your child formed a negative attitude toward reading during his early years in school, that negative attitude can hinder his reading progress long after the causes of this poor attitude have disappeared.

5. *Dyslexia* is a term frequently associated with severely reading-disabled children. Despite its prevalent use in literature on reading, however, dyslexia does not describe a specific reading problem. Though this term is sometimes used to describe a condition where a child sees printed words in a reversed manner, it is also used in a variety of other ways. It may be best for you to think of *dyslexia* simply as a catch-all word describing a very few children who have severe difficulty learning to read, despite good instruction, proper motivation, adequate intelligence, and intact senses.

6. *Physical and mental handicaps* can be so severe that some children will never learn to read well. These children need professional help, guidance, and an extra amount of love and patience from their parents. Even though the potential for these children is low, it is an extremely valuable accomplishment to guide these children toward the fullest use of their capabilities.

A word of caution...

Before we suggest ways that you might help your child overcome his reading difficulties, a word of caution is in order. There are two major disadvantages parents may face in helping their own children work through reading difficulties:

1. Many parents simply do not have the patience to work with their own children. Reading progress for a good reader is very slow and rarely observable on even a week-to-week basis. Progress for a child who is already having problems is even slower. For example, if your child is in the fifth grade and is reading at the third grade level, you have to realize that *it may take months to notice a significant improvement.*

2. The emotional investment that parents and children have in each other may interfere with a healthy teacher-student relationship. Some parents find that trying to help their own child with reading is so charged with emotion that neither parent nor child can relax, and a relaxed setting is the key to a good reading program.

The Home Reading Program

This home reading program is directed primarily to parents who have elementary school children with reading difficulties. Assistance for junior high (middle school) or high school students with reading problems will be discussed in a separate section of this chapter (see page 98).

This home reading program can also be useful for parents whose children read well, but who want to help their children in reading better still. They will find these parts of this section most useful:

- A reminder about home environment—page 88
- Helping your child find a good book—page 88
- The 40-minute scheduled program—page 90

BACKGROUND WORK TO A HOME READING PROGRAM

Now is the time to make sure you have considered all of our previous suggestions:

1. *Talk with the teacher about your child's reading problem.*
Find out if the teacher has any insight as to why your child is not reading well.

Learn what specific recommendations the teacher has concerning how you can help at home.

Inquire about special programs or instructional aids at the school that could help your child.

2. *Consider whether your child has shown any signs that might indicate some sort of physical problem.*
It is not necessary to take every child with reading difficulties to an eye, ear, or speech specialist, but if your child shows some of the symptoms described in the earlier section, take her for a thorough exam.

3. *Consider whether you have the patience and proper rapport with your child to work with him on a daily basis.*
A HOME READING PROGRAM CONDUCTED BY A TENSE, ANGRY, OR FRUSTRATED PARENT IS MORE DAMAGING THAN NO PROGRAM AT ALL.

4. *Consider sending your child to a reading clinic*, a private reading instruction center outside of the school.

If your child is having severe reading problems, or you just feel that you cannot work effectively with him, this might be an option for you.

Reading clinics can be found through school referrals or by looking in the Yellow Pages of your phone book. (We discuss diagnostic testing by reading clinics on page 83.)

Reading clinics vary too much in the kinds of instruction given and success in improving reading skills for us to generalize about them. Your best bet is to visit several and see them in operation. Ask the clinic for references and then call a few parents whose children have attended that clinic.

Rates currently vary from $10 to $20 an hour, primarily depending on how many children the instructor will work with at any one time. Usually, one to three children will work with each instructor. In almost all cases, reading clinics provide individualized programs.

SETTING THE TONE

• BE WARM AND FRIENDLY TOWARD YOUR CHILD WHEN YOU DISCUSS A HOME READING PROGRAM WITH HIM. If your child feels she is being punished for not reading well, she will not benefit by reading at home.

• BE UNDERSTANDING ABOUT YOUR CHILD'S CONCERNS. And you can be *sure* that your child *is* concerned. Tell him that you know he has been working hard, and that you are sure there have been times when he has perhaps become angry or frustrated. It is very important you acknowledge your child's feelings. He may say that the reason he's "no good at reading" is because he "hates it." You might respond by saying you're sorry he feels that way and that you hope to show him that reading can be fun and rewarding.

• BE POSITIVE ABOUT HELPING YOUR CHILD. Once you begin the program, it does no good to bemoan the fact that your child is having difficulties.

• ASK YOUR CHILD HOW HE FEELS ABOUT READING. Find out what he enjoys most about it, what he dislikes most about it. Listen closely whenever your child talks about his feelings toward reading.

• DON'T BE DISCOURAGING. If your child feels good about the progress she is making, then encourage those feelings. Never put down a child's positive feelings—even if *you* don't see the progress you expect. Comments like "Unfortunately, you're not doing as well as you think you are" can do only harm.

The evidence shows that children who are given some kind of organized remedial instruction do benefit from it. YOU *WILL* HELP YOUR CHILD. It is important that your child knows not only that you can help him, but that he can help himself. Convince him that he has only begun to tap his reading potential.

• TELL YOUR CHILD THAT YOU THINK READING IS SO IMPORTANT AND CAN BE SO ENJOYABLE THAT YOU'D LIKE TO START A READING PROGRAM AT HOME—*A PROGRAM FOR BOTH OF YOU.*

The Home Reading Program

HOME ENVIRONMENT

We have said before that a positive home environment is *essential* in aiding children's reading progress.

• *Make sure that your child has plenty of reading material around that interests him.* His own personal bookshelf is a great idea. Comic books and magazines stir up interest in reading. Many children have been turned on to reading through *Superman* comics or some movie star magazine. Use what works!

• *Keep reading stories aloud to your child.* Just because your child is learning to read doesn't mean you should quit reading to her. Children in *all* grades love to be read to. It stimulates their imagination, it gets them excited about the pleasure that comes from reading, and it's a type of sharing that strengthens the bond between parent and child.

• *Take your child to the public library.* Show him where the dinosaur, pet, and hobby books are. Even children who are not enthusiastic about the library get pretty excited when they find books that deal with things they enjoy.

• *Set up situations where your child can succeed.* If there are some things that he does exceptionally well, go out of your way to praise those accomplishments. Success has a tonic effect. Children who do well in one area tend to carry over those feelings of confidence into other fields. A child who comes to feel pride in his skating ability will carry over some of that "I can do it" feeling to reading and any other task he undertakes.

HELPING YOUR CHILD FIND A GOOD BOOK

Your child needs an enjoyable book for this program. It should not be a textbook or a basal reader, but it should be at the appropriate grade level for your child. Finding a book that is at the proper level of difficulty for your child takes time. We suggest you follow these steps:

1. Look at the reading selections that you used to evaluate your child (found on pages 66 through 81). Concentrate on the last readings that he completed successfully. Read the selection over to get a *general* idea of the level of difficulty. You want your child to read a book that is written on approximately the same level.

2. Contact the teacher and tell him about your home reading program. Ask if he can help your child find a book that interests her and that would be suitable to bring home. This is one of your best bets for finding a good reading book. If your child does bring a book home from school, you still need to find out how well she can read it.

3. Go to a library or bookstore and ask the librarian or salesperson to guide you to some good, high-interest books at the reading level you are looking for. Ask your child to choose some books that he'd like to read. Ask him to try to find a book he thinks he can read fairly well.

After your child has chosen several books, skim over them yourself. If a book is obviously too difficult, it's fine to bring it home for your child's personal enjoyment, but it's *not* one you want for your program.

4. When you find a book that seems OK, open the book and ask your child to read a paragraph or two. Before she begins, pronounce any unusual names that might be in the paragraph. The story should not be so easy that she reads it perfectly, nor so difficult that she begins to show frustration. This simple evaluation technique is meant to give you some general guidelines. Don't be too rigid. Use these suggestions, your child's enthusiasm, and your own common sense to help you and your child select a good book.

If you must choose between a book that you feel is too easy and one that is too hard, get the one that is too easy. It's very important that a child with reading problems not be reading a book at a level of difficulty that frustrates him or makes him feel incompetent.

At the end of this chapter, we provide a list of favorite books for children in elementary school. These books were recommended by librarians, teachers, and reading specialists (and children!). The books are divided by reading levels from first through eighth grade. Remember, however, that these grade level designations are approximate and do not mean the book could not be enjoyed or read by children in other grades. In all cases, you will still want to check to make sure that the book is at the appropriate level for your child and that he is interested and motivated to read it.

SELECTING THE TIME

Our basic, parent-assisted home reading schedule takes about 40 minutes a session. We recommend that you use this program three days a week.

It is important that you establish certain times of the day and week for this program and then *keep to your schedule*. You and your child should agree on the best time for both of you.

• A reading session should *not* be right after school, right before dinner, or right before bed.
• Children who are hungry, sleepy, or have not had time to play are not primed to sit down and start reading.
• Some *good times* are a couple of hours after school lets out or shortly after you've finished the evening meal.

You need to spend this 40 minutes with your child in a comfortable setting with few, if any, interruptions and as little background noise as possible.

The 40-Minute Schedule

We realize that it's not easy for busy parents to set aside time for a home reading program. In fact, it's hard for most parents to find time for their own reading enjoyment. It will take commitment to coordinate this schedule with your child and stick to it. We can promise you one thing: ONCE YOU MAKE THE EFFORT, YOU'LL BE GLAD YOU DID.

THE SCHEDULE

15 Minutes	Parent/Child Silent Reading Time
5 Minutes	Discussion of Reading Material
15 Minutes	Reading Aloud/Correcting Reading Errors
5 Minutes	Positive Visiting Time
Optional time period	Extended Silent Reading

PARENT/CHILD SILENT READING TIME (15 MINUTES)

The first part of your program is basic and simple. While your child reads silently for fifteen minutes, you read something of your own for the same length of time.

It takes a great deal of concentration for some children to read *silently and continually* for just fifteen minutes, especially children with reading problems. Tell your child that concentration is a skill. Explain that building concentration is like building a muscle. The more you exercise your concentration, the better it becomes.

Children are all different: some learn and read more easily when moving around, others like holding onto something, and yes, some even learn better with something in their mouth.

If your child has trouble getting through his silent reading period, here are some tricks that might help:

• Let him nibble on an apple, a piece of cheese or some other healthy snack.

• Place some sort of comfortable object near your child, such as a pillow, or blanket, or favorite stuffed animal.

• Let him read in any position he feels comfortable with—whether it's curled up in the corner of a couch, or lying on the floor, or moving from one position to another. As his concentration increases, begin moving your child toward a posture that is assumed in most school classrooms, sitting upright in a chair.

While reading silently, your child will come across words that she cannot pronounce or understand. During this specific time period, she is to continue reading *without* asking you for assistance.

Why read something of your own while your child is reading? While you should be in the room to see that your child is reading, no one likes someone reading over his shoulder or waiting for him to finish. Your reading eliminates this problem. It also lets your child see you enjoy reading. Children need to see their parents read; your reading during this time provides a terrific model for your child to follow.

90

For this part of the program to work effectively, you need to be familiar with the material your child is reading. In order to ask meaningful questions and determine whether your child is grasping the main idea, you should skim his books and stories before he begins reading them.

When the 15-minute silent reading time is over, take a minute to get up and stretch. During this time, tell your child about what you've been reading. *This is important.* If you are reading a story, keep him up on the plot; if it's a magazine article, tell him why it is interesting to you.

Then ask your child about what he just read. If he's reading material at the proper level of difficulty, he should be able to summarize a fair amount of what he has just read. After he finishes telling about the story, you should ask a few questions about what he has read. Following are four types of questions you should ask your child:

1. A question about some *detail*:

Example: "What type of food did Red Riding Hood pack in her basket?"
    or
"Why was Red Riding Hood going to Grandmother's house?"

2. A question about the *order of events*:

Example: "Who arrived at Grandmother's house first?"
    or
"What happened after Red Riding Hood said, 'Grandmother, what big teeth you have!'?"

3. A question about the *main idea*:

Example: If your child has completed a chapter or story in his book, you might ask: "What important thing happened in this chapter?"
    or
"What can we learn from this story?"

4. A question of *speculation* (that goes beyond the story):

Example: "Do you think the story of Red Riding Hood could really happen? Why or why not?"

If your child cannot remember much of what he has just read—

Reevaluate your child's ability to read the material. (Use the methods described on pages 88–89.)

• If the material is too difficult, choose a new book that is at a better level.

If you still believe that the original book you chose is at the proper level of difficulty, then you need to spend more time working on comprehension.

• Extra time for working on comprehension can be fit into the oral reading part of this program. How to give your child that extra help is described in Reading Aloud to Your Child, page 93.

READING ALOUD/CORRECTING READING ERRORS (15 MINUTES)

This section is divided into three categories:

—READING ALOUD TO YOUR CHILD (with extra help on comprehension)

—LISTENING TO YOUR CHILD READ ALOUD

—HELPING YOUR CHILD CORRECT READING ERRORS

You can divide up the 15 minutes for this section evenly, between all three categories, or better yet, vary the time spent on each according to the mood and needs of your child.

> You can help your child read better.
> It doesn't take much time.
> It doesn't have to be a chore.
> It can be an activity that both you
> and your child look forward to.

Before you begin—a word on reading aloud:

In general, everyone has more difficulty reading aloud than reading silently. Everyone reads more slowly when he reads aloud. Also, it is common to mispronounce familiar words. Everyone must concentrate on punctuation marks to make the reading make sense. People are more nervous reading aloud than reading silently. Your child is no different.

It is important for you to understand these added difficulties that come with helping your child read aloud. With this caution in mind, however, you should also realize that this is the only way for most parents to assist their children with direct reading instruction.

This is your time for direct reading instruction. This one-to-one instruction time is extremely important.

Ask your child to show you where he last stopped reading silently and use this as a starting point for your reading. Sitting next to your child, read to him for a couple of minutes.

Reading aloud to your child has a number of wonderful benefits, but in the home reading program, you'll focus on three.

1. It lets your child hear how oral reading is supposed to sound. Your reading serves as a model to your child on how to use expression in his voice and how paying attention to punctuation marks helps the reading make sense.

2. This gives you an opportunity to provide some extra help on reading instruction.

3. It reinforces for your child that reading must sound like language. Many children with reading difficulties concentrate so much on individual words that they forget that their reading is supposed to flow and be understood—it's supposed to make sense.

Helping children who need extra practice on comprehension

Listening comprehension leads to reading comprehension. Children who have trouble with reading comprehension can benefit by listening to oral reading.

After you finish reading to your child, ask him to recall information from the pages you just read. Ask him the types of questions listed earlier on page 91. As your child learns to recall and think about what he is listening to, his understanding of what he is reading will also increase.

LISTENING TO YOUR CHILD READ ALOUD

Ask your child to read aloud from the pages he just read silently. Being familiar with what he's reading will give your child confidence and allow him to read better. Remind him to read at a relaxed pace. Hurried reading leads to carelessness.

When your child reads aloud:

1. Be attentive. Keep your mind from wandering.

2. When he has problems with a word, give him four or five seconds to figure it out and then tell him what it is.

3. As your child goes on reading, quickly write the problem word and page number down on a piece of paper. Do not stop the flow of his reading by teaching him how to figure the word out—you'll do this later.

Some advice to anyone helping their children with reading: Remember—

- *Always find opportunity for praise.*
- *Be supportive.* You are working with your child to help her read better, not to find fault with her.
- *Don't expect change overnight, "overweek," or even "overmonth."* If you are pleasantly surprised at the rate of growth you observe, that's wonderful. But generally, *reading progress is slow.* Just keep faith and hang in there, because progress *will* take place.

Recording word errors

After your child gets done reading to you, praise him for his efforts and tell him to take a little break.

Now look over the words you wrote down while your child was reading. If there aren't more than a couple, the book is probably not challenging enough for your child. Put a star by the words you feel are most important for your child to learn, because you probably won't have time to help him with them all. Try to choose common words that you feel your child will face regularly in his reading. If you must choose between *money* or *currency*, choose *money*.

Write these words down on 3 × 5 cards one word to a card. On the back of the card write the page number the word came from. If the meaning of the word isn't clear to your child, add a short definition to the back of the card as well. These are the words that you will help your child with.

The next step is direct instruction. You will review the words one at a time, helping your child with each word before moving on to the next. Before teaching your child how to figure out the word, have him reread the sentence that contains it.

Consider the following: If the average school reading period is an hour in length and if the teacher divided his time equally among 30 students, each student would receive just 2 minutes of individualized instruction a day, or just ten minutes a week. You exceed this 10 minutes a week in just *one evening* of your home reading program.

If your child is having difficulties with a word, you have several ways to help.

1. <u>Break the word into syllables and use phonetic decoding.</u> Though this sounds complicated, it is what many parents do naturally. This is what you are doing when you ask your child to sound out the word. Use this method sparingly. If you ask your child to sound out too often it will take the fun out of reading.

banana   *becomes* ba • nan • a
continental *becomes* con • ti • nen • tal
reservation *becomes* res • er • va • tion*

We suggest you do not use this method with first and second graders. (Refer to page 57 in "The Beginning Reader" section for a detailed explanation.)

2. <u>Show him that the word is actually made up of two words, that it is a *compound word*.</u>

airplane   *becomes* air • plane
schoolhouse *becomes* school • house
football   *becomes* foot • ball

3. <u>Show him that the word is actually a beginning or ending—a *prefix* or *suffix*—</u> added to a simpler, *root* word.

incomplete *becomes* in COMPLETE
rewrite   *becomes* re WRITE
sailing   *becomes* SAIL ing

*(with a reminder that "-tion" is pronounced "shun.")

4. You can simply *pronounce* the word for your child and ask him to memorize it. Do this when you come upon words that are not sounded out easily or that cannot be explained simply and quickly.

Example: debt, whistle, half, phony, laugh

5. Teach your child to *reread* the full sentence for clues as to what the unknown word might be. *For example:* Read the following sentences, leaving out the underlined words.

The astronaut put on his spacesuit.
The monkey ate a bunch of bananas.

You can see that even if your child does not recognize words like *astronaut* or *bananas*, he can probably figure out these words just by filling in the word that makes the sentence make sense. This is called using *context clues*.

Your child can also use context clues to figure out the meaning of some words he can read but not understand.

Example:
Sam put on his galoshes so he wouldn't get his feet wet.

Suppose your child read this sentence and hesitated as she read the word *galoshes*. If she isn't sure what galoshes are, ask her to read the sentence over using context clues. Once she does, it will become clear that galoshes are something worn on the feet to keep them dry.

6. Check to see if your child is substituting a word of similar meaning.

Example:
The *sentence reads*: "The elephant was very angry."
Your *child reads*: "The elephant was very upset."

This type of error is really nothing to be concerned with. In fact, it shows that your child is looking for meaning when he reads, which is a sign of a good reader.

7. Check to see if your child is making errors that show he is not making sense out of what he reads.

Example:
The *sentence reads*: "Mother said, 'Please *whisper* so you won't wake the baby.' "
Your *child reads*: "Mother said, 'Please *wish* so you won't wake the baby.' "

This type of error is an indication that your child still isn't reading for meaning. The word *wish* doesn't make sense in this sentence. If your child could not read the word *whisper*, he should have stopped and attempted to figure it out.

Substituting a word that has no place in a sentence is a serious problem. You can help your child correct this type of error by teaching him to use context clues. You should also spend more time reading aloud to him so he can hear how reading must sound like language. You cannot emphasize this enough to your child.

TELL YOUR CHILD:

Reading is language: It should make sense *to you*. If it doesn't make sense, stop and figure out why—ask for help!

There are two other, more general, types of reading problems that you can help your child correct.

1. *Repetition.* If your child reads part of a sentence, pauses, and then goes back and repeats two or more words, she is making a repetition error.

Example:
> *The sentence reads*: "Suddenly, the cat pounced on the mouse."
> *Your child reads*: "Suddenly, the cat— suddenly, the cat pounced on the mouse."

Many times children repeat words to allow them thinking time to figure out a difficult word that they see coming up. This type of word repetition is *not* something to be concerned about. In fact, it is a sign that your child is trying to make sense out of what she reads.

Some children, however, get into the habit of frequently repeating themselves, even when there is no apparent reason for it.

One way to help correct repetition problems is through something called *echo reading.* Tell your child that you want him to read aloud in a moderately slow voice. As he begins to say each word, say it with him. As soon as it appears that he is going back to repeat himself, then say the next word for him to get him back on track without letting him repeat. If repetition is a problem for your child, we suggest you practice echo reading for a couple of minutes each night. This will help your child read with more flow and less repetition.

2. *Child loses his place.* Some children have a difficult time following along a printed line. They lose their place and become frustrated. The most natural reaction for children when they find themselves losing their place is to begin *finger-pointing* at each word.

While finger-pointing isn't really something to become concerned about, you can help your child's reading to flow a little more smoothly by encouraging him to use a book marker to keep his place. Have him place the bookmarker *above* the line he is reading so it won't interfere with his switching down to the next line. If your child continues to have problems keeping his place, have his vision checked.

A FINAL NOTE—
try to keep a
word file.

Try to keep a word file. At the very end of your oral reading session, review the words that you worked on for that day. Then choose three words to enter into an ongoing "word file." (You can keep the word cards in a special box.) Next, review the words that were entered into the file from previous days. Circle any words your child can't remember so you can continue to work on them more the following day.

After your child recalls a word and its meaning, for several days in a row, remove it from the file. Try to keep the word file down to about a dozen words. Long word lists are unmanageable and seldom used. It's a good idea to make a game out of the words with a little reward for learning them. This may encourage your child's interest in words.

POSITIVE VISITING TIME . . .
(5 minutes)

It is important that when the reading is done you spend five minutes visiting and sharing with your child in a warm and positive way. Because:

• Children with reading difficulties can be prone to developing poor self-concepts.
• A poor self-image can aggravate a reading problem.
• If you can improve a child's self-image, you can often improve his inclination and motivation toward reading.

A program based at the Los Angeles County Education Office, Equal Opportunities in the Classroom, showed conclusively that reading scores dramatically improved in classrooms where the teacher was specifically trained to develop feelings of competence and self-worth among students.

Sometimes the lives of parents become so filled with the day-to-day necessities that we forget to make time for the most basic and yet most rewarding experiences of family life. Some suggestions for positive visiting time with your children:

• Ask your child about his favorite interests, his friends, his worries, his enjoyable times at school.
• Ask imaginative questions about wishes, desires, and daydreams.
• Ask speculative questions like "What would you do if . . . ?"
• Find areas that you can praise and give your child support.

You also need to share something of yourself—your childhood experiences, your daydreams, happy reflections about things you and your child have done together, even concerns that you had when you were young that are similar to ones your child presently faces.

EXTENDED SILENT READING
(optional time period)

Children learn to read by reading. The more time your child spends reading silently, the better reader he will become.

A child's attention span increases with age. If your child is in the third grade, or younger, she probably will not be too thrilled about extending her home reading program past 40 minutes. Don't push it, but if the desire is there, encourage it.

Children in the upper elementary grades should be encouraged to develop extended silent reading periods. Eventually, these periods will be necessary for your child to become a good reader. If your child resists, though, know when to let up. A 40-minute program, three times a week is an accomplishment for a struggling reader to be proud of. If your child faithfully keeps to your home reading program schedule, don't make him feel inadequate because he doesn't want to extend it further. As your child sharpens his reading skills, he will become much more inclined toward extended silent reading.

Many times, however, even below-average readers can move toward 30–45 minutes of silent reading—if the book is of high interest and at the proper reading level. By the time your child can read at a fourth or fifth grade level, he should be able to improve greatly his own reading skills by sitting down and reading for half an hour or more at a stretch. Encourage these periods of silent reading in your youngster and reward his efforts with praise and perhaps some special treat. You might want to schedule loosely these silent reading times for evenings when you don't have your home reading program. You might even want to make a family activity out of it. Desire, enthusiasm, and practice are the best teachers in the world.

Helping Teenagers with Reading Difficulties

If you remember nothing else from this section, remember the following facts:

- Most teenagers who take part in a structured, individualized reading program improve their reading skills significantly.

- Most teenagers with reading difficulties are of average intelligence—they are intellectually capable of becoming good readers.

Obviously, the time to form good reading skills and to catch and correct reading difficulties is during your child's early years in school. Unfortunately, many children leave elementary school taking their reading problems with them. To make matters worse, many parents and schools simply shrug and say, "It's too late to do anything for the child now."

Well, it's *not* too late! If you have a child in junior high or high school with reading difficulties, you can help him improve. But before going further, you need to understand some important information.

Why do reading difficulties persist past elementary school?

- *Some children with reading difficulties are not given the proper remedial instruction.* Remedial instruction is the special, individualized instruction that a child needs to help him learn something he's having difficulties with. It is possible that your child has had teachers who have not, for whatever reasons, provided him with the kind of extra help he needs to learn how to read better.

- *The home environment has not encouraged reading.* This is one of the major causes of reading difficulties. Perhaps there have been just too many things going on at home for your child to concentrate on reading—a divorce, lack of parental supervision, a death in the family, no structured quiet times, too many distractions, etc. If you feel that somehow your home environment has not been supportive of reading, there are a few adjustments that you can make that might prove helpful.

- *A physical problem that interferes with reading has gone undetected.* While this is possible, it is not very likely. Most children with visual or hearing problems have had these problems detected and diagnosed before leaving elementary school. If your child still reads poorly, make sure you have had her vision and hearing thoroughly checked.

- *Some children will never be capable of reading well.* There are some children who have permanent mental or physical handicaps that will always keep them from becoming good readers. Even though the potential for these children is low, every effort should be made to help each individual reach his full capability. Remember: these children account for only a small part of those teenagers with reading difficulties.

By the time most children leave elementary school, they have learned the basic rules of phonics. This is true even for many children with reading difficulties. At the intermediate and secondary levels, the problem isn't so much that the student can't recognize individual words, it's what happens when he puts them all together. Some common difficulties are:

- The student cannot understand the materials he's given to read
- The student reads too slowly and with difficulty
- The student does not like to read

Why do reading difficulties become harder to correct?

While it is true that most teenagers who are given structured, individualized instruction improve their reading skills, it is also true that reading difficulties *are harder to correct* in teenagers than in younger children. We do not list these problems to make you pessimistic, but to be realistic. Thus you can better understand how to help.

• A pattern of failure has been set that is difficult for the teenager to break. The child has convinced himself, or has been convinced by others, that he is not smart enough to be a good reader. Rather than beat his head against a wall, the child acknowledges defeat, thus ensuring he will not be able to read well.

• Teenagers have a need to become more independent of their parents and so become more reluctant to be helped or to show they need help.

• Academic problems caused by reading difficulties sometimes lead to behavior problems. Some students deal with their lack of success in school by adopting a "who cares" attitude. It is their way of protecting their pride. Unfortunately, this attitude can lead to behavior problems, and obviously it is difficult to help someone who says he "couldn't care less" about being helped.

• The teenager's reading difficulty has become an emotionally charged topic for her parents. With other subjects, like math, the child can have difficulties and her parents do not consider her dumb or themselves failures. But with reading, parents immediately think there's something very wrong with their child, or they look upon themselves as failures. This emotionalism keeps parents from effectively aiding their children.

• Finally, the structure and emphasis of junior high and high school works against students with reading difficulties. In elementary school your child's math and science teacher was also his reading teacher. The teacher knew if the math problems or the history book were too difficult for your child to read, and often the necessary adjustments were made. The structure of education after elementary school does not allow each one of your child's five or six teachers to understand him as a "whole person." The often-heard remark "In elementary school teachers teach children, and in high school teachers teach subject matter" is not too far from the truth. The consequences for a child with major difficulties in reading can be disastrous if they go unchecked.

A child who leaves elementary school with reading difficulties faces a profound disadvantage not only in reading, but in English, social science, foreign language, science, and even math. There are very few classes of any kind where reading is not part of the course work. Unfortunately, there are very few teachers who will be aware of your child's reading difficulties or know how to give him special assistance in that area.

CLASSROOM READING INSTRUCTION FOR TEENAGERS

Reading specialists across the nation have fought a long, uphill battle to bring reading programs into the junior high and high schools. Gradually, more schools began offering reading classes to students as an elective in their course of studies. Some junior highs (or middle schools) have now gone beyond just remedial reading and now *require* a period of reading for every student, each day. Today, there is a good chance that your child will attend a school that offers reading instruction.

Some reading programs at the intermediate and secondary level are outstanding; some are good; and, unfortunately, some are almost a waste of time. The problem is, there are still too many educational administrators who do not take reading classes at this level seriously, and, therefore, do not insist upon high standards.

Here are some things to look for in a good *reading program:*

- The teacher has either reading specialist credentials or is taking classes toward their completion.
- The teacher is excited about the program.
- The students' reading abilities are all individually evaluated at the beginning of the program and reexamined throughout.
- The program is individualized to meet each student's needs.
- The class size is no more than 25 (and even this is sometimes too high).
- Progress charts are kept up to date so each student can verify his accomplishments.
- The feeling in the classroom is *warm* but *serious.*
- When you visit the classroom, you see students reading.

Here are some signs of a poor *reading program:*

- The teacher lacks enthusiasm.
- The teacher has no special background in reading. (Credentialing in English does *not* qualify the instructor to teach reading.)
- The class size is over 25 students per instructor.
- The classroom does not offer structured individualized instruction, but instead is essentially a "free reading period." (Watch out for this one, because it's all too common.)
- The teacher does not work at building the students' self-esteem, but rather treats them all as "problem readers."
- When you visit the classroom, you see students visiting or doing other things that don't involve reading.

If your school does not seem to offer a good reading program, go to the principal and express your concern!

THE PARENT'S ROLE—
WHAT YOU CAN DO TO HELP YOUR TEENAGER

If the school has a good reading program, suggest to your child that he enroll in it. You should suggest the program to your child, not force it on him. A child who does not want to work at learning how to read better will not benefit from any reading program; he might disrupt it for others. With time, he may come around.

It's important to tell your teenager that a good school reading program can help her read better. Some high schools are reporting that their students gain an average of two years in reading ability for every year they are in the program.

If the school does not have a reading program, or does not offer what you consider a good reading program, *enroll your child in a private reading program* (or a commercial reading clinic) *if your child is willing and you can afford to do so.* Reading clinics, or reading programs run by the business community, have been very successful in helping teenagers read better. Make sure you review the information we've already presented about these reading programs and follow our advice carefully while choosing one for your child (see pages 83 and 87).

A child who spends close to an hour a day in a good school reading program may get overloaded if he is also enrolled in a private reading clinic at the same time. Be careful about applying too much pressure, but if your teenager wants to be in both programs, terrific.

Assisting your child at home

Most reading specialists advise *against* parents giving their teenagers direct reading instruction (such as the kind described for elementary school children on pages 86–97.) They find that emotions get in the way of parents and teenagers working well together in the area of reading instruction.

If for some reason you feel the relationship with your child will allow you to give direct assistance, then we suggest you rearrange our Home Reading Program in a way that will be beneficial to your teenager.

There are many ways, however, that you can give indirect reading assistance to your child. Though this assistance does not involve actually teaching your child how to read, it can still lead to very real growth in her reading ability.

Encouraging Reading

• Help your teenager feel good about himself. Teenagers can get very down on themselves about not reading well. At this point, just the thought of reading probably makes your teenager tense. This negative tension really interferes with learning—try to get rid of it. Let your teenager know he's OK. He's not stupid or slow; he simply has difficulties with reading—difficulties that can be worked with and corrected. Find other things to praise your child about and build his self-esteem and feelings of competence.

• Set up an after-dinner quiet time at home. Set aside a half hour each night when all the noise stops and you read. If your teenager doesn't want to read, don't force it. Remember, though, that the more a young person sees his parents read, the more inclined she will be to read.

• Keep reading aloud to your teenager. Read him interesting articles from magazines or newspapers. Read him letters. Read passages from books. Read to him about his favorite hobbies or other interests. Stress the idea that reading lets you find out what you want to know.

• Buy magazines for your teenager that appeal to his special interests. Consider magazines like: *Sports Illustrated, Road & Track, Seventeen, Ebony, Field & Stream, People,* and *Life*.

• Buy books for your teenager that are of high interest and comfortable for her to read. Your librarian can help you find some favorites. We suggest some sure-fire winners at the end of this chapter in a recommended book list. Remember, provide the books, but do *not* insist that your child read them.

• Give your child money to buy her own books or magazines. Try not to criticize what she chooses—if she reads it, she's learning.

• Check the textbooks your teenager uses in his different courses. Ask him if he can read them. If he is having problems with a class because he can't read the material, it will just increase his negative feelings toward reading. Ask your child to explain the situation to the teacher (or you can see the teacher yourself if your child prefers) and request special assistance.

• Spend time talking with your teenager. Reading, and especially reading comprehension, relies heavily on *language experience.* The more subjects your teenager can talk about and understand in conversation, the more subjects she will be able to understand and read about easily. Through conversation, try to broaden your teenager's vocabulary and her knowledge of the world around her.

• BE POSITIVE. Many parents feel guilty if their child doesn't read well. Seeing this guilt only aggravates your teenager's tensions and worsens the situation. Be encouraging and show you'll help him in any way you can.

THE GOOD READER

Elementary School

If your child reads at (or above) his grade level, you can consider him a good reader. Does this mean you no longer have to monitor his progress? Is the reading he does at school adequate? The answer to both these questions is *no*.

Follow your child's progress in reading all the way through school. You should be able to see growth in her ability each year. If your child is reading above grade level in the fourth grade, you should still see her above grade level in the sixth grade. Certainly, there are many children who show a great deal of talent in their early years of schooling yet end up with rather mediocre skills because they are left to coast too long on their early advantages.

Make your own expectations clear to your child. You may find that your expectations exceed those of the school. It is your role as a parent to set goals which you feel your child can reasonably achieve. You may not feel satisfied with the amount of reading or quality of reading that the school requires. If this is the case, add your own standards to those of the school.

By the time a child can read well at the fourth grade level, she'll usually improve at reading in direct proportion to the time she spends reading. Children who read well in elementary school will certainly benefit from taking part in the Home Reading Program. Most good readers by fourth grade, however, should be doing more than 15 minutes of silent reading, three days a week. It is reasonable to ask a child of this age, with good skills, to spend half an hour a night reading silently.

Cut down on your child's TV time and encourage him to entertain himself with reading. Reading engages the mind, and it requires continual alertness and thought—especially compared with watching TV, which is usually a passive activity requiring little thought or imagination. There is no doubt that it's a challenge for parents to get their kids turned off television and turned on to reading. Accept the challenge.

Almost all children will very soon learn to enjoy reading at home when they sit down with a book that holds their interest. Your major challenge as a parent is to find a book that will get your child involved and excited about reading. (You can break up the routine some days by reading the book aloud to your child.)

The first time that you mention setting aside a silent reading time every night, you're probably going to catch a lot of flak:

"None of my friends have to."

"If it's so important, how come the teacher didn't assign it?"

"I've got things I have to do."

"I hate reading."

"I don't have time."

"What a stupid idea!"

Explain what the benefits are, compromise a little, but hang in there!

Junior High and High School

Beware!

In April 1981, a National Assessment of Educational Progress compared the reading abilities of today's youth with those of children five and ten years ago. The study concluded that while nine-year-old children are reading better than in the prior ten years, the same is not true of older children. It appears that the improvement in young children levels off by age thirteen, and that by age seventeen, today's "best" students fail to read as well as their counterparts of ten years ago.

Why?

The study did not focus on why students don't keep up the reading momentum from their earlier education. It was suggested, however, that reading time is facing increased competition from TV, a wide variety of teenage recreational activities, and an increasing number of high school students taking after-school jobs.

It isn't easy to get teenagers to sit down and read. By the time your child is a teenager, the expectations he has for himself and the study habits he keeps will have been fairly well determined. As he enrolls for classes in junior high and high school, encourage him to take courses that require reading in order to complete the assignments. Check from time to time to see how much actual reading is assigned in classes.

If you find your child is reading less and less at home, you should make some attempt to remedy the situation. Do not, however, force your child to read if she does not want to. Try a few of these suggestions:

• Subscribe to a newspaper and encourage your child to read it by involving him in discussions centered around news articles.

Example:
"Did you see that article about how Fernando Valenzuela finally got to pitch for the Dodgers?"
or
"What do you think about that article on teenage runaways?"

• Set up a time in your home, after dinner, when all the TV's, radios, and record players go off. Take the time to do some pleasure reading and suggest to your child that he do the same.

• Next time you're at a shopping center, give your child some money to buy a book of his choice.

For College-Bound Students

Universities across the nation are reporting that more and more incoming freshmen do *not* have the reading skills necessary to be successful in college.

Make your teenager aware of the growing concerns of university professors. It should be possible to convince him that a commitment to high standards today will serve him well in the future.

Being able to pronounce words on a printed page is not enough. To succeed in college, a student must strengthen and refine his skills. Ask yourself these questions:

Can my child read—

• *efficiently*, with a minimal amount of effort?
• *rapidly*, so that he doesn't feel like he's plodding along?
• *continually*, for an hour or two without tiring?
• *and with understanding*, so that he will not be overwhelmed by the enlarged vocabulary and complex ideas of a college text?

NEVER STOP READING TO YOUR CHILD

Never stop reading to your children. They love it and need it too. The benefits it provides your children are numerous.

1. *It keeps beginning readers from getting turned off to reading.* Many young children look forward to learning how to read because they learned the joy of books from having been read to. But some children soon find their school reading books boring compared to the stories they're used to listening to. The reason is clear. Textbook writers tailor the words of their stories to the child's ability to read them. What happens is that the early reading books end up without the types of words that make a story exciting to children, because words like *gorgeous*, *monstrous*, or *lickety-split*, while loved and understood, are too difficult to read.

One way to work around the first and second grade "this-book-is-boring-so-who-wants-to-read" blues is to read to your child. Keep up your child's enthusiasm for reading until he can begin to read for himself books that stir his thinking and imagination.

2. *It challenges the mind and imagination of the advanced reader.* Listening to a story forces the mind to visualize what it is hearing. Thus listening to a story is a creative process because the listener puts part of himself into the story to *see* what he's hearing. The imagination acts much more freely picturing the "lost boy" in the story as opposed to seeing the "lost boy" on TV where nothing is left to the imagination. For example: a ten-year-old black child can imagine the "lost boy" in the story to be much like himself but viewing the boy on TV might leave him no choice but to see him as a white teenager.

3. *It keeps problem readers excited and enthusiastic.* The more difficult it is for a child to learn to read, the more important it is to emphasize the value and pleasure of reading. For the poor reader, the joy of listening to a wonderful story encourages him to keep working so that some day she'll be able to read that story for herself.

4. *It builds comprehension and critical thinking skills and helps to clarify values.* After you read a story to your child, talk about what you have read. Ask questions that require real thought from your child:

"What made the Velveteen Rabbit become real?"
"Can you remember all the things Charlotte did to save Wilbur's life?"
"Do you think it was right for the soldiers to force Geronimo and his people onto the reservation?"

Children who learn to think about stories in the ways described above become much more competent and insightful readers than those who learn to react to literature on just the surface level.

5. *It is sharing a meaningful experience with your child.* Reading a story with your child builds closeness and understanding. Your twelve-year-old needs that kind of bonding now, just as much as when she was five.

RECOMMENDED BOOKS

The following books are recommended by children's librarians, teachers, and especially kids. Titles are listed according to readability level. If you are trying to find a book that will hook your young reader, this is a good place to start.

ELEMENTARY SCHOOL

First Grade

Are You My Mother?
P. D. Eastman

Albert the Albatross
Syd Hoff

"The Berenstain Bears" (series)
Stanley and Janice G. Berenstain
The Bear's Picnic
Old Hat, New Hat
The Bear's Vacation

The Cat in the Hat
Dr. Seuss

The Clumsy Cowboy
Jean Bethell

Come to the Pet Shop
Ruth M. Tensen

Curious George Flies a Kite
Margaret Rey

The Day I Had to Play with My Sister
Crosby N. Bonsall

Whose Mouse Are You?
Ruth Kraus

Willie's Adventures
Margaret Wise Brown

Second Grade

But No Elephants
Jerry Smath

The Case of the Cat's Meow
Crosby N. Bonsall

Curious George
Margaret Rey

Frog and Toad Are Friends
Arnold Lobel

George and Martha
James Marshall

Goggles!
Ezra Jack Keats

The Homework Caper
Joan M. Lexau

Hooray for Pig!
Carla Stevens

Leo the Late Bloomer
Robert Kraus

Nate the Great
Marjorie W. Sharmat

Third Grade

Alexander and the Terrible, Horrible, No Good, Very Bad Day
Judith Viorst

Amelia Bedelia
Peggy Parish

Do You Love Me?
Dick Gackenbach

Encyclopaedia Brown Takes the Case
Donald J. Sobol

Freckle Juice
Judy Blume

The Great Custard Pie Panic
Scott Corbett

Lyle, Lyle, Crocodile
Bernard Waber

McBroom Tells the Truth
Sid Fleischman

Ramona the Pest
Beverly Cleary

Sylvester and the Magic Pebble
William Steig

Fourth Grade

And Now Miguel
Joseph Krumgold

Dracula's Cat
Jan Wahl

Encyclopaedia Brown Lends a Hand
Donald J. Sobol

James and the Giant Peach
Roald Dahl

Little House on the Prairie
Laura Ingalls Wilder

The Master Puppeteer
Katherine Paterson

Miss Pickerell on the Moon
Ellen MacGregor and Dora Pantell

Misty of Chincoteague
Marguerite Henry

Ramona and Her Mother
Beverly Cleary

Superfudge
Judy Blume

Fifth Grade

The Cay
Theodore Taylor

Charlie and the Chocolate Factory
Roald Dahl

Charlotte's Web
E. B. White

The Great Brain
John D. Fitzgerald

Harriet the Spy
Louise Fitzhugh

It's Like This, Cat
Emily Neville

Julie of the Wolves
Jean Craighead George

The Lion, the Witch and the Wardrobe: A Story for Children
C. S. Lewis

The Summer of the Swans
Betsy Byars

A Wrinkle in Time
Madeleine L'Engle

Sixth Grade

Are You There God? It's Me, Margaret
Judy Blume

The Black Stallion
Walter Farley

Caddie Woodlawn
Carol Brink

From the Mixed-Up Files of Mrs. Basil E. Frankenweiler
E. L. Konigsburg

Island of the Blue Dolphins
Scott O'Dell

Ronnie and Rosey
Judie Angell

The Secret Garden
Frances Hodgson Burnett

A Swiftly Tilting Planet
Madeleine L'Engle

Tintin (series)
Herge

Where the Red Fern Grows
Wilson Rawls

JUNIOR HIGH
Seventh Grade

And This Is Laura
Ellen Conford

Beat the Turtle Drum
Constance C. Green

The Cat Ate My Gymsuit
Paula Danziger

"Choose Your Own Adventure" (series)
  By Balloon to the Sahara
  D. Terman
  Journey Under the Sea
  R. A. Montgomery
  Sugarcane Island
  Edward Packard

"Chronicles of Prydain" (series)
Lloyd Alexander

The Dark Is Rising
Susan Cooper

The Great Gilly Hopkins
Katherine Paterson

Jenny Kimura
Betty Cavanna

The Transfigured Hart
Jane Yolen

The Upstairs Room
Johanna Reiss

Eighth Grade

*Can You Sue Your Parents
For Malpractice?*
Paula Danziger

Deathwatch
Robb White

Deenie
Judy Blume

The Diary of a Young Girl
Anne Frank

I Am the Cheese
Robert Cormier

The Iceberg Hermit
Arthur Roth

Killing Mr. Griffin
Lois Duncan

108

The Pinballs
Betsy Byars

The Pigman
Paul Zindell

A Ring of Endless Light
Madeleine L'Engle

HIGH SCHOOL

Here are some high interest books for older
readers who read *below grade level*. (These
books are written below eighth grade readability.)

Durango Street
Frank Bonham

Face-Off
Matt Christopher

Honey
Cavanagh

A Lantern in Her Hand
Bess Aldrich

The Rocking Chair Rebellion
Eth Clifford

Run
William Sleater

Tennis Champ
Evelyn Luneman

The Testing of Charlie Hammelman
J. Brooks

The Two-Minute Mysteries
Donald J. Sobol

*We Interrupt This Semester
for an Important Bulletin*
Ellen Conford

Following are some favorites recommended
for *successful high school readers.*

All Quiet on the Western Front
Erich Maria Remarque

Animal Farm
George Orwell

Call of the Wild
Jack London

The Catcher in the Rye
J. D. Salinger

The Chocolate War
Robert Cormier

Death Be Not Proud
John Gunther

Fahrenheit 451
Ray Bradbury

Flowers for Algernon
Daniel Keyes

The Old Man and the Sea
Ernest Hemingway

The Red Badge of Courage
Stephen Crane

A Separate Peace
John Knowles

To Kill a Mockingbird
Harper Lee

Magazines

Most of these kid's favorites are available at your local library. A gift subscription to a magazine is also a good way to encourage the reading habit.

- *Boys' Life* (ages 9–12)
- *Cobblestone* (ages 8–13)
- *Cricket: The Magazine for Children* (ages 8–12)
- *Dynamite* (ages 8–12)
- *Ebony Jr.!* (ages 8–12)
- *Electric Company* (ages 7–10)
- *Highlights for Children* (ages 6–10)
- *Humpty Dumpty's Magazine* (ages 4–8)
- *Mad* magazine (junior high)
- *National Geographic World* (ages 8–11)
- *Ranger Rick's Nature Magazine* (ages 9–12)
- *Sesame Street* (preschool)
- *Stone Soup* (ages 8–12)
- *Tiger Beat* (junior high)

CHAPTER 4

. I would think that the home atmosphere is
some importance. Is there some correlation
tween bad writing and home attitudes of
srespect for books and writing?

—*Arthur Miller*

The Writing Chapter

Last year 36,000 books were published in the United States—not to mention magazines, pamphlets, brochures, and a ton of advertising copy. Add to that the millions of words written annually on birthday greetings, postcards, and letters. Then consider the everyday scrawls: shopping lists, notes for school, phone messages, checks, invitations, instructions for the repairman. Let's face it—we can't get through a day without writing.

The better a person's command of the written language, the better she will function in our society. Whether we like it or not, we are judged by what we write and how well we write it. That's *us* written down on that paper.

Our children will need to write in every class they take, from kindergarten through college. They will have to write outside of school and long after the schooling years are over. It would be difficult to find a job that does not require some form of writing. Besides this, writing can add a quality to your child's life that's difficult to measure. The right words written at the right time can land a job, stop a fight, or mend a heart.

Despite the fact that writing is fundamental to our lives, most young people are not competent writers when they finish school. Writing is not taught well; nor do children have enough opportunities to practice writing outside of school. This is a serious concern among both educators and parents.

Schools are now trying to solve the problem—but that's not enough. Parents need to help their children learn to write. Your involvement in the "second *R*" can make an incredible difference in your child's education.

THE DECLINE IN WRITING SKILLS

Although writing has never been America's long suit, it continues to decline. More and more people are unable to express ideas in writing *clearly and correctly*.

To understand the depth of the problem, it is important to see how the current decline in writing has been determined. Much of the information comes from the following three sources:

• *The Scholastic Aptitude Test (SAT)*. The verbal scores on the SAT have been declining since 1965. Granted, a greater cross section of students is now taking college entrance exams. Nevertheless, the "top" students today can't match the "top" students twenty years ago.

• *National Assessment of Educational Progress*. This test has shown a steady decline in writing skills for the past ten years. The scores stabilized in a number of areas in 1979, indicating things may have hit bottom.

• *College English Placement Tests*. These essay tests, given to incoming freshmen at many colleges and universities, have been a major indicator of trouble for some time now. At Temple University in Pennsylvania, there was a 50 percent increase in the number of students taking remedial writing from 1968 to 1975. In 1981, at the University of California at Irvine, 80 percent of the freshman class did not pass the writing competency test.

Coupled with the test findings is the fact that many business and government employers can no longer find employees who write well enough to fill out the application—let alone to handle the job. Errors that previously were made by high school graduates are now being made by college graduates.

How has all this come about? We need to look at both *schools and society* for the answer.

114

Why Don't Schools Teach Writing Well?

1. *It is difficult to measure writing skills*. Unlike reading and math, writing progress is not easily measured. Your child may read at the fourth grade level or score 89 percent on his fractions test. Evaluating his short story on dragons is much more difficult. One teacher might give him an "*A*" for creativity; another would assign a "*C*" because of the spelling errors. Writing refuses to fit into neat categories.

2. *Schools depend on standardized tests*. Faced with the problems mentioned above, schools have moved toward measuring writing ability with multiple choice tests. Most statewide "English" tests check mechanical and grammatical errors only, and require *no real writing*. Take a look at a couple of test questions for high school students from the California Test of Basic Skills:

A. Carl laughed as the fat lady _____ around the circus tent.

1. walked   2. whisked   3. waddled   4. wandered

B. If what the directions on the package say is true, you only need ⅛ cup detergent for each load.

In the above sentence, "on the package" modifies:
1. the load 2. the need 3. the directions 4. you

There is tremendous pressure on school districts to do well on tests such as these. The trouble is that *the kind of teaching that leads to higher test scores does not necessarily lead to better writing*.

3. *Teachers are not trained to teach writing.* Elementary education classes emphasize reading. Secondary classes emphasize literature.

4. *English classes are too large.* A high school English teacher who teaches five classes of 35 children has a total of 175 students! There is no way those kids can write an essay a week and the teacher stay sane. This reality is not going away; in fact, it's getting worse.

5. *English teachers don't write enough.* It is hard to imagine a Spanish teacher who does not speak Spanish or a band director who is tone deaf. But being a good writer has never been a necessity for teaching English. Many English teachers are not comfortable with writing and do not do much of it in or out of class.

6. *Teachers rely on workbooks too much.* Since many teachers don't know how to teach writing and school districts are pushing "short answer" tests, workbooks fill the bill. They emphasize short, quick answers — but little real writing. Students may be asked to put commas in a sentence correctly, but they *do not write sentences* themselves. Publishers also contribute to this situation, as there is no money to be made in the most effective writing materials: blank paper and pencils.

7. *Schools emphasize reading over writing.* Experts feel that the amount of time and energy devoted to reading over the past decades has been done *at the expense of writing.* There is more research on reading (as far back as the eighteenth century), more materials available, and it's easier to teach. School districts spend $100 on reading for every dollar spent on writing. This is not to say reading is not important; writing just needs a larger share of the pie.

8. *The back-to-basics movement often stresses grammar.* In an attempt to stop the writing decline, many concerned folks have focused on the "icing" of writing (grammar, spelling, and penmanship) and not the "cake" (content, ideas, something worth saying). Both aspects of writing are important. *A perfectly executed paper that says nothing important is not good writing.* The problem is not that kids aren't diagramming sentences enough—it's that they're not *writing sentences* enough.

9. *Language arts and school electives often ignore writing.* The term "language arts" usually means reading, spelling, handwriting, and workbook exercises. Few such programs include a structured writing program.

In a similar way, many high schools have been offering students their choice of English courses (such as "Mystery Stories" or "Analyzing Films"), very few of which stress writing.

10. *Classes other than English do not require writing.* As a rule, writing is not taught or even noticed except in English and language arts. Teachers in other areas do not know how to teach writing either and, in any case, "can't be bothered."

11. *Teachers use writing as punishment.* We've all had teachers—and they're still out there—who assign writing as punishment for bad behavior. (Write "I will not chew gum in class" 100 times or a 500-word essay on "Why I Should Not Disturb Others.") It's hard to imagine a teacher saying, "I've had it with you, Vince—go read a story." Such methods reinforce the idea that writing *is not fun.*

12. *Changes in the teaching of writing are slow to take place.* Although much new information is available on how to teach writing, it is slow to filter down to the actual classroom teacher . . . sometimes as long as twenty years!

These facts about schools and how they teach (or do not teach) writing are not new. Along with this, we need to look at the changes that have occurred in our society over the past fifty years.

How Does Our Society Discourage Writing?

- *Television.* TV itself is a passive activity that does not require reading or writing. More important, it takes away time that used to be spent doing other things—like writing.
- *Telephones.* Increased use of the telephone has replaced an old habit: letter writing. Now that you can dial Mombasa, Kenya, directly, why bother to send a note to your cousin in Des Moines?
- *The Family.* In the "old days," more teaching went on in the home. Both the lifestyle and makeup of families has changed this pattern. More and more parents, due to economic pressures, are out of the home for longer periods of time. It is harder for parents to devote the time and energy to help their children learn.
- *The Ready-Made Approach.* With greeting cards for every occasion and computerized letters, it is possible to "communicate" with people without putting pen to paper. There are fewer opportunities to *practice* writing.
- *Adult Examples.* Fewer children today see people who are close to them writing or taking writing seriously. Furthermore, you don't have to look far to see poorly written books, songs, and film scripts become best sellers.

Why Parents Must Get Involved

Although, as we have seen, there are not enough opportunities to write in school or outside school, the need for writing continues—but within a society that does not support it; that is the dilemma. There is hardly a job that does not require writing, from lawyer's briefs and police reports to business proposals and automotive repair statements. Employers in every field insist on good writing, but aren't getting it.

What all this means is that your child is going to have to learn to write despite many obstacles. It can be done—but not by the schools alone. Much of writing development will have to take place in the home.

Although the schools do teach writing—and there are some wonderful teachers out there—it is still not enough. If you leave it solely to the schools to teach your child how to write, chances are he will not be where he should at graduation. Yes, he may be "average," *but it is important to remember that the average high school graduate today is not a competent writer.*

Consider these responses to a national survey on writing given to high school seniors:

- 67 percent occasionally or never received comments on how to improve their work.
- About 25 percent had done little or no writing during the six weeks prior to taking the test.
- 50 percent said little or no time was spent on writing instruction in English classes.
- Only 8 percent had taken an actual composition course.
- 75 percent wrote less than once a week.

WHAT EVERY PARENT SHOULD KNOW ABOUT WRITING

Whether you think the schools *should* be able to teach writing is beside the point; given the realities we've discussed, they can't. If your child has several strong teachers, you may only have to supplement what's being done at school. If your child's teachers do not stress writing, you may have to do a lot of writing with your child at home. *Either way, your child will not receive enough writing instruction in school to learn to write well.* He must have your help.

What Is Writing?

If you are going to accept the challenge of helping your child learn how to write, you need to be aware of some basic information plus knowledge about what works and what does not. Let's start at the very beginning.

Human communication can be illustrated as follows:

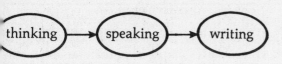

Writing begins in the head as thinking. We experience things and store them up in our mind. We usually do not *think* about an experience as it happens; we simply act and react. It is only afterward that our minds begin to mull over the experience and give it meaning.

The next step is speaking. If we look upset, a friend may ask what's wrong. We then have to find words to communicate the mass of feeling going on inside our heads. Talking about our thoughts forces us to make sense out of them. However, talking also allows us a lot of freedom—to ramble, to start a sentence but not to finish it, to stutter, to use a lot of "uh's." We can also add facial expressions and body language to speech to make our meaning clear.

The final stage is writing. Writing is speech put down on paper, but in a much more solid way. The hesitations, the ramblings, and the "I dunno's" disappear. Nor does writing have additional help from a distraught face or waving arms. Writing your thoughts down really means coming to terms with them to a degree not possible in conversation. They must stand alone with only the written symbols to convey all the meaning.

> "If I could not write, I could not write to my friends who move far away."
> Fred Wenzlaff, grade 6

How Does a Child Learn to Write?

This is the usual sequence that a child goes through when he first learns to put his thoughts down on paper. These steps almost always take place from about preschool (age four) through the third grade.

1. The child tells the adult (parent or teacher) the thought he wants written down. This is referred to as *dictation*.

a. The child may start with one or two words to use as labels ("My dog," or "trucks").

b. The child then begins to dictate a whole sentence; this will usually be done in connection with a drawing the child has made ("That is a car crashing into another car").

c. The child *observes* at this stage how the adult writes thoughts down (capital letters, shapes of letters, shapes of words, periods, etc.).

2. The child dictates his message to the adult and then tries to copy part of the message (the child writes "Dear Mom and Dad" and "Love, Kirsten" on a letter; the adult prints the rest of the letter).

3. The child dictates his thoughts to the adult, who writes them down. The child then copies the entire message in his own writing. (In school, often a whole group of children will suggest thoughts for a group letter, for example.)

4. The child begins to write his own words and short sentences with a lot of help from the adult ("Our cat is black" or "This is my Mom"). This is the beginning of independent writing.

5. The child begins to write on his own with less help, but still seeks out an adult when needed.

6. The child writes on his own and uses self-help aids more and more (personal dictionary, word lists, etc.).

What about . . .

GRAMMAR?

Many parents are concerned that their kids aren't learning enough grammar—that "they just don't teach it anymore." Before you get too upset, it is important to understand that the study of grammar *by itself* does not improve writing.

What grammar can do. It gives us a set of terms (such as noun, verb, adjective, etc.) which are useful when we want to talk about writing:

"Notice the colorful adjectives Mark Twain uses."

"Try not to start every sentence with a noun."

What grammar cannot do. It cannot substitute for writing. Too often teachers (and parents) get caught up in the teaching of grammar because it's easier to judge. But this is like insisting a long distance runner spend hours studying charts on how her muscles work. A brief discussion may be fine—but then she's got to get out and run.

And your child must get out and write!

Studies have shown that there is no relationship between studying grammar, as a separate activity, and improved writing. Many weak writers can get an *A* on a grammar test, yet there are excellent writers who don't know a "gerund" from an errand.

How grammar should be used. If your child can write clear, complete sentences, he does not need to spend much time naming the parts of those sentences. However, if his writing is dull or vague, he may benefit from a study of adjectives (words that describe things) and how they can work for him. Remember: grammar is like a warm-up. Don't confuse it with the main event.

CREATIVE WRITING?

Creative writing usually refers to writing that is fun and original; one of its main purposes is to get students excited about writing.

Unfortunately, creative writing has gotten a bad name in recent years. Many experts feel it has contributed to the decline of writing skills. It is not creative writing itself that has been criticized, but the *way it has been handled*.

Too often creative writing has been an "anything goes" exercise. It did not have to be organized, to be neat, or to have structure. Such rules, it was felt, would inhibit children's creativity. Creative writing became an excuse for lazy writing.

Children need to do creative writing, but it must be done well. Here are some guidelines for looking at creative writing assignments from school and writing practice you give your child at home:

1. Just because your child has written down what he "feels" does not necessarily mean it is good writing. Even though your child may be "inspired," he still may need direction to get his work into a form that will also inspire others.

2. To be good, writing must communicate. If your child is the only one who can make sense of what he's written, there is no point to the writing. Only a personal diary need not speak to anyone but the writer.

3. Creative writing should not be set apart from other kinds of school writing. A report or an essay needs to be colorful and original. In the same manner, poems need structure and short stories must make sense.

4. Contrary to the opinion that your child will be frustrated if she has to think about rules is the belief that having a grip on the basic skills actually frees your child to write. She can then say what she wants without constantly worrying about rules.

5. Your child should be encouraged to get his ideas down first without worrying too much about form or rules. *Then* you or your child's teacher can help him present his ideas in the best way possible. Your child should realize that his creative efforts *deserve to be written well*. To say that spelling doesn't matter in a short story is to say that the short story isn't as important as "real writing." This just isn't so.

> "I like to write because it's an excellent way to express my innermost feelings that are not easily spoken."
>
> Tom Parks, grade 10

WRITING INSTRUCTION?

Although we have seen how much reading has had the upper hand in education, writing is now competing for equal time.

One of the most impressive attempts to improve the teaching of writing is the National Writing Project, which started at the University of California at Berkeley. Under this program, classroom teachers are retrained in how to teach writing and, in turn, return to their schools to teach others.

As a result of such projects, many schools around the nation are trying some new methods. You should be familiar with them and what they are trying to accomplish.

WRITING INSTRUCTION?

1. *Peer grading*. The children in the class read each other's writing. In this manner, students have an opportunity to write for someone besides the teacher. It is also believed that children can help each other improve, along with the teacher's help.

2. *Emphasis on content and then mechanics*. Students are encouraged to get their ideas down first and worry about writing skills second. This approach is based on the belief that many children, especially from the fourth grade on, have developed "blocks" to writing that need to be removed.

Studies have shown that many writing skills improve on their own when children become more relaxed about writing.

3. *Grading a paper for one thing only*. A paper may be graded on the basis of one main aspect, such as organization or use of varied sentences. If that "one thing" is done correctly, the paper is a success. Other errors not being judged are overlooked at this time. This way a student is not presented with an overwhelming amount of red ink but can zero in on one problem at a time. It's more effective and less frustrating.

DIALECTS?

Many children in the United States speak a dialect which differs from standard English. These differences can be noted in vocabulary, pronunciation, and the way sentences are put together. Although there are a number of different dialects, the most prominent is Black English.

Since language is, above all, communication, it would be pointless to expect a child to give up his style of speaking with his friends and family. Nevertheless, more opportunities will be open to the child who can use standard English as well. Therefore, most writing experts today *encourage a child to maintain his own dialect, but also to become comfortable in the common "code" used by society at large*. Parents can help their children accomplish this goal:

1. Whenever your child does creative work (poems, short stories, and personal experiences), have him write them in his own dialect. If your child is dictating a story, write down *exactly* what the child says. The older child also writes his words down as he would speak them.

However, it is important that your child follow the rules that apply to all good writing: complete sentences, descriptive words,

good spelling, and ideas holding together.

2. When your child has to write reports, letters, and the like (that are designed to reach a wider audience), you should encourage him to use standard English.

Remember: teach your child to use the style of English most appropriate for the situation.

SPELLING?

Although there is absolutely no connection between spelling and intelligence, people are still judged on how well they can spell. Since bad spelling is considered "dumb" in our society, anyone who wants to make it—in college or in a job — had better figure a way to beat the system.

Your child may feel spelling rules make no sense at all. In many cases, he's right. Nevertheless, at some point he's going to have to learn to spell or his writing will be dismissed. There are basically four ways he can realistically do this:

1. He can be a "natural-born speller" (congratulations!).

2. She can become a good speller by memorizing words.

3. He can rely on a dictionary or word-book (these will not help, however, if he has no idea how to spell the word).

4. She can rely on other people to tell her how to spell.

A weak speller will probably need to use a combination of methods 2, 3, and 4—with a heavy emphasis on #2. The more words your child can spell on his own—without a friend or a dictionary—the better off he will be. On most school exams, he will not be able to use outside help. He will need to rely on himself first.

First of all, don't make a big deal about every misspelled word or you will drive your kid nuts. Try to work on words that you feel someone your child's age should know how to spell. Use our spelling charts and common sense to help with this. Then take off from there.

Tips for helping your child to spell

1. When your child is first starting to write, have him get his words down as well as he can—take a stab at any words he doesn't know how to spell. Then go back and correct the spelling later. This keeps the flow of writing going.

2. If your child continues to spell a word wrong, correct her and help her with it. Allowing her to write the same word wrong over and over will simply reinforce the bad spelling.

3. If a very young child is having difficulty with a word, write the word in large print and have him trace the letters of the word with his finger.

4. A parent must be as tolerant with spelling as with early attempts to speak. It takes time and it's difficult. Just because *you* were a good speller does not mean it will come easily to your child.

5. Help your child see the cause of his spelling error, especially in cases like these: writing *there* for *their* is a meaning problem; writing *Febuary* for *February* is a pronunciation problem.

6. The important thing is to help your child learn useful words she will *need* in her writing. Don't spend time working on a word like *kaleidoscope* when more common words are still being misspelled.

7. Spelling must be stressed in *all school work*, not just English classes. Insist on good spelling for the science report *and* the book report.

8. Remember, the ability to tell the difference between certain sounds is a skill that grows with your child. First graders may have difficulty hearing the difference between *glass* and *class* or *try* and *dry*. Spelling errors can result. Again, be patient.

9. Help your child learn how to attack a problem word:

   a. say the word aloud

   b. write the word

   c. say the syllables of the word and point to them (con - ver - sa - tion)

   d. write the word without looking at the original one

   e. check the word against the original

10. One of the best ways to learn to spell a word is to figure out a trick that will help your child remember it. Here are a few:

believe—you can't believe a *lie* (be*lie*ve)

weird—*we* are weird (*we*ird)

dessert—the more calories, the more *s*'s

friend—there is no *end* to friendship (fri*end*)

Obviously, the trick should center on the part of the word that's causing the problem.

11. In general, try to develop a *spelling conscience* in your child. He needs to look upon spelling as manners—a polite way of presenting his writing. It is both unnecessary and lazy to burden writing with a lot of misspelled words.

The Home Environment and Writing

Good writing is the result of a home environment that encourages communication in al.
forms—speaking, listening, reading, and writing. The more your family uses words, the
more natural it will be for your child to write.

Talk at Home

• Talk, talk, talk to your child! Carry on meaningful conversations, even with small children. Discuss your frustrating day with your three-year-old. She may not understand every word, but notice how she listens!

• Encourage your child to speak clearly and to make sense. Don't interpret for him. However, it is important that you do not constantly correct his speech. The flow of ideas is what's important. Insisting on perfect speech will make any child clam up.

• Try to eat some meals with your child and use these as times to talk. An amazing research study showed that children whose parents talked to them at breakfast (before they went to school) did better in reading and writing.

• If you must correct your child, *wait until she's finished speaking* and then suggest a better way of saying it.

Remember: speaking well comes before writing well!

Read at Home

• Read aloud to your children no matter how old they are. In this manner they hear how words fit together and how powerful good writing can be. When you read something that's good, mention the writing and what makes it work: "Can you believe the details she uses? Can't you just feel the cold?"

• Reading builds vocabulary that children can later transfer to their own writing. Studies show that the best readers are the best writers.

Write at Home

• Pay attention to everything your child writes—from kindergarten scribbles to high school term papers. Children must get a response to what they have written in order for them to feel it's worthwhile.

• React first to *what* your child has written—not *how* it is written. Your child wrote the paper to say something, so deal with content first. Try to help your child prevent errors before they happen. If he's going to write birthday thank-you notes, for example, provide him with a list of words he'll need to know—*handkerchief, stationery, o. calculator.*

• Always focus on significant error only! (It's understandable that a fourth grader may misplace a comma, but he should know where a period goes; misspelling *doesn't* is a more serious error for a tenth grader than leaving an *r* out of *occurred*. Limit the amount of corrections you make on any one paper. Zero in on the major ones, but let smaller ones go. Otherwise your child will get too discouraged.

• Accept your child's writing level even if *you* could make it sound much more brilliant! If a second grader uses *awful*, don' suggest a word like *grotesque*. A child should sound like a child—not a college graduate.

• Let your child's teachers know the value your family places on writing. It may not result in any miracles, but it can't hurt.

122

To encourage writing in general—

A flat, smooth surface to write on and good lighting
A variety of paper—lined, plain, large, small
Various things to write with—pencils, pens, chalk, crayons, felt pens
Erasers and/or "white out" liquid eraser

To encourage letter writing—

Stationery of different types (large sheets, postcards, notes)
Envelopes—large and small
Stamps and child's own address book
• Child's own address stickers

To encourage good writing by example—

Jack and Jill magazine (ages 6–12)
Cricket magazine (ages 8–12)
• *Stone Soup* magazine (written entirely by children, ages 6–12)

To encourage good spelling and word usage—

Provide a dictionary—at least by fourth grade
• Any good first dictionary (grades 1–3)
• *Macmillan's Dictionary for Children* (grades 4–6)
• *Thorndike Barnhart Handy Dictionary* (junior high)
• *American Heritage Dictionary*, college ed. (high school)
• *Roget's Thesaurus* (a book of synonyms to help your child use different words instead of the same ones over and over)
• *Webster's New World 33,000 Word Book* (an alphabetical list of words and how to spell them; much quicker to check spelling than a dictionary)

Miscellaneous gift ideas—

• pencils with child's name
• personalized stationery
• rubber stamp and ink pad
• magnetic alphabet letters
• funny-shaped erasers
• typewriter (a used one is fine)

"I write to express my thoughts and to communicate to the busy world around me."

Annalee Andres, grade 7

WRITING-READINESS ACTIVITIES (PRESCHOOL & KINDERGARTEN)

Before your child begins the first grade, there are many things she will be doing to prepare for writing. Some activities may begin as early as age two when your child scribbles away in her first coloring book. Others will occur in your child's nursery school and still more during kindergarten.

Clear Speaking

More and more evidence indicates that there is a *very strong* relationship between how a child speaks and how she writes. Spoken English must follow the same rules that later will be used in written English:

- complete sentences
- proper verb tense

- sensible statements
- use of descriptive words

- ability to persuade
- sticking to the point

Since speech is so important, let's look at some facts about children's speaking habits. These will give you some ways to measure your own child's ability.

1. A child's basic grammar (the words he chooses, the verb tense, how he puts sentences together) is formed by age 3½! Listen to the speech of a talkative three-year-old and you'll realize the staggering amount he's learned in thirty-six months.

2. A normal three- or four-year-old is a *big talker*. One study showed that a three-year-old stopped talking for only 19 minutes of his waking hours. (This will come as no surprise to many weary parents.) These talking machines have clocked in at 7,600 words per day!

3. The most advanced talker is the only child because he converses most with adults. Not surprisingly, the least advanced talkers usually are twins.

4. If language growth is proceeding normally, you will be able to tell by the *length* of your child's sentences:

18 months: (1 and 2 words)—"Want cookie"
3½ years: (4 words)—"I want a cookie."
5 years: (5 words)—"I want a chocolate cookie."

5. Girls often will use more words than boys and speak in complete sentences sooner. Boys, however, tend to ask more questions and use more slang.

Encouraging speech at home—

• *Encourage vocabulary development* because a large speaking vocabulary leads to more descriptive writing. Ask your child questions about what he says. (Example: "What size dog did you see? What color was he? What did his bark sound like?")

• *Encourage your child to tell a whole story on his own* because organizing thoughts will be very helpful later in writing. (Example: "Tell me about a teddy bear and a rabbit who go to the doctor.") You can start by telling a story yourself and letting your child finish it.

• *Discourage baby talk* because pronunciation has a lot to do with future spelling.

• *Read the same stories or poems* over and over again to your child (even though it may drive you mad). Somehow this builds a child's speaking ability. (Notice that your child will ask you to do this—you won't have to suggest it!)

• *Be sure your child spends time playing with toys that encourage speaking,* such as toy phones, figures for dramatic play (little people, doll houses, cars, etc., to "act out" with), playground equipment used with other kids.

• *Be sure your child does not do non-talkative activities only* (painting, watching television, observing activities but not participating).

• *Do things aloud that your child will later write down,* such as lists, stories, "favorite" things, etc.

Dictation

Dictation is an important step in the writing process. It is in this way that your child learns how his ideas can be put down on paper with symbols, and then read exactly as he said them. It gives children the idea of writing and makes them excited about learning to write themselves. Here are some tips on doing dictation successfully with your child:

• Have your child tell you something about a picture he has drawn. You can encourage this by asking your child, "What's happening in this picture?" or "Tell me about this farm." *Don't* say: "What's this supposed to be?"

• Try for a complete thought. Instead of writing down "monster eating," push for "This is a monster eating another monster." (Unpleasant, but complete.)

• Encourage your child to come up with several sentences eventually. To do this, ask your child more questions about her drawing: "What is this dinosaur doing over at the side of your picture?" "Is this daytime or nighttime?"

• Print your child's words in large, clear letters—not handwriting. Try to come close to the kind of printing he will be doing in school (lowercase letters with uppercase at the start of the sentence or for someone's name).

• Read your child's words back to her and have other people read them too. This shows that writing something down makes it last, and that each person can read exactly what was said.

> "I think writing is useful because it helps people express their feelings toward one another."
>
> Nia Cooper-Willis
> grade 6

Home Writing Activities

Even though your preschooler or kindergarten child does not write yet, there are a number of pre-writing activities you can do besides speech and dictation. The purpose of these activities is to get your child excited about the idea of writing and to build up his coordination for the act of writing.

___ Encourage your child to add something of his own to letters you write—some scribbling or a drawing. Have him "sign" his name on a birthday card along with other members of the family.

___ Encourage activities that develop the muscular coordination that will eventually be needed to write: hammering, shaping clay, dialing a phone, using crayons, etc.

___ Encourage activities that require the coordinated use of pen or pencil: connect-the-dots, tracing, or coloring.

___ Occasionally move your finger along the words as you read to your child. This develops the idea that writing goes from left to right.

___ Make a big deal about early scribblings and attempts to write. Put them up on the refrigerator or bulletin board and point them out to others. ("Look what Marcos wrote yesterday!")

___ Ask your child what her scribblings say when she pretends to write. This way she connects writing with meaning.

___ Provide your child with *experiences*: pets, trips, TV specials, movies, etc. Try to include your little one in other family members' activities whenever possible: sister's soccer game, older brother's musical show, grandpa's Veterans Day parade, Dad's fishing trip. *The more your child has done, the more he will have to write about.*

___ Help your child make a book. He can either draw his own pictures for it, cut them out of magazines, or use actual photographs. Paste the pictures on pages and have your child dictate captions to go with each one. Then staple the pages together and "read" the new book to your child. Have others read it too.

By the end of kindergarten, your child should be able to—

1. Speak clearly and with ease—without mumbling, repeating, or using baby talk.

2. Recognize most letters of the alphabet and a few words, such as his own name or a word like *stop* on a traffic sign.

3. Show an interest in words and try to write things. You should frequently hear: "What does that say?"

4. Communicate ideas and stories through drawing; this is the first real step toward writing.

5. Enjoy books and printed materials of all kinds; she should begin to understand that books and the like *are writing*—and she will be able to do that too.

6. Tell a story that makes sense; it should have a beginning, a middle, and an end. Your child should not lose his train of thought while telling it.

7. Print her name (although not well) and a few other letters; most children do not have the muscular coordination to do much writing at this age.

Remember: the times when your child does these things will vary, depending on his own rate of growth, his nursery school, and his kindergarten.

WRITING SKILLS (GRADES 1–12)

The following charts can give you a general picture of where your child's writing ability should be at different grade levels in school. They are divided as follows:

- 1–3: early elementary
- 4–6: upper elementary
- 7–9: junior high
- 10–11: high school

Different skills are covered at each grade level, such as types of writing done, paragraphs, sentences, word usage, grammar, capitalization, punctuation, spelling, and style.

The writing skill charts are divided differently than either reading or math charts because it is much more difficult to say exactly what a child should be doing in *each* grade. Thus, the skills are divided into three-year blocks. Still, these are only general guidelines. Many teachers may introduce a certain item (such as quotation marks) sooner than fourth grade because the children are writing the types of stories that need them. Others may teach something later for the same reason. Keep that in mind as you compare your child's schoolwork with our writing guidelines.

Furthermore, a skill may be introduced at one grade level, but not mastered until later. For example, the apostrophe to show ownership ("Laura's doll") is usually taught in the third grade, but many children do not become comfortable with this skill until fifth or sixth grade. (There are probably some high school teachers out there who'd like a nickel for every apostrophe left off.)

As we indicated, some skills will be taught on a different timetable from the one we've shown here. But, by and large, these skills match up with many district learning guides and writing texts. *This does not mean your child will be able to do them when he should.* Many bright high school kids are struggling with skills they should have learned in the fifth grade (that's why there's a writing problem). However, knowing what your child *should* learn is the first step to solving the problem.

The writing skills charts are designed to be used in a number of different ways, depending on your child's needs and how closely you wish to monitor his writing progress. A few suggestions follow.

How to use the charts

1. You can look over the grade-level skills each fall before your child starts school. This will give you some idea of what skills he should be learning and what skills he should already know.

2. You can compare any writing your child does with the writing skills presented on the charts. For example, if he is not capitalizing the first word of a sentence in the second grade, a look at the charts would indicate it's OK to help him with this. On the other hand, if he's not using quotation marks correctly in the second grade, you will know not to be too concerned.

3. During the school year, you can check with your child's teacher if you feel there are some basic writing skills (such as paragraph writing) that are not being covered at school.

4. At the end of the school year, you can browse through the chart and see if your child seems to be on target. Obviously, it will be easiest to measure your child during the final grade covered on the skill chart. (For example, by the end of third grade, your child should know all the skills taught in first, second, *and* third.)

Writing Skills (Grades 1–3)

It is during these years that your child will learn the basics of writing: how to form letters, words, and sentences. He will discover that ideas which form in his head can be put down on paper for others to read. Children at this age usually like to write and seldom need to be pushed.

WHAT TO EXPECT OF YOUR CHILD

During the first, second, and third grades, your child should:

1. Be gaining confidence about writing.
2. Be getting her ideas down on paper. (Concerns about how she puts her ideas down will be dealt with gradually.)
3. Begin to understand that there are rules of writing—capital letters, periods, spelling, and similar basics.
4. Be doing a good job on small amounts of writing. Trying to write too much too soon can lead to frustration and a dislike of writing.
5. Be writing from one to two pages a week. (This would be an estimate of all their single sentences put together; this does not mean one to two pages at one time.)
6. Be able to write clear, original sentences with no help and be working on the paragraph by the end of the third grade.

> "I like to write because it's fun and beautiful. Life would not be fun if I could not write because I would be scribbling all the time."
>
> Maggie Mason, grade 2

TYPES OF WRITING

____ can write short stories—first only a few sentences in length and then moving up to a paragraph in length; some children can use several paragraphs to tell a story.

____ can write a simple, friendly letter

____ can address an envelope properly

____ can write a short summary of a book (six or seven sentences)

____ can put titles on stories, reports, or poems

____ understands the idea of rhyme and can write simple poems

____ knows the proper heading for school work (name, date, teacher)

____ can read something in a book or magazine and write a few sentences about it (beginning of "report writing" skills)

____ can begin simple editing of own work (check for spelling, capital letters, periods, or words left out)

____ can begin to write paragraphs with a topic sentence, supporting ideas underneath, and a "wrap up" sentence, as in the following example:

My Brother

My brother is the most fun to play with. He builds me things out of blocks. He also lets me read his comic books. Sometimes he watches TV with me and other things. I love my brother a lot.

SENTENCES

___ knows the term *sentence*
___ knows a sentence is a complete thought which tells or asks something
___ can write all four kinds of sentences:

statement: Harold is a boy.
question: Is Harold a boy?
exclamation: Harold is some boy!
order: Don't hit Harold.

___ can identify a subject and a predicate in a sentence:

The family / took a vacation

(subject)   (predicate)

___ can make an incomplete sentence ("running down the street") into a complete one ("The boy was running down the street.")
___ can write sentences that *average* six words in length by the end of the third grade

WORD USAGE

___ understands the idea of opposites (war/peace)
___ understands the idea of synonyms, that is, different words with the same meaning (*bad, awful, terrible*)
___ begins to use more and varied adjectives to describe things ("A *bad* ghost . . ."/ "A *horrible* ghost . . .")
___ begins to use more and varied words to describe action (adverbs) ("He ran *rapidly* . . ." / "She looked *fearfully* . . .")
___ asks about how to spell words or uses own word list
___ starts using a children's dictionary
___ uses simple plurals (*horse/horses; dress/dresses*)
___ uses simple endings (*sing/singing; dance/danced*)
___ uses correct forms of most words ("He *brought* this." NOT "He *brung* this.")

GRAMMAR

___ can make nouns and verbs agree ("The girls *are* nice." NOT "The girls *is* nice.")
___ knows how to spell and use personal pronouns (*I, me, you, he, him, she, her, it, we, us, they, them*)

CAPITAL LETTERS

___ to begin a sentence ("This is my snake.")
___ for people's or pets' names (Rosita, Fido)
___ for the name of a school (Venado Middle School)
___ for the names of cities, states, and countries (Houston, Kansas, Spain)
___ for the word "I" ("The work I did was difficult.")
___ for names of streets (Fremont Avenue)
___ for special titles: Mr., Miss, Ms., Mrs.
___ for months and days of the week (April, Tuesday)
___ for holidays (Hannukah, Christmas)
___ for the first word of a letter ("Dear Gabriel . . .")
___ for words in a title of a report or story ("My Vacation")
___ for names of books or magazines (*Stuart Little, Highlights*)

PUNCTUATION

Periods
___ at the end of a sentence
___ after numbers when making a list
___ after someone's initial (John F. Kennedy)
___ after abbreviations (Ave., Nov.)

Commas
___ in dates (December 10, 1981)
___ words on a list ("I like dogs, cats, and snakes.")
___ between city and state (Koloa, Hawaii)
___ after a greeting ("Dear Holly,")
___ after a letter closing ("Love, Dave")

Apostrophes
____ in contractions (is not = isn't;
I am = I'm)

Colons
____ in writing the time (1:30 PM)

Question Marks and Exclamation Marks
____ at the end of a sentence ("Can you go to the party?" "My mom won't let me!")

KNOWLEDGE OF ALPHABET LETTERS

____ should know the names of all alphabet letters and be able to say and print them
____ be able to pick out words starting with the same letter
____ put words into alphabetical order by first letters
____ begin handwriting

SPELLING

Spelling at this level is very difficult—every word is new. Try to work with your child on words that he is going to need frequently in his writing (see chart below). The more of these words he can master, the easier writing will be for him.

Spelling Chart #1—100 most commonly used words (grades 1–3) in order of frequency of use

1. I	21. at	41. do	61. up	81. think
2. the	22. this	42. been	62. day	82. say
3. and	23. with	43. now	63. much	83. please
4. to	24. but	44. can	64. out	84. him
5. a	25. on	45. would	65. her	85. his
6. you	26. if	46. she	66. order	86. got
7. of	27. all	47. when	67. yours	87. over
8. in	28. so	48. about	68. know	88. make
9. we	29. me	49. they	69. well	89. may
10. for	30. was	50. any	70. an	90. again
11. it	31. very	51. which	71. here	91. before
12. that	32. my	52. some	72. them	92. two
13. is	33. had	53. has	73. see	93. send
14. your	34. our	54. or	74. go	94. after
15. have	35. from	55. there	75. what	95. work
16. will	36. am	56. us	76. come	96. could
17. be	37. one	57. good	77. where	97. dear
18. are	38. time	58. know	78. no	98. made
19. not	39. he	59. just	79. how	99. glad
20. as	40. get	60. by	80. did	100. like

Writing Skills (Grades 4–6)

In the upper elementary years, your child will be putting his newly acquired writing skills to work—writing paragraphs, reports, and short stories. Despite the fact that much has been learned, there's still a long way to go in terms of writing ability.

Often, around the fourth grade, teachers may begin to separate language drills (workbooks, grammar work sheets, etc.) from actual writing situations. Because of this, it is possible that your child will not be writing as much or as often as you would expect at this level.

WHAT TO EXPECT OF YOUR CHILD

During the fourth, fifth, and sixth grades your child should:

1. Continue to gain confidence as a writer. It is easy to get frustrated by all the new and more difficult writing demands.

2. Reinforce and enlarge the basic skills learned in the first three grades (see pages 128–130) so he can move on to higher ability levels.

3. Increase her vocabulary in order to say all the things she wants to say.

4. Have a firm handle on the basic spelling words needed in his writing. This will give him confidence and help the writing flow.

5. Be able to proofread her own paper for major errors.

6. Get used to the idea that writing is rewriting. Your child should begin doing rough drafts and then the final copy.

7. Be writing about two to three pages a week (all work combined should equal this).

8. Be able to write a fully developed paragraph with a topic sentence, supporting details, and a concluding sentence. This may sound easy, but it's no small task!

> "Life would be pretty dull if I could not write because there are some feelings I do not want to share. Yet I want to get it out somehow so writing would be the best thing."
>
> Mia Greenfield, grade 4

TYPES OF WRITING

___ reports: this is the age when your child learns the many skills needed in doing a basic report—
1. make an outline:
   I. Fantasy Games
      A. Dungeons & Dragons
         1. why it is fun
         2. how it makes you think
2. take notes: after reading some information in a book or magazine, your child can write it down *in his own words*.
3. use an index or table of contents in books and magazines.
4. use the card catalog in the library.
5. write up a simple bibliography: Stewart, Paul, *Judo*, Lippincott, 1976

___ basic business letters—can write a simple letter asking for a brochure or the like

___ poetry—can understand some of the methods used in poems and can write several different types of poems

___ book reports of one, two or three paragraphs in length (depending on the child)

PARAGRAPHS

_____ write a full paragraph with topic sentence, supporting details, and a concluding sentence.

For example, a paragraph on "Cats" might begin with the topic sentence:

Cats are wonderful pets.

This is followed by three or four ideas that support or prove the topic sentence:

1. Cats are clean animals.

2. Cats can take care of themselves.

3. It is an old belief that cats are lucky to have around the house.

4. Cats keep people from feeling lonely.

Concluding with a wrap-up sentence:

Wouldn't you like to own a cat?

_or_

You couldn't have a better pet than a cat.

_____ indent at the beginning of each new paragraph

_____ begin to use simple transitions (or connecting words) between ideas or paragraphs:

First, we went to Lake Tahoe.

Next, we visited my grandma in Oregon.

Finally, we got to Seattle.

SENTENCES

_____ begins to spot a run-together sentence and correct it:

Leslie is my older sister, she's in high school. (Put in "and" or a period after sister)

_____ no longer writes incomplete sentences:

I had to use binoculars. _To see the eagles._ (incomplete)

_____ makes writing interesting by varying sentence length (routinely writes sentences of eight words or more)

WORD USAGE

_____ uses a dictionary in new ways:

to find more than one meaning for a word

to be quite good at alphabetical order (puts _bleed_ before _blend_)

knows approximate position of a word in the dictionary (_company_ near the front; _thief_ near the back)

_____ avoids errors in words that sound alike but are spelled and used differently. The big ones are:

to, two, too

there, their, they're

here, hear

know, no

lose, loose

quit, quite, quiet

chose, choose

break, brake

new, knew

forth, fourth

_____ begins to use similes (comparisons) in writing:

Kim swims _like a dolphin_

The trees looked _like soldiers standing in a row._

GRAMMAR

Grammatical terms are introduced and used to talk about writing: noun, verb, adjective, adverb, preposition, conjunction, pronoun.

CAPITAL LETTERS

_____ for organizations (Boy Scouts, Future Farmers of America)

_____ for nationalities and race (Russian, Mexican, Italian)

_____ with brand names (Cheerios, Hot Wheels, Kool-Aid)

_____ with companies (Goodyear, Sears)

_____ for names of geographical areas (Sahara Desert, Rocky Mountains, Lake Michigan)

_____ for first word of a quote: Carlos said, "Move out of the way."

PUNCTUATION

Commas

___ used before a quote: Bill said, "What's for dinner?"

___ to make a sentence's meaning clear: After we rested, Susan left the park (comma after *rested*)

___ in a series of things: We took sleeping bags, tents, and rafts on the trip.

___ after an introductory phrase: Until it's summer, we can't go to the pool.

Colon

___ in a business letter—Dear Sir:

___ for a list—Bring the following: cookies, napkins, forks, and mustard.

___ in a play—Sue: Where's the boat?
　　　　　　Ed: I sold it.

Quotation Marks

___ for dialogue to indicate exactly what someone said: "I hate this shirt!" screamed Rick.

___ for the names of stories, poems, or magazine articles: I read "The Brothers Lionheart" in my magazine.

Hyphen

___ to separate words that don't fit on one line:　We are all on the party com-mittee this year at school.

Underlining

___ for book titles: I read <u>Little House on the Prairie</u>.

Apostrophes

___ consistently used to show ownership: Jim's house.

SPELLING

Children will often merely memorize words for a spelling test and then promptly forget them. Be sure your child *really* knows these words!

Spelling Chart #2—100 commonly used words (grades 4-6)

1. accident	21. choice	41. good-bye	61. money	81. said
2. address	22. climb	42. guess	62. much	82. Saturday
3. airplane	23. clothes	43. half	63. never	83. says
4. almost	24. color	44. hear	64. none	84. seems
5. always	25. country	45. height	65. often	85. shoe
6. American	26. decide	46. hope	66. once	86. since
7. answer	27. didn't	47. hour	67. past	87. some
8. around	28. different	48. hungry	68. peace	88. stop
9. arrive	29. dining	49. hurry	69. perhaps	89. story
10. beautiful	30. doctor	50. instead	70. piece	90. straight
11. because	31. doesn't	51. interesting	71. plan	91. sure
12. begin	32. don't	52. it's	72. possible	92. through
13. build	33. early	53. just	73. prove	93. together
14. busy	34. easy	54. know	74. purpose	94. too
15. buy	35. enough	55. lady	75. raise	95. trouble
16. can't	36. every	56. later	76. read	96. until
17. careful	37. excellent	57. library	77. ready	97. weather
18. carrying	38. February	58. lying	78. realize	98. which
19. certain	39. friend	59. many	79. really	99. woman
20. children	40. future	60. minute	80. safe	100. write

Writing Skills (Grades 7–9)

By this stage, your child's writing should begin to match his speaking ability. In other words, he should have little difficulty writing what it is he thinks and feels. Having learned words, sentences, and paragraphs firmly in elementary school, he is now ready to write papers of three paragraphs or more on a frequent basis.

WHAT TO EXPECT OF YOUR CHILD

During seventh, eighth, and ninth grades your child should:

1. Develop a foundation of standard English usage. From such a base, he can then try more creative forms of expression should he so desire.

2. Be able to concentrate far more on the *content* of his work now that his basic skills have been established.

3. Practice choosing a topic and developing ideas around that topic.

4. Begin to realize the *power* of writing and its ability to affect people.

5. Begin to master commonly used but often misspelled words (see page 138).

6. Be able to proofread his own paper for most errors.

7. Be writing about three to four pages a week (at least).

8. By the end of the ninth grade, be able to write an essay (or composition) consisting of at least three paragraphs. He should also be able to write reports of five or six pages in length without any problem.

9. Realize that it may take several drafts before the final paper is written. Your child needs to remember that writing is a *process*.

TYPES OF WRITING

____ business letters—can now write an effective business letter using the proper form

____ forms and applications—can now complete almost any kind

____ rough drafts—is beginning to use a rough draft for almost all work (which he then edits before submitting a final copy)

____ poetry—understands more advanced ideas about poetry such as different types of rhyme

____ outlines—can now use outlines to a fairly detailed degree:

I. My Grandma Zelda
   A. Childhood
      1. birthplace
      2. houses lived in
      3. brothers
   B. Jobs held
      1. nursing
         a. training
         b. hospitals worked in
      2. bakery

____ proofreading—be able to evaluate a piece of writing for clarity, good writing, and emotional impact

____ dialogue—can write about half-page dialogue between two people

____ essays/compositions—
by the end of ninth grade, be able to write a 300- to 400-word essay

be able to narrow a topic down (Example: not "Whales," but "Migration Habits of the California Gray Whale")

be able to take a stand on a topic and defend it with some important facts

PARAGRAPHS

___ be able to organize material into properly structured paragraphs (see page 132); knows what information belongs where

___ be able to write transition (or "connecting") sentences to join paragraphs: "*In contrast*, dogs are much different from cats."

SENTENCES

___ seldom writes incomplete (fragment) or run-together (run-on) sentences

___ can write sentences that average about ten words by the end of the ninth grade, as well as sentences of varying length

WORD USAGE

___ is able to use a thesaurus (a book of synonyms, or words that are similar in meaning to other words)

___ starts using words that show shades of meaning or a certain degree, rather than absolutes:

absolutes	*more thoughtful words*
always	sometimes
never	usually
totally	occasionally
	almost

___ writing becomes increasingly descriptive—your child tries hard to find "just the right word" to use instead of tired, overused words

GRAMMAR

___ continues to use grammatical terms to discuss writing (the same terms as used in grades 4–6—plus a few new ones, such as *prepositional phrase*)

___ if sentence diagramming is used, it is usually introduced at this grade level

PUNCTUATION

Commas

___ masters the use of commas with introductory phrases: After the game, we went out for pizza.

___ uses commas in phrases that are "set off" from the rest of the sentence:

Tom Wills, the mayor of Weston, is my uncle.

Yes, you may go to the party.

Parentheses

___ used when phrase is not really part of the main sentence:

When you look at the facts (see graph A), it is obvious that we need better food in the cafeteria.

Underlining

___ with books and magazines:
I read Call of the Wild.
Sarah enjoys Seventeen magazine.

SPELLING

Begin working on the commonly used but often misspelled words listed on page 138 of the high school section.

> "I really enjoy writing. It lets my feelings escape and above all it's fun."
> Matt Otto, grade 9

Writing Skills (Grades 10–12)

Although writing ability has been largely determined by this age, it is still possible to make significant improvements. More students at this level understand the *need* for good writing—especially with college looming before many of them.

If this new motivation can be met with some good instruction and structured writing situations, much can happen. Unfortunately, few high schools have been able to offer students what they really need at this point. Nevertheless, let's take a look at what students should be doing for maximum progress.

WHAT TO EXPECT OF YOUR CHILD

During tenth, eleventh, and twelfth grades, your child should:

1. Be doing *all types* of writing: book reports, essays, character sketches, poetry, descriptions, and even research papers.

2. Be aware of what type of writing is appropriate for each assignment (this is called "audience"). A childhood memory, written for other students in the class, will be quite different from an essay for a college application.

3. Be able to use his writing time well—to decide on a topic, organize the paper, and get ideas down quickly. Those who are going to college will need to do this in all essay examinations.

4. Be developing an attitude about writing errors: that they are an *annoyance* that interferes with what is being communicated. The reader reading a paper is like a jogger moving along at a smooth, comfortable pace. Spelling errors, run-together sentences, and bad grammar are like obstacles placed in the runner's path. They break up the runner's movement. By this age, they are unacceptable!

5. Make every attempt possible to learn how to spell the commonly misspelled words (see page 138). It will be an enormous time-saver from here on out and every bit as useful as learning multiplication tables.

6. Be aware that real writers don't sit down and write a final copy. Writing a paper requires preparation time, a rough draft, someone to read the rough drafts, and perhaps several rewrites. A rewrite is more than simply correcting the spelling.

7. Be reading some of the well-known classics during these years: *Red Badge of Courage, The Scarlet Letter, Of Mice and Men, A Separate Peace, Death of a Salesman, To Kill a Mockingbird, All Quiet on the Western Front, The Old Man and the Sea, Hiroshima.* (For others, see the reading list on page 108.)

8. Be able to write an essay consisting of a number of paragraphs, with both an introduction and a conclusion. There should be no major writing errors of any kind. Above all, it should be well organized, clear, and make sense.

TYPES OF WRITING

___ reinforce the types of writing done in grades 7, 8, and 9—essays, book reports, poems, outlines, dialogues, etc.

___ write the three most common forms of essays:

narrative—an essay that tells what happened—very much like a story (sample topics: My Memorable Seventeenth Birthday, The Tale of Inspector Robbins, Mark Twain's Visit to a Gold Rush Town)

descriptive—a composition that describes a place, a person, or something of interest (sample topics: My Uncle Robert, The Grand Canyon at Sunrise, A Unique Invention)

expository—an essay that presents an idea or an opinion; this is the most "basic" kind of composition done in the upper grades and in college (sample topics: Teenage Drinking, The Causes of the Civil War, Why I Love Skiing)

___ write a 400- to 600-word essay (two to three pages) without much difficulty; some will be writing considerably longer papers

___ write a paper over a two-week (or more) period of time, such as a term paper—or can write a pressure paper during a 50-minute class period

___ type fairly well by now and turn in some typed papers

___ do a critique, or an evaluation of an article or piece of fiction such as a short story, play, or novel.

___ do a research paper using a number of sources, the library, footnotes, bibliography, etc. (not all students will have an opportunity to do this in high school)

PARAGRAPHS

___ write well-structured paragraphs without any difficulty; everything in the paragraph should clearly relate to the topic sentence

___ use more complicated transitions (or connections) between paragraphs: *on the other hand, in a similar manner, consequently, nevertheless*

SENTENCES

___ uses a variety of sentences and sentence patterns:
I really prefer to backpack on the Olympic Peninsula.
The Olympic Peninsula is my favorite backpacking area.

___ writes sentences of various lengths:
The Ancient Inn was located off a rugged dirt road about five miles outside of Lone Pine. It was well named. (seventeen words and four words)

___ writes sentences averaging about thirteen to fourteen words by the end of the twelfth grade.

WORD USAGE

___ tries to use new and more challenging words (even if not sure of the spelling)

___ uses a wordbook (for spelling) and a thesaurus (to help with word choices) frequently

___ is aware of connotation, or the feeling, certain words have:
he was thrifty/he was cheap
she was discriminating/she was picky

___ is aware of euphemisms, words used in place of other words that make us feel uncomfortable:
saying "passed away" for *died*
saying "intelligence gathering" for *spying*
saying "relocation center" for *concentration camp*

GRAMMAR

should be familiar with the parts of speech (verb, noun, etc.) and be able to understand and use the terms when talking about ways to improve writing.

CAPITALS AND PUNCTUATION

knows how to use all forms of capitalization and punctuation correctly—although there may be some slipups now and then, especially with the semicolon:
I couldn't stand Suzy; she was selfish and conceited.

STYLE

____ begins to work on the way thoughts are expressed—to get a feeling or point across in the most effective way.

____ reads different types of writing to get a feeling for the "style" of an author

____ can write in a straightforward, natural style that does not sound forced, awkward, or dull

____ avoids extra words or phrases that "clutter" up the paper; writing has been trimmed of all "fat"

____ writing is lively and interesting—it should hold the reader's interest

____ all writing is written with a particular "audience" in mind

SPELLING

continues to work on the list of 100 commonly used but often misspelled words. Many students this age still have great difficulties with some of these words. It will be a *great* time saver to learn them.

Spelling Chart #3—100 commonly used and misspelled words (grades 7–12)

1. accommodate
2. achievement
3. acknowledge
4. acquaint
5. acquire
6. affect
7. amount
8. annually
9. apparent
10. argue
11. argument
12. article
13. athletic
14. beautiful
15. believe
16. benefit
17. breathe
18. business
19. chief
20. choose
21. chose
22. college
23. commitment
24. committee
25. conscience
26. conscious
27. definitely
28. dependent
29. description
30. dessert
31. disappear
32. disappoint
33. disastrous
34. effect
35. embarrass
36. environment
37. exaggerate
38. existence
39. experience
40. explanation
41. fascinate
42. foreign
43. forty
44. height
45. interest
46. involve
47. loose
48. lose
49. marriage
50. necessary
51. ninety
52. occasion
53. occur
54. occurred
55. occurrence
56. opinion
57. opportunity
58. parallel
59. particular
60. performance
61. personal
62. personnel
63. possession
64. possible
65. practical
66. practice
67. preferred
68. prejudice
69. prepare
70. principal
71. principle
72. privilege
73. probably
74. procedure
75. proceed
76. psychologist
77. pursue
78. quiet
79. quit
80. quite
81. recommend
82. repetition
83. rhythm
84. sacrifice
85. safety
86. separate
87. similar
88. studying
89. succeed
90. succession
91. surgeon
92. surprise
93. than
94. thorough
95. transferred
96. unique
97. unnecessary
98. weird
99. write
100. writing

HELPING YOUR CHILD TO WRITE

If your child is to become a competent writer, he needs help with his schoolwork. He also needs to do many types of writing at home, in addition to the writing he does for school.

This section is designed to help you assist your child with both her school writing and her home writing. Each grade block contains the following:

- Helping with Schoolwork
- Special Problems
- Proofreading Guide for Children
- Home Writing Activities

A parent needs to show interest in what his child writes and provide opportunities for him to write at home. Along with this you need a combination of patience and firmness. *Patience* for the difficulty and time it takes to learn to write. *Firmness* in insisting on good writing habits. Most kids will live up to the standards you set for them.

Learning to write doesn't just happen. It's going to take some of your time and energy to pull it off. But you couldn't give your child a better gift.

Follow These Steps

Your Writer (Grades 1-3)

In the first years of school, your child will be learning the basics of writing. Since this is al
new, there will be lots of mistakes. Be very patient. Your main role during these grades is t
be positive about your child's early attempts to write. Here are some tips to help the proces
along—

HELPING WITH SCHOOLWORK

• *Always find something good to say* about your child's school writing. ("You really did remember a lot about our vacation!")

• *Keep some of your child's papers* that were written early in the school year — say October. Then bring them out in March to show him the improvement he's made.

• *Tell your child how to spell any word she asks.* Do not tell a child of this age to "go look it up." It takes too long to do this at this age and slows down the writing process.

• *Keep a list of words your child needs in his writing*, but has trouble spelling. They can be kept in a small notebook (alphabetized—a page for each letter) or a file box. Gradually encourage the use of these helpers.

• *Have your child make all his own correc*tions. You can tell him how it should b written, but let him erase it and write over.

• *Help your child develop her vocabular* by suggesting new words to replace over used words like *good* or *thing*. ("You'v used *good* here four times—how about *in teresting* or *fun?*")

• *Don't teach formal grammar* at this point A child of six, seven, or eight needs to hea and use language—not analyze it.

• *Insist that your child speak clearly.* Don' interpret for him because "you know wha he really means."

• *Have your child read books* appropriat for her age level. (See our book list, pr 106–107.)

SPECIAL PROBLEMS

PROBLEM: Writing that sounds short and choppy ("Dick and Jane" writing).

EXAMPLE: "I went to the park. There were trees. There were flowers. I saw ducks. I saw a kite. It was fun."

WHAT TO DO:

1. Be sure your child is reading something *other* than his school reading book. Basal readers tend to have this choppy sound, and children will imitate it.

2. Help your child *combine* a few of his thoughts.

"There were trees *and* flowers."
"I saw ducks *and* a kite."

3. Help your child add words to his sentences:

"I saw a *bright, red* kite."

PROBLEM: Child cannot write complete sentences, or runs them together.

EXAMPLE: "Running down the street." "I went to the park, there were trees, I saw a kite."

WHAT TO DO:

1. Write a simple, complete sentence on a strip of paper and then cut up the individual words. Mix up the slips of paper and have your child put them back together again in the original sentence, thus showing what words make up a sentence.

2. Have your child read sentences in a book and stop and look at you *at the end* of each sentence.

3. Dictate two sentences to your child and have her write them down, putting in capital letters and periods.

4. Be sure your child does not think a new line on the paper means he must start a new sentence.

5. Have your child complete parts of a sentence:

"_____was running down the street."

"When my grandma comes . . ."

PROBLEM: Child has so much trouble with spelling that he gets frustrated trying to write anything.

EXAMPLE: Child will write a few words and then must seek out an adult for spelling help. He then writes two more words and comes to another word he can't spell. And so it goes—till he gives up.

WHAT TO DO:

1. First of all, remember that some kinds of "bad spellings" show that the child is thinking—such as writing *frend* for *friend*. He is trying to sound out!

2. Provide child with words he may need before he begins to write. If he's doing thank-you notes, write down *birthday*, *grandma*, *calculator* or whatever ahead of time.

3. Have your child take a stab at a word he's unsure of and then check it with you later. This at least keeps the flow of writing going.

4. Have your child leave a space for the word he doesn't know and you can help him fill in all of them later.

5. Show your child how to use his wordbook, word file, or picture dictionary if he can do this quickly without frustration.

PROBLEM: Your child's ideas are way ahead of her writing ability. (This is a problem for *most* children at this age!)

EXAMPLE: The best way to tell this is to have your child first tell a story and then write the story. If the difference is amazing, she's probably frustrated at not being able to write what she's thinking.

WHAT TO DO:

1. Have your child try to say her sentence first and then copy it down. This still may be too difficult, however.

2. Have your child begin the story, and then you finish the writing, while she dictates. This method keeps up her interest in the story enough to finish it.

3. Have your child tell her story into a tape recorder and then slowly write it down with her.

PROBLEM: Child just can't get started with what he wants to write about.

EXAMPLE: When faced with a writing task, your child will say "I don't know what to say" or "I can't write anything."

WHAT TO DO:

1. Talk about the topic with your child first:

"Well, what can you say about your rabbit? Do you remember where we got him? How about the day we got him? Didn't your friend Tom go with us? Do you remember how you and Dad built the hutch?"

This helps your child recall facts about the topic and gives him ideas about what he can say.

2. If your child gets stuck while he's writing, ask questions about the topic. "What does your rabbit eat? You can mention that. Or how about how his fur feels?"

3. If your child is writing a story, help him think the whole thing through first.

4. For a very young child who gets stuck, start the sentences off for him, and let him finish them in his own words.

"We got our rabbit . . ."
"His fur . . ."
"He likes to eat . . ."

PROBLEM: Your child is writing more and more with his left hand.

WHAT TO DO: It is generally agreed today that it is unwise to try to make a left-handed child into a right-hander once he clearly favors one hand over the other. Parents can encourage the infant and very young child to use his right hand—but after he's made up his mind, you should go along with the decision.

Eleven percent of children become left-handed and they assume a wide variety of positions to write. When a child first starts to write, parents and teachers can try to discourage the left-hander in several ways from "hooking"

his arm around:

Have your child place his paper on the left side of the desk or writing surface and tilt it slightly toward the right.

Have your "lefty" hold his pencil farther back than the right-handed child would. This allows him to see what he has written much more easily.

In any case, your child will have decided on his "style" of writing by the fourth grade and it is damaging to try and change him after that point. Even if it's a wild and crazy "hook," so be it. There is no correlation between *how* a child writes and *what* he writes.

HOME WRITING ACTIVITIES (GRADES 1–3)

Make Lists

___ Shopping lists
___ Gifts your child wants
___ Lists of gifts for others
___ Items to take on a family trip
___ Names of friends and relatives and their phone numbers
___ Favorite toys
___ Best friends
___ Favorite TV shows and when they're on
___ Favorite foods
___ What I might be for Halloween
___ Favorite books
___ What I like to do the most
___ Animals we saw in Yellowstone Park

Leave Notes

___ Write messages on pieces of paper ("Feed the cat," or "I'm over at the Nelsons") for your child to read.
___ Encourage your child to leave notes, too ("I went to Donny's house" or "Wash my baseball shirt please!").
___ Use magnetic letters to write notes on the refrigerator.
___ Leave notes on your child's bulletin board ("Clean your room or else!").

Letters, Cards, Invitations

Letters and the like are a wonderful form of "first" writing. They have both a structure children can follow and a purpose.

___ Have child send her own greeting cards for various occasions (Valentine's Day, Christmas, Hanukkah, birthdays).
___ Have child write out his own birthday party invitations rather than using the ready-made ones.
___ Child should address envelopes as well.

"I like to write because it makes my mom happy at Seattle. Writing is useful for writing sentences."

Tecumseh Strong, grade 3

Creative ideas

___ Start a story and let your child end it (either aloud or in writing).
___ Finish sentences: "When I am twelve . . ." or "If I were a boy . . ."
___ Write or draw to music (suggested records: "Carnival of the Animals" or scary Halloween sounds).
___ Make "senses" charts—
At the beach, list what you would see, hear, taste, smell, and touch.
___ Give your child six words that he must use in a story (Example: cowboy, gallop, gun, quick, robber, bank, brave).
___ Encourage your child to come up with descriptive comparisons by having him finish phrases like these:

She ran fast as a _____
Daddy's snoring sounds like a _____

___ Write about a secret wish.
___ Make word lists for topics your child likes to write about:

Monsters	*Hawaii*
scary	vacation
teeth	beach
blood	surf
scream	waterfall
dragon	ocean
Dracula	

Other Ideas

___ Have child keep a record of a long-term activity (growing a garden).
___ Take pictures and then let your child write captions for them in the family album ("This is Matt building a sand castle.").
___ Play category games with your child (this helps him to organize his thoughts); put words on cards such as truck, apple, show, pear, car, train, dress, banana. Put cards under headings such as *clothes, transportation, food.*

PROOFREADING GUIDE FOR CHILDREN
(GRADES 1–3)

_____Have I said what I wanted to say? Does it make sense?

_____Have I used many different kinds of words, and not the same words over and over?

_____Can I add any words to make my writing more colorful or give a better description?

_____Is each sentence complete? Does it make sense when read by itself?

_____Does each sentence start with a capital letter and end with a period, question mark, or exclamation point?

_____Did I put in all my apostrophes? (for words that I make shorter, like "I'm," or words that show someone owns something, like "Susan's.")

_____Are there any words I'm not sure how to spell?

_____Did I leave any words out?

_____Does my paper need a title?

_____Is my printing or handwriting neat enough that every word can be read?

_____Am I proud of this paper?

WE SUGGEST THAT YOU PHOTOCOPY THIS CHECKLIST AND PUT IT ON YOUR CHILD'S BULLETIN BOARD OR SCHOOL NOTEBOOK.

Your Writer (Grades 4–6)

Each time your child takes a jump in writing levels, there will be an increase in errors as he tries out new forms of expression. Prepare, then, to see your child's writing skills vary in quality during this period of time.

As the demands on your child's ability become greater, he may develop a fear and dislike of writing. Parents need to offer much *support and encouragement* at this time. Here are some things you can do—

HELPING WITH SCHOOLWORK

• *Try to look over your child's schoolwork before it's due.* This allows time for discussion, correcting errors, and recopying, if necessary.

• *Continue to help your child write interesting and varied sentences.* Perhaps nothing else at this time will have more effect on the quality of his writing.

• *Help your child add details to her writing.* If she writes "It was a pretty day," try for, "It was a crisp windy day that smelled like fall."

• *Help your child with the idea of paragraphing*—when writing is moving to a new topic or idea. Be sure all his paragraphs are indented, with a topic sentence.

• *Don't hang over your child* while he is writing something. (How would *you* like it?)

• *Show your child what a "rough copy" of something is* and how it differs from the "final copy" he presents to the teacher.

• *Insist that all work turned in for school is neat and is your child's best effort.* Develop good attitudes *now*.

• *Do not write your child's papers for her.* Even if she's in a jam, let her face the music.

• *Help your child learn the spelling words* needed for this grade level (page 133).

SPECIAL PROBLEMS

PROBLEM: Student tries to write longer sentences, but ends up running them together.

EXAMPLE: We went to Vermont, we could only ski for an hour, it was so cold!

WHAT TO DO: Help your child see that these are three complete thoughts.

Complete thoughts must be joined by more than a comma.

"We went to Vermont. We could only ski for an hour *because* it was so cold."

Here are ways to join two ideas run together—

1. use a period between the two ideas

2. use a connector word (conjunction) between the two ideas (*and, because, or, but, yet,* etc.)

PROBLEM: Using too many *and*'s, especially to start sentences.

EXAMPLE: We went to Disneyland. And we saw the big castle, and then we went on a pirate ride and the Matterhorn. And then it was time for lunch. My sister and I had hot dogs. And my dad had a hamburger.

WHAT TO DO: There are several ways to help this kind of writing:

1. join some of the *and*'s to the sentence in front of it (example: "We went to Disneyland *and* saw the big castle.")

2. take away some of the *and*'s (example: "Then we went on the pirate ride and the Matterhorn.")

3. substitute other words for some of the *and*'s (example: "*When* it was time for lunch, my sister and I had hot dogs.")

PROBLEM: Your child has trouble writing an organized, clear paragraph about a topic.

EXAMPLE: I went fishing this summer and also horse-back riding. I did this in Wyoming. We also took a raft trip on the Snake River. We saw a moose and some deer on the river banks. I want to do this again next summer. It was hot and sunny every day too.

WHAT TO DO: To help a child write paragraphs, you must move very slowly. First talk about the paragraph, *then* outline it. *Then* write it.

Talk about the paragraph:

1. What is the main idea I want to write about?

2. What facts do I have to back up my main idea?

3. How can I end my paragraph *and* state my main idea once again?

Outline the paragraph:
(introduction) Main Idea: The Wyoming trip was my best vacation.
(body) Facts to back this up:
   1. horseback riding
   2. fishing
   3. good weather
   4. raft trip (saw moose and deer)
(conclusion) Main idea again: The trip was so good that I want to go again.

Write the paragraph:

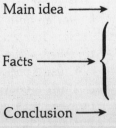

Main idea ⟶ Our trip to Wyoming was the best vacation I ever had. It was hot and sunny every day. We got to go fishing and Facts ⟶ horseback riding. We also got to go on a raft trip where we saw a moose and some deer on the river banks. I can't Conclusion ⟶ wait to go to Wyoming again next summer!

Games

— Have your child prepare a "treasure hunt" for a friend or another member of the family; write each clue in complete sentences on slips of paper ("Look behind the television for Clue #4.).

— Play Junior Scrabble with your child (available at all toy stores).

— Purchase simple crossword puzzle books for your child (helps with building vocabulary and spelling).

— Have your child imagine switching places with someone else (mother, father, an astronaut, a favorite TV hero).

— Have your child write a story about having special abilities or strengths— like Superman or Wonder Woman.

Ideas to do with books

— Have your child continue to read books appropriate for her age (see our Book List, page 107).

— Have your child keep a "Book List" of what he has read and include a short summary of the book as well.

Example: *Charlotte's Web*—this book was about a spider named Charlotte and a pig named Wilbur. Charlotte becomes friends with Wilbur and ends up saving his life.

Letters and cards

____ Have your child write Christmas or Hanukkah letters instead of sending ready-made cards. It can be a very brief message or poem of his own creation.

____ Write all thank-you notes and address envelopes

____ Write own party invitations and address envelopes

____ Write letters sending for things (catalogs, vacation information, etc.)

Creative Ideas

____ Show your child interesting photographs, magazine pictures, or paintings and have him write how it makes him feel.

____ Have your child write to music ("Nutcracker Suite," Beethoven's Fifth Symphony, or something similar).

____ Have your child write about imaginary situations such as:

If I were five inches tall . . .

If I were invisible . . .

If I were a wolf . . .

"I love to write because I can express myself in poems and plays."

Kira Jorgensen, grade 5

PROOFREADING GUIDE FOR CHILDREN
(GRADES 4–6)

_____When I read my writing out loud, does it make sense and say what I want to say?

_____Do I have a good topic sentence that tells what the paragraph will be about? If I have more than one paragraph, does each one have a topic sentence?

_____Do I have a wrap-up sentence at the end to tell the reader that the paper is finished?

_____Have I tried to use different words—not the same words over and over?

_____Is there any place in my paper where I can add more details or descriptive words?

_____Is there any place where I can combine two sentences to make my writing sound less choppy?

_____Is each sentence complete? Have I run any sentences together, instead of using a "connector word" or a period?

_____Are there any words I'm not sure how to spell?

_____Have I put in all my capital letters, periods, commas, and apostrophes?

_____Do I have an original title that fits my paper?

_____Does my paper appear neat when I look at it? (no big cross-outs, smudges, or obvious eraser marks?)

_____Did I make a rough draft first, correct and improve it, and then write my final copy?

_____Am I proud of this paper?

WE SUGGEST THAT YOU PHOTOCOPY THIS PAGE TO PUT ON YOUR CHILD'S BULLETIN BOARD OR SCHOOL NOTEBOOK.

Your Writer (Grades 7–9)

The junior high years are often difficult at best! Your child is going through lots of changes—physical, emotional, and social—during this period of time. This is an ideal time to get a child hooked on writing because it can serve as one form of release for all the turmoil going on inside.

A child at this age tries to assert himself in various ways. One is to rebel against "silly rules"—such as those used in writing. Now is the time to be patient, but firm. Encourage your child to express his new ideas and feelings. At the same time, emphasize the importance of writing in a "code" that everyone can understand. Some tips for helping the seventh, eighth, and ninth grader follow.

HELPING WITH SCHOOLWORK

• *Help your child see the purpose of a rough draft.* These copies are just that—*rough*. They can be messy, with cross outs, notes in the margin, arrows, and spelling errors. This is the "work" copy and should look it.

• *Insist that your child's final copy look sharp.* All words should be right, all errors corrected, and any last-minute changes erased cleanly or "whited out."

• *Help your child with the use of paragraphs.* Have him read each sentence of his paragraph to be sure it belongs.

• *Say something positive* whenever you see that your child has done something correctly that she used to have trouble with. Research has shown that positive comments have more effect on developing good writing habits than negative statements do.

• *React positively to the use of new and colorful vocabulary words.* "Glorious—what a great word to describe a sunset!" This is more effective than telling your child he's got a lot of dull words in his essay. Make a big deal about the unique words.

• *Go through the report-writing process once with your child.* Help him narrow his topic; show where to find sources, how to take notes, how to organize the material into paragraphs or chapters; write a first draft; go over it; make the final copy. Hang in there—this will pay off!

SPECIAL PROBLEMS

PROBLEM: Your child continues to write short, choppy sentences that make her writing sound immature and dull.

EXAMPLE: I went to my grandma's for Christmas. She always invites us to her house. It took us eight hours to drive there.

WHAT TO DO: Try to help your child combine ideas into one sentence without using *and*.

Sue played hard, *but* Bill didn't try at all.

Joe was a man *who* tried to help his family.

PROBLEM: Your child continues to write run-together sentences or incomplete sentences.

EXAMPLE: Logan owns the boat, he's really a good captain. (run-on)

or

In fact; no one knew the answer to the question. (fragment)

WHAT TO DO: The same methods are used for grades 7–9 as for grades 4–6 (see page 145).

HOME WRITING ACTIVITIES (GRADES 7–9)

____ Have your child write down the words of a favorite song.

____ Have your child try to write down a joke. (This is a tricky activity and much harder than it sounds!)

____ Have your child write a letter to a famous person she admires (musician, author, public official, or sports figure). Mail it!

____ Encourage your child to write letters to relatives or friends who are far away.

____ Let your child pick out postcards while on vacation and send them to his friends back home.

____ Have your child write a story about a photo or picture you've chosen for him.

____ Have your child write a short paper on how she would spend $100.

____ Have your child write an imaginary conversation between himself and a famous person (the President, an astronaut, a visitor from outer space).

____ Have your child write a story starring himself as a super hero of some sort—Wonder Woman, Spider Man, Bionic Woman, etc.

____ This is a perfect time to introduce your child to the idea of a diary or journal. You might buy one for a gift just before a big family trip.

____ Put your child in charge of the vacation scrapbook or family photo album. Have him write captions or short sentences to go with the pictures and souvenirs.

____ Help your child with research skills by giving him a Secret Spy Assignment:

Example: You have been assigned to find out the following information about Amelia Earhart:

1. Where and when was she born?
2. What did she do on June 21, 1928?
3. She was the first woman to do what?
4. How did she die?

____ Continue having your child keep a book list of what he's read. Have him write a short summary of each book—but now have him include some of his own *feelings* about the book.

Example: The Call of the Wild by Jack London. This book was about a dog named Buck and his adventures in the Yukon during the Gold Rush. Only one man, John Thornton, ever really tamed Buck. I really liked this book because it made me look at animals in a new way. It also made me wonder how much "wild" dog is still in my own dog, Ginger.

PROOFREADING GUIDE FOR STUDENTS
(GRADES 7–9)

____Is my paper clear and does it say what I want it to say?

____Is it well organized with a clear introduction?

____Does each of my paragraphs have a topic sentence? Does every sentence in my paragraph have something to do with the topic sentence?

____Do I have a concluding sentence or paragraph at the end of my paper?

____Have I used words that really describe things well? Have I used lots of different words?

____Have I combined sentences where I could?

____Are all my words spelled correctly?

____Have I put my commas and apostrophes where they should go?

____If there's any dialogue in my paper, do I have my quote marks placed correctly?

____Do I have a unique title to fit my paper—different from everyone else's?

____Is my paper neat (margins wide enough, no cross-outs or smudges)? Have I used an eraser or "white out" where needed?

____Did I spend time *rewriting* the paper to make it as effective as possible? Did I prepare at least one rough draft?

____Is this the best job I could have done?

WE SUGGEST THAT YOU PHOTOCOPY THIS CHECKLIST AND PUT IT ON YOUR CHILD'S BULLETIN BOARD OR SCHOOL NOTEBOOK.

Your Writer (Grades 10–12)

You need to be as involved in your child's writing now as you were when he was in elementary school. As writing assignments become more difficult, it may be harder to help your child. But there are still a number of things you can do.

HELPING WITH SCHOOLWORK

• *Encourage your child to experiment* with different writing styles. She may have a few disasters, but now is the time for practice. It is important that she try new ways to make her writing more interesting—even if she slips up occasionally.

• *Engage your child in "pre-writing" activities.* This involves talking or reading about a topic and lets your child ask questions and throw out ideas. A parent can be of great help during this "brainstorming" period.

• *Always encourage your child to write about subjects that he is deeply interested in.* He will enjoy the process more, he will learn something he wants to know, and, lo and behold, he will write a better paper.

• *Read the papers your child writes for school!* It is surprising how many parents do not do this. Talk about them, compliment them, make a photocopy to send to a relative.

• *Make a lot of noise about good writing.* If your child does well on a piece of writing, let him know you're proud.

• *Encourage your child—always—to read good books.* Give books for gifts; offer rides to the library; read aloud from books you are reading. There is no substitute for reading good writing.

• *Visit your child's English teacher each school year.* Let him or her know that you care about your child's writing. You might mention this concern to teachers in other subject areas as well.

SPECIAL PROBLEMS

PROBLEM: Your child frequently gets low grades on her writing papers, but does not know how to improve.

EXAMPLE: Your child's paper has a few comments like this: "Doesn't hold together" or "Be concise."

WHAT TO DO: There are several possible steps to take here.

1. First, insist that your child talk with her teacher and try to find out exactly what "doesn't hold together" means, for example. Have your child ask the teacher what she *could* have done differently.

2. If the teacher explains what your child is having difficulty with, you can try to help her at home. If sentences ramble too much, perhaps you can work with her on cutting out useless words, etc.

PROBLEM: Your child's writing sounds immature due to limited vocabulary and short, choppy sentences.

EXAMPLE: I think the food at lunch is terrible. It is not good for your body. I don't want to eat there. I'd rather go to McDonald's down the street.

WHAT TO DO:

1. First, encourage your child to use bigger, more specific words—even if he doesn't know how to spell them. Insist he use a wordbook and thesaurus (see page 123).

2. Use the method of combining sentences recommended for the earlier grades. This gives writing a more mature sound:

I think the food at lunch is terrible because it's not nutritious. Instead of eating in the cafeteria, I'd rather go to McDonald's.

PROBLEM: Your child's writing sounds stilted and phony. She is obviously trying to sound literary.

EXAMPLE: Mr. Howard partook of alcoholic beverages habitually to an excess.

WHAT TO DO: Although writing is different from speaking, it might help at this point to have your child say aloud what she wants to get across. Have her try to match her natural speaking style more closely.

Mr. Howard drank too much.

PROBLEM: Your child's writing is error-free, but does not have much feeling or personal touch.

EXAMPLE: The first quality I would like to possess is musical talent. I feel music is an important part of life and has enriched mankind through the ages. If I could play an instrument well, I would feel fulfilled in many ways.

WHAT TO DO: Writing like this isn't bad, but it's lifeless. Any student could put his name on the paper and turn it in. There is nothing that ties the paper to the student. It doesn't reach us or make us feel anything.

A few suggestions that may help with style:

1. Don't try to sound "smart"—try for a natural, relaxed writing style

2. Try to write as sincerely and honestly as possible—if you don't believe it, the reader won't either

3. Use comparisons whenever possible to help the reader understand more clearly what it is you're trying to say

4. Try to find ways to make the reader feel as deeply as you do about your topic

5. Remember—great writing with a few mistakes is better than average writing that is grammatically perfect.

A BETTER WAY TO WRITE IT: The first quality I would love above all others is musical talent. Last weekend my folks took me to hear Itzhak Perlman play the violin. It was magnificent! I only wish I could hold the bow that was making those incredible sounds.

HOME WRITING ACTIVITIES (GRADES 10–12)

___ Encourage your child to write personal letters and also letters about concerns she has: to the school paper, the local paper, government officials, school board, etc.

___ If your child has writing talent, encourage him to keep a collection of his best examples—put poetry in a book, etc.

___ Encourage your child to write poems or stories for special family occasions.

___ Have older children help younger ones with their writing.

___ Encourage your child to enter school writing contests—or contests advertised in young people's magazines.

___ Have your child help you write messages on the family Christmas card or greetings for other occasions.

___ If your child is taking a special tri (with the choir on tour or a schoo backpacking trip) or a long vacatio over the summer, encourage him t keep a record of the experience.

___ Make bets with your high school stu dent about words: "I'll bet you a quarte you can't spell *occurrence*.

___ Play Scrabble with your kids.

___ To encourage a wide knowledge c books, play "literary charades," usin book titles only.

Another lifesaver for parents is a little classic entitled *The Elements of Style* by William Strunk and E. B. White. Run, don't walk, to your nearest bookstore.

PROOFREADING GUIDE FOR STUDENTS
(GRADES 10–12)

_____Is the content of my paper solid? Does it have lots of specific facts or ideas?

_____Is my paper written for the audience that's going to read it?

_____Does my paper have feeling in it? Does it reflect the way *I feel*?

_____Have I tried to write this paper in such a way that it is uniquely mine?

_____Does each of my paragraphs have an appropriate topic sentence? Does each sentence in my paragraph relate to the topic sentence?

_____Have I used transitional sentences between my paragraphs?

_____Have I combined sentences where I could?

_____Are there any run-together sentences or incomplete sentences?

_____Do I need to check the spelling of any words?

_____Is all my punctuation (commas, apostrophes, colons, semicolons, quotation marks) where it should be?

_____Have I capitalized words that need it (such as *English*)? Are all book or magazine titles underlined?

_____Have I picked an original title for my paper?

_____Does my paper look sharp?

_____Did I make several drafts of this paper? Did I go over my rough drafts with someone to see how my writing comes across?

_____Do I feel good about this paper?

IT MAY BE HELPFUL TO PHOTOCOPY THIS CHECKLIST FOR YOUR CHILD'S BULLETIN BOARD OR SCHOOL NOTEBOOK.

CHAPTER 5

Would you have a man reason well, you must . . . exercise his mind . . . nothing does this better than mathematics.

—John Locke

The Math Chapter

From counting change to balancing a checkbook, from doubling a recipe to figuring out your income tax, using basic arithmetic is a necessity of life. True, there are thousands of occupations that require an understanding of higher mathematics. The future engineers, chemists, and economists will not only need to know basic arithmetic, but statistics, trigonometry, and calculus as well. However, most adults rarely use any math skills beyond those usually taught in junior high, and the majority could get by fairly well using arithmetic skills we learn in the first six grades of school.

All children study math in elementary school. Math continues for all youngsters in junior high. High school students complete an additional one to four years of math, depending upon their interest. Those going on to college usually complete two years of algebra and one year of geometry.

This chapter will tell parents how they can help make the first six grades of arithmetic successful for their children. Helping your child learn the basic skills not only aids him in becoming a competent adult, it also boosts his pride and lets him feel he is a capable student. For those youngsters who will go on to professions that use higher mathematics, a successful foundation is where it all begins.

One final note before we begin: even for those not "mathematically inclined," learning to use math can be a rewarding experience. It can provide a way of thinking about and understanding the world around us. It teaches us to be accurate and orderly. It encourages us to be logical and helps us make comparisons, measure growth, and check progress. It is important, therefore, that math develop a "good reputation" among as many youngsters as possible. And, if taught properly, almost every child *can* feel successful in learning the basic arithmetic skills.

GETTING READY FOR ARITHMETIC

When is a child ready to learn arithmetic—that is, at what age can he really begin to understand the use of numbers? Not usually until the ages of six or seven, or even eight—which may surprise most parents.

Because preschoolers can imitate the ways that adults use numbers, adults too often assume their young child understands numbers the same way they do. For example, there are many preschoolers who can count to 20, tell you their ages, or regularly use numbers in speaking. However, it is not usually until the first grade that most will understand what numbers actually mean (that the number 9 can stands for 9 balls, 9 pounds, 9 miles, or 9 minutes) and not be confused by the size or shape of the things they are measuring or counting.

You can check your child's understanding of numbers and measurement yourself. Try this:

1. Collect two dozen pennies or 24 other items.
2. In front of your child, count them out loud into two equal sets, counting each object, 1 through 12, as you lay it down.

Row 1:   • • • • • • • • • • • •
Row 2: •   •   •   •   •   •   •   •   •   •   •   •

3. The sets should be placed in rows as shown above.
4. Now, with the two sets laid side by side, ask your child: "Which row has more?"

You'll probably find that your four- or five-year-old will point to the second set—the one that is stretched out. If you ask your child the same question when she is seven or eight, she'll probably wonder why you asked and will tell you they are both the same.

Does this mean that you are just wasting your time if you provide math-type activities for your preschooler? Not at all! You can provide experiences for your young child that will form the basis for understanding what will come later. The stronger the foundation you provide, the more certain the growth that follows.

Math-Readiness Activities (Ages 3–6)

Most parents will find they already do many of these activities with their young children. Parents are natural teachers.

There are hundreds of activities your preschooler can do that involve thinking mathematically. We have listed only a few, just to give you an idea of the types of things that build a good math foundation.

REMEMBER:
• These activities are supposed to be fun.
• Some of the suggestions may be too difficult for your three-year-old and too easy or boring for your six-year-old.
• If your child doesn't want to do an activity, skip it and try it again later.
• These are just a few suggestions. You can think up dozens more on your own—if you haven't already.

Don't worry, then, about trying to teach your preschooler to count to 100, or how to add 3 + 5, or subtract 6 − 2. What is important is that you provide experiences that introduce your child to the concepts of arithmetic. The better your child can use these ideas, the more easily he will begin using numbers in a way that makes sense to him. That's what learning arithmetic is all about!

TRY ACTIVITIES LIKE THESE WITH YOUR CHILD

SORTING

Sorting helps your child understand that objects can be divided into groups.

Separate coins into stacks of pennies, nickels, dimes, and quarters.
Put away the kitchen utensils (knives, forks, spoons) in their proper slots.
Sort out building blocks by shape, marbles by color, or books by size.

COMPARING

Comparing exposes your child to what numbers can help us do, and how to judge differences.

What weighs more, a beach ball or a soccer ball? a sponge or a plate?
What's bigger, a mouse or a rabbit? my room or your room?
What are there more of, grapes (in a bunch of grapes), or bananas (in a bunch of bananas)?
What's longer, this piece of rope or the sofa? this crayon or this pencil?
What contains more water, this wide, short glass or this tall, skinny glass? (Let your child play with water, pouring from one container into another.)

PATTERNS

Patterns help your child look for relationships among objects; learning patterns is the basis for understanding the rules of arithmetic.

String beads in a pattern—two red, one green, two red, one green, etc.
Arrange blocks in a pattern—tall on the outside, short in the middle, etc.
Set the table.

MEMORIZING

Memorizing the numbers 1 to 10 gives your child the language skills to further explore numbers.

• Read beginning counting books to your child.
• Make up a tune or verse to count the first ten numbers.
• Watch *Sesame Street* on TV—they always have fun with numbers.
• Buy a set of wooden or plastic numbers at the store (they usually come along with letters of the alphabet) and make up games with them.

USING NUMBERS IN SPEECH

Using numbers in speech helps your child begin to understand what numbers mean and are used for.

• "Bring me two cookies, please."
• "Put five napkins on the table."
• "Count how many stuffed animals you have."

ORDERING

Ordering numbers helps your child understand the relationship between numbers.

• Play the card game "War" and have your child say which wins, the 5 card or the 7 card.
• Play a game of toss with bean bags and have your child figure out who got the most in the basket (other lightweight objects can be used for this).
• Practice using "ordinals"—*first, second, third,* etc. Put this shirt in your third drawer, turn to the second page, etc.

Help your child see that numbers are everywhere—

• street addresses   • recipe books   • baseball uniforms

• store receipts   • on traffic signs

CHECKING YOUR CHILD'S PROGRESS
(GRADES K–6)

We have provided you with what educators call a *continuum* of math skills. This show you, in an easy-to-follow chart, the arithmetic skills that are taught at each grade level.

Of the three *R*'s taught in elementary school, arithmetic is the one parents can most easi help their children with. It is also the area in which parents can most easily judge whether not their child is learning what is expected.

Obviously, the teaching of arithmetic varies from classroom to classroom and from on textbook to another. However, after reviewing the most up-to-date, widely used textbook and comparing the math guidelines from school districts around the nation, we found goa and expectations to be similar regardless of area and what textbooks are used. The ma charts are based on these findings.

For each grade, we list the skills that are to be learned by the *end* of the school year. B cause there is some variation, the math skill charts are presented in this manner:

LEVEL 1: the skills that almost all the school systems and textbooks agree should be taught and understood by the end of the year. These are the *baseline skills* for each grade.

LEVEL 2: the skills that the typical textbook publisher and school feel a child of that grade *should probably learn.*

LEVEL 3: the *more advanced skills* that some districts and textbook publishers feel should be introduced or taught.

IMPORTANT:
There are certain minimal standards that are well established across the nation. If your chil achieves the *baseline standards*, grade by grade, he will learn all the basic arithmetic skills b the end of the sixth grade. *Terrific!*

Using the Math Skill Charts

You should expect the teacher to help your child learn the common, baseline skills we have listed for each grade. If your child has normal capabilities, you should expect and help him to learn these baseline skills by the end of each year.

Follow these steps in using the charts:

1. At the beginning of each year, review the skills your child should have learned in the previous grade. Check to see that your child has these skills, using the sample problems we've provided and similar ones of your own creation.

Remember, skills that are not practiced can be forgotten. If your child has difficulties, see if a few simple hints can get him back on track. Watch to see if he is making careless mistakes or really doesn't understand how to work the problem.

If your child hasn't learned these skills, he needs special help from you at home (see pages 188–190) and extra assistance from his teacher.

2. Next, look at the skills that are to be taught by the end of the current grade.

3. When you talk with your child's teacher during the first part of the year, find out what expectations she has for your child in math. Then, working with the teacher, determine which of the three "skill levels" your child should be working toward.

4. Now, using the Arithmetic Operations Guide (pages 198–216), study the specific skills your child must learn by the year's end.

5. With this information, you can check to see if your child is making appropriate growth in his arithmetic skills as the year progresses.

6. If your child has not learned these skills by the end of the year, use the guidelines on pages 191–197 to help him catch up over the summer.

KINDERGARTEN

YEAR END SKILL	WHAT TO EXPECT FROM YOUR KINDERGARTEN CHILD
Reading & Writing	Reads and writes numbers 1 through 10
Shapes	Learns the basic shapes circle square triangle (maybe rectangle)
Telling time	*Begins* learning to tell time to the *hour*
Understanding money	Learns the value of a penny, nickel, and dime
Ordinals	*Begins* learning ordinals first through fifth 1st 2nd 3rd 4th 5th
Vocabulary	Learns to use words of comparison: larger–smaller, taller–shorter, longest–shortest
ADDITION & SUBTRACTION	Prepares for addition and subtraction using blocks and other objects to show "one more than," "one less than," etc.

LEVEL 1

164

FIRST GRADE

EAR END SKILL	WHAT TO EXPECT FROM YOUR FIRST GRADER

.eading and writing
umbers (place value)

Reads and writes numbers up to 99 or 100

hapes

Knows shapes

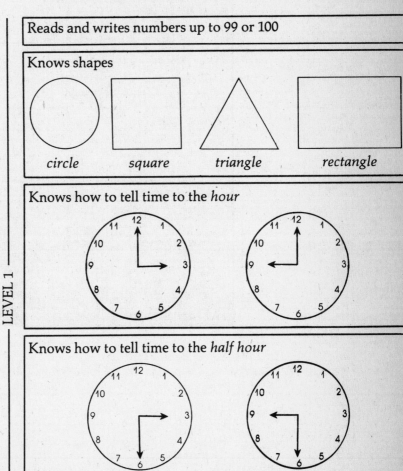

elling time

Knows how to tell time to the *hour*

Knows how to tell time to the *half hour*

LEVEL 1

Jnderstanding money

Knows the value of a penny, nickel, dime, and perhaps quarter

Ordinals

Knows ordinals first through fifth, perhaps up to seventh
1st   2nd   3rd   4th   5th   6th   7th

Counting

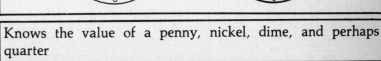

Begins to count by 2's (2–4–6–8) and 10's (10–20–30)

ADDITION

LEVEL 1	Learns addition "facts" through sums of 10

$$5 \atop +5 \above 0pt 10 \qquad\qquad 8 \atop +2 \above 0pt 10$$

$$
\begin{array}{c}
5 \\
+5 \\
\hline
10
\end{array}
\qquad\qquad
\begin{array}{c}
8 \\
+2 \\
\hline
10
\end{array}
$$

LEVEL 1

Learns to add 2-digit numbers that don't require carrying (regrouping)

$$
\begin{array}{c}
32 \\
+46 \\
\hline
78
\end{array}
\qquad
\begin{array}{c}
20 \\
+50 \\
\hline
70
\end{array}
\qquad
\begin{array}{c}
41 \\
+42 \\
\hline
83
\end{array}
$$

LEVEL 2

Learns addition facts through sums of 12 and begins learning sums up to 18

$$
\begin{array}{c}
6 \\
+6 \\
\hline
12
\end{array}
\quad
\begin{array}{c}
7 \\
+5 \\
\hline
12
\end{array}
\quad
\begin{array}{c}
8 \\
+8 \\
\hline
16
\end{array}
\quad
\begin{array}{c}
9 \\
+8 \\
\hline
17
\end{array}
\quad
\begin{array}{c}
9 \\
+9 \\
\hline
18
\end{array}
$$

Learns to add 3 numbers at one time, up to sums of 10, 12, or 18 (depending on how far they get in learning "facts")

$$
\begin{array}{c}
6 \\
3 \\
+1 \\
\hline
10
\end{array}
\qquad
\begin{array}{c}
7 \\
4 \\
+1 \\
\hline
12
\end{array}
\qquad
\begin{array}{c}
6 \\
3 \\
+9 \\
\hline
18
\end{array}
$$

LEVEL 3

Learns addition facts through 18

$$
\begin{array}{c}
8 \\
+9 \\
\hline
17
\end{array}
\qquad\qquad
\begin{array}{c}
9 \\
+9 \\
\hline
18
\end{array}
$$

SUBTRACTION

LEVEL 1

Learns subtraction facts through 10

$$\begin{array}{r} 10 \\ -5 \\ \hline 5 \end{array}$$

Knows how to subtract numbers which don't require carrying (regrouping)

$$\begin{array}{r} 68 \\ -43 \\ \hline 25 \end{array} \qquad \begin{array}{r} 90 \\ -40 \\ \hline 50 \end{array} \qquad \begin{array}{r} 74 \\ -14 \\ \hline 60 \end{array}$$

LEVEL 2

Learns subtraction facts through 12

$$\begin{array}{r} 12 \\ -6 \\ \hline 6 \end{array}$$

Begins learning subtraction facts up to 18

$$\begin{array}{r} 18 \\ -9 \\ \hline 9 \end{array}$$

LEVEL 3

Knows all subtraction facts through 18

$$\begin{array}{r} 18 \\ -9 \\ \hline 9 \end{array}$$

SECOND GRADE

YEAR END SKILL	WHAT TO EXPECT FROM YOUR SECOND GRADER
Reading & writing numbers (place value)	Reads and writes numbers up to 999
Telling time	Learns how to tell time within 5 minutes 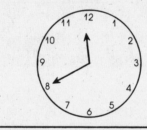 
Understanding money	Reviews value of penny, nickel, and dime; learns quarter and half dollar
Ordinals	Knows ordinals first through tenth 1st 2nd 3rd 4th 5th 6th 7th 8th 9th 10th
Counting	Knows how to count by 2's, 5's, and 10's
Vocabulary	Learns what is meant by *odd* and *even*
ADDITION	Memorizes addition facts through 18
	Adds 2-digit numbers not requiring carrying (regrouping)

LEVEL 1

$$\begin{array}{r} 22 \\ +\ 43 \\ \hline 65 \end{array} \qquad \begin{array}{r} 47 \\ +\ 12 \\ \hline 59 \end{array} \qquad \begin{array}{r} 62 \\ +\ 24 \\ \hline 86 \end{array}$$

ADDITION

LEVEL 2

Adds 3-digit numbers not requiring carrying (regrouping)

```
   436          623          124
 + 251        + 176        + 233
 ─────        ─────        ─────
   687          799          357
```

Adds 2-digit numbers with last number carrying over (regrouping)

```
    64           71           94
 +  83        +  83        +  61
 ─────        ─────        ─────
   147          154          155
```

Begins learning to carry (regroup) from 1's to 10's toward the end of the school year

```
    ₁            ₁            ₁
    68           29           78
 +  29        +  23        +  12
 ─────        ─────        ─────
    97           52           90
```

LEVEL 3

Learns to carry (regroup) from 1's to 10's

```
    ₁            ₁            ₁
    67          258          428
 +  14        + 135        + 243
 ─────        ─────        ─────
    81          393          671
```

169

SUBTRACTION

LEVEL 1

Knows subtraction facts through 18

```
   18
 −  9
 ────
    9
```

Subtracts 2-digit numbers, no carrying (regrouping)

```
   38          47          64
 − 12        − 13        − 32
 ────        ────        ────
   26          34          32
```

LEVEL 2

Subtracts 3-digit numbers with no carrying (regrouping)

```
  874         798         675
− 251       − 444       − 321
─────       ─────       ─────
  623         354         354
```

Subtracts 2-digit numbers from 3-digit numbers

```
  105         128         147
−  63       −  76       −  77
─────       ─────       ─────
   42          52          70
```

Begins learning to carry (regroup) from 10's to 1's toward the end of the year

```
  ⁶⁷2         ⁴⁷0         ⁵⁷1
 − 13        − 24        − 22
 ────        ────        ────
   59          26          39
```

LEVEL 3

Learns carrying (regrouping) 10's to 1's

```
  ⁸⁹4         ⁶⁷3         ⁵⁶4
 − 28        − 38        − 47
 ────        ────        ────
   66          35          17
```

MULTIPLICATION

LEVEL 1	Begins learning what multiplication is
LEVEL 2	Learns first multiplication facts of 2's, 3's, and 5's (up to 2×9, 3×3, and 5×5)
LEVEL 3	Memorizes multiplication facts up to 2×9, 3×3, and 5×5

FRACTIONS

LEVEL 1

Begins to recognize parts of a whole using ½, ⅓, ⅔, ¼, ²⁄₄, ¾

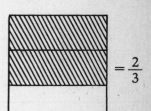

$= \dfrac{3}{4}$ $= \dfrac{2}{3}$

THIRD GRADE

YEAR END SKILL			WHAT TO EXPECT FROM YOUR THIRD GRADER
Reading & writing numbers (place value)	LEVEL	1	Reads and writes numbers up to 9,999
		2	Reads and writes numbers up to 99,999 or 999,999
		3	Reads and writes numbers up to 999,999 or 9,999,999
Telling time	LEVEL 1		Begins learning to tell time to the nearest minute 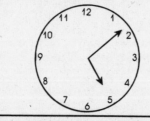 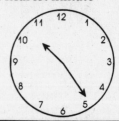
Understanding money			Knows the value of penny, nickel, dime, quarter, and half dollar
Counting			All third graders should know how to count by 2's, 5's, and 10's
Ordinals			All third graders should know ordinals first through tenth 1st 2nd 3rd 4th 5th 6th 7th 8th 9th 10th

ADDITION

LEVEL 1

Begins adding 3-digit numbers using regrouping

```
  1 1              1 1
  675              394
+ 529            + 538
 1204              932
```

LEVEL 2

Begins adding 4- and 5-digit numbers with regrouping

```
  1 1 1            1 1 1
  5864             93859
+ 3967           + 75486
  9831            169345
```

Begins learning more difficult column addition

```
   46               1 1
   52               268
+  30               504
  128             + 691
                   1463
```

SUBTRACTION

LEVEL 1

Subtracts 3-digit numbers with regrouping

```
   6 13
   7̶4̶0
 - 263
   477
```

LEVEL 2

Begins subtracting 4- and 5-digit numbers with regrouping

```
   7 12             5 10 10
   5̶8̶3̶6            6̶2̶1̶1̶4
 - 3569           - 39576
   2267            22538
```

Learns to check subtraction problems with addition

```
   6 13
   7̶4̶0
 - 263
   477
 + 263
   740
```

173

MULTIPLICATION

LEVEL 1 — Knows multiplication tables up to 5 × 5

LEVEL 2 — Memorizes all multiplication tables up to 9 × 9 and begins to regroup in multiplication problems that require carrying only once

$$\begin{array}{r} {\scriptstyle 3} \\ 24 \\ \times\ 8 \\ \hline 192 \end{array} \qquad \begin{array}{r} {\scriptstyle 1} \\ 36 \\ \times\ 2 \\ \hline 72 \end{array}$$

LEVEL 3 — Knows how to multiply using regrouping (carrying only once in the problem)

$$\begin{array}{r} {\scriptstyle 2} \\ 74 \\ \times\ 6 \\ \hline 444 \end{array}$$

DIVISION

LEVEL 1 — Begins division and learns divison facts up to

$$\begin{array}{r} 5 \\ 5\overline{)25} \end{array}$$

LEVEL 2 — Learns division facts up to

$$\begin{array}{r} 9 \\ 9\overline{)81} \end{array}$$

Begins dividing 1-digit numbers into 3-digit numbers (no regrouping)

$$\begin{array}{r} 321 \\ 3\overline{)963} \end{array}$$

LEVEL 3 — Knows how to divide 1-digit numbers into 3-digit numbers

$$\begin{array}{r} 321 \\ 3\overline{)963} \end{array}$$

Begins to use simple "remainder"

$$\begin{array}{r} 4r2 \\ 4\overline{)18} \end{array} \qquad \begin{array}{r} 3r5 \\ 7\overline{)26} \end{array}$$

FRACTIONS

LEVEL 1 — Begins learning to compare by sight fractions up to ¾ (which is larger, ⅓ or ¼?)

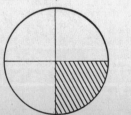 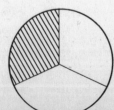

Third grade math skills you may wish to review. . . .

FOURTH GRADE

WHAT TO EXPECT FROM YOUR FOURTH GRADER

LEVEL 1	
	Reads and writes numbers in the millions
	Knows how to tell time to the minute 
	Is able to apply arithmetic skills to problems involving money
	Knows how to add using 5-digit numbers and how to do column addition

Knows how to add using 5-digit numbers and how to do column addition

$$\begin{array}{r} \overset{1\,1\ \ 1}{62857} \\ +39435 \\ \hline 102292 \end{array} \qquad \begin{array}{r} \overset{1\,1}{461} \\ 854 \\ 366 \\ +510 \\ \hline 2191 \end{array}$$

Knows how to subtract using 5-digit numbers (during the first part of the school year)

$$\begin{array}{r} \overset{3\,1\ \,8\,1}{74391} \\ -53748 \\ \hline 20643 \end{array}$$

175

MULTIPLICATION

LEVEL 1

Knows all multiplication tables up to 9 × 9

Multiplies 1 digit times a 2- or 3-digit number using regrouping

```
    5              7 7
   38             489
 ×  7            ×  8
  266            3912
```

LEVEL 2

Multiplies 2 digits times a 2-digit number using regrouping

```
    2              2
    3              4
   86             75
 ×45            ×48
  430            600
  344            300
 3870           3600
```

Begins learning to multiply 2-digits times a 3-digit number

```
    1 1
    2 3
   458
 ×  24
  1832
   916
 10992
```

LEVEL 3

Learns to multiply 2 digits times a 3-digit number

```
    1 2
      1
   624
 ×  73
  1872
  4368
 45552
```

DIVISION

Knows division facts to 9

$$9\overline{)81}$$ with quotient 9

Divides 1 digit into a 3- or 4-digit number (no regrouping)

$$2\overline{)122}$$ with quotient 61

$$3\overline{)1209}$$ with quotient 403

Divides 1 digit into 3- or 4-digit number using both regrouping and remainders

$$8\overline{)4903}$$ with quotient $612r7$

$$5\overline{)5230}$$ with quotient 1046
5
02
0
23
20
30
30
0

Begins learning 2 place division (near the end of the year)

$$13\overline{)52}$$ with quotient 4
52
0

$$25\overline{)125}$$ with quotient 5
125
0

Divides 2 digits into a 2- or 3-digit number with a 1-digit answer, no remainder

$$13\overline{)52}$$ with quotient 4
52
0

$$25\overline{)125}$$ with quotient 5
125
0

Begins learning to divide 2 digits into 3-digit number to get a 1-digit answer with a remainder

$$24\overline{)174}$$ with quotient $7r6$
168
6

177

FRACTIONS

LEVEL 1

Identifies fractions as part of a whole up to $^{10}/_{10}$

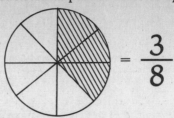

$$= \frac{3}{8}$$

LEVEL 2

Adds fractions with "like" denominators (during the last half of the year)

$$\frac{3}{5} \quad + \quad \frac{1}{5} \quad = \quad \frac{4}{5}$$

$$\frac{3}{5} + \frac{1}{5} = \frac{4}{5}$$

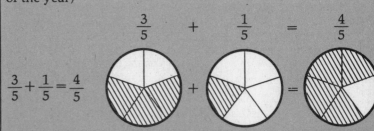

LEVEL 3

Subtracts fractions with like denominators

$$\frac{5}{7} \quad - \quad \frac{3}{7} \quad = \quad \frac{2}{7}$$

$$\frac{5}{7} - \frac{3}{7} = \frac{2}{7}$$

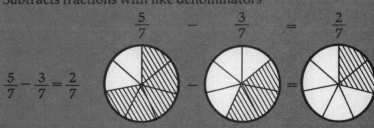

Begins learning to recognize *equivalent fractions*

$$\frac{1}{2} \quad = \quad \frac{3}{6} \quad = \quad \frac{4}{8}$$

$$\frac{1}{2} = \frac{3}{6} = \frac{4}{8}$$

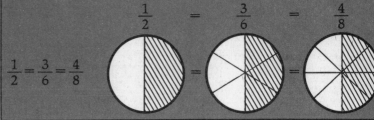

DECIMALS

LEVEL 1

Begins learning about decimals and relating decimals to fractions (place values of 10 and 100)

$$.7 = \frac{7}{10} \qquad\qquad .21 = \frac{21}{100}$$

Fourth grade math skills you may wish to review. . . .

FIFTH GRADE

YEAR END SKILL		WHAT TO EXPECT FROM YOUR FIFTH GRADER
Reading & Writing Numbers (place value)	LEVEL 1	Reads and writes numbers up to hundred millions 120,000,000
	LEVEL 2	Reads and writes numbers in the billions 14,000,000,000
	LEVEL 3	Reads and writes numbers in the trillions 8,000,000,000,000

Telling time		All fifth graders should know how to tell time
Understanding money	LEVEL 1	All fifth graders should be able to apply arithmetic skills to story problems involving money
ADDITION		In the fifth grade addition is practiced and reviewed
SUBTRACTION		In the fifth grade subtraction is practiced and reviewed

MULTIPLICATION

LEVEL 1

Multiplies 2 digits times a 3-digit number

```
  6 4
  8 6            1                1
  897           763              804
× 79          × 22             × 13
 8073          1526             2412
 6279          1526              804
70863         16786            10452
```

LEVEL 2

Multiplies 3 digits times a 3-digit number

```
  7 4
  6 4           2 1
  5 3           1 1               1
  785           243              102
×986          ×641             ×613
 4710          243              306
 6280          972              102
 7065         1458              612
774010       155763            62526
```

LEVEL 3

Multiplies 3 digits times a 4-digit number

```
  2  1         3 2 3
  1            1 1 1            3 3 3
  1            3 2 4            1 1 1
 6412          5758             7999
×  733        ×  425           ×  142
 19236         28790           15998
 19236         11516           31996
 44884         23032            7999
4699996       2447150         1135858
```

DIVISION

LEVEL 1

Divides 1 digit into a 4-digit number to get a 3-digit answer (with or without a remainder)

```
      609              353r4
   7)4263           5)1769
     42                15
     06                26
      0                25
     63                19
     63                15
      0                 4
```

Divides 2 digits into a 3-digit number to get a 2-digit answer (with or without remainder)

```
       41               15r29
   21)861            37)584
      84                37
      21               214
      21               185
       0                29
```

<table>
<tr><td rowspan="1">LEVEL 1</td><td colspan="2">Divides 2 digits into a 3-digit number to get a 1-digit answer (with or without remainder)</td></tr>
</table>

LEVEL 1

Divides 2 digits into a 3-digit number to get a 1-digit answer (with or without remainder)

```
        3               5r21
   45)135          82)431
      135             410
    ─────           ─────
        0              21
```

LEVEL 2

Divides 2 digits into a 4-digit number to get a 3-digit answer (with or without remainder)

```
      216r2            162r15
  24)5186          43)6981
     48               43
    ────             ────
     38              268
     24              258
    ────             ────
    146              101
    144               86
    ────             ────
      2               15
```

Divides 2 digits into a 4-digit number to get a 2-digit answer (with or without remainder)

```
      77r10             67
  47)3629          20)1340
     329             120
    ────             ────
     339             140
     329             140
    ────             ────
      10               0
```

LEVEL 3

Divides 2 digits into a 5-digit number to get a 3-digit answer (with or without remainder)

```
      527r34            603
  70)36924          25)15075
     350              150
    ────             ────
     192                7
     140                0
    ────             ────
     524               75
     490               75
    ────             ────
      34                0
```

Divides 2 digits into a 5-digit number to get a 4-digit answer (with or without remainder)

```
      1266             1102r1
  23)29118          49)53999
     23               49
    ────             ────
     61               49
     46               49
    ────             ────
     151              09
     138               0
    ────             ────
     138              99
     138              98
    ────             ────
       0               1
```

FRACTIONS

LEVEL 1

Changes fractions to lower terms (reducing)

$$\frac{8}{12} = \frac{4}{6} = \frac{2}{3}$$

Finds equivalent fractions

$$\frac{4}{7} = \frac{\boxed{16}}{28} \qquad\qquad \frac{1}{4} = \frac{\boxed{4}}{16}$$

Adds and subtracts with like (same) denominators

$$\frac{2}{5} + \frac{1}{5} = \frac{3}{5} \qquad\qquad \frac{7}{8} - \frac{4}{8} = \frac{3}{8}$$

Adds and subtracts with unlike (different) denominators

$$\begin{array}{r} \frac{3}{5} = \quad \frac{12}{20} \\ + \frac{1}{4} = + \frac{5}{20} \\ \hline \frac{17}{20} \end{array} \qquad\qquad \begin{array}{l} \frac{3}{8} - \frac{1}{4} = \\[4pt] \frac{3}{8} - \frac{2}{8} = \frac{1}{8} \end{array}$$

Changes mixed numbers to improper fractions

$$1\tfrac{1}{5} = \frac{6}{5} \qquad\qquad 1\tfrac{2}{7} = \frac{9}{7}$$

Changes improper fractions to mixed numbers

$$\frac{16}{5} = 3\tfrac{1}{5} \qquad\qquad \frac{17}{4} = 4\tfrac{1}{4}$$

LEVEL 2

Multiplies fractions (proper and improper)

$$\frac{1}{2} \times \frac{3}{5} = \frac{3}{10} \qquad\qquad 2\tfrac{1}{3} \times 1\tfrac{1}{5} =$$

$$\frac{7}{\cancel{3}_{1}} \times \frac{\cancel{6}^{2}}{5} = \frac{14}{5} = 2\tfrac{4}{5}$$

LEVEL 3

Begins dividing with fractions

$$\frac{2}{5} \div \frac{7}{3} = \frac{2}{5} \times \frac{3}{7} = \frac{6}{35}$$

DECIMALS

Reads and writes decimals to the 1,000th place

45.038   Forty-five and thirty-eight thousandths

Adds and subtracts decimals and knows how to line up decimals correctly

$$6.2$$
$$29$$
$$+ \quad .55$$

$$6.2 + 29 + .55 = \overline{35.75}$$

$$7.20$$
$$- \quad .61$$

$$7.2 - .61 = \overline{6.59}$$

Multiplies whole numbers times a decimal

$$\overset{2}{3.4}$$
$$\times \ 5$$
$$\overline{17.0}$$

$$\overset{2 \ 3 1}{\underset{3 \ 4 1}{4.462}}$$
$$\times \ \ 67$$
$$\overline{31\ 234}$$
$$267\ 72$$
$$\overline{298.954}$$

Multiplies a decimal times a decimal

$$\overset{1}{\underset{3\ 1}{40.62}}$$
$$\times \ \ 3.6$$
$$\overline{24\ 372}$$
$$121\ 86$$
$$\overline{146.232}$$

$$\overset{3\ 1}{\underset{7\ 2}{6.931}}$$
$$\times \ \ 4.8$$
$$\overline{5\ 5448}$$
$$27\ 724$$
$$\overline{33.2688}$$

Changes decimals to fractions

$$.26 = \frac{26}{100} = \frac{13}{50}$$

Changes fractions to decimals

$$\frac{3}{5} = 5\overline{)3} = 5\overline{)3.0} = .6$$
$$\underline{30}$$
$$0$$

Divides a whole number into a decimal

$$\begin{array}{r} .05 \\ 25\overline{)1.25} \\ \underline{0} \\ 125 \\ \underline{125} \\ 0 \end{array}$$

$$\begin{array}{r} .19 \\ 9\overline{)1.71} \\ \underline{9} \\ 81 \\ \underline{81} \\ 0 \end{array}$$

183

SIXTH GRADE

YEAR END SKILL	WHAT TO EXPECT FROM YOUR SIXTH GRADER
Reading & writing numbers (place value)	Knows how to read and write numbers into the billions or trillions
Telling time	All sixth graders should know how to tell time
Understanding money	All sixth graders should be able to apply arithmetic skills to story problems involving money
ADDITION	Addition is practiced and reviewed
SUBTRACTION	Subtraction is practiced and reviewed
MULTIPLICATION	Multiplies 4 digits times a 3-digit number

LEVEL 1

```
      6 2 3                          4 1 2
      1 1                            5 2 3
      7 2 4                          1
      6935                           3624
    ×  728                         ×  792
    ───────                        ───────
     55480                           7248
     13870                          32616
     48545                          25368
    ───────                        ───────
    5048680                        2870208
```

DIVISION

Divides 2 digits into a 5-digit number

```
        521                      1576r18
  67)34907                 56)88274
     335                      56
     ───                      ──
     140                      322
     134                      280
     ───                      ───
      67                      427
      67                      392
      ──                      ───
       0                      354
                             336
                             ───
                              18
```

Divides 3 digits into a 5-digit number

```
         59                      138r509
  847)49973                532)73925
     4235                     532
     ────                     ───
     7623                     2072
     7623                     1596
     ────                     ────
        0                     4765
                             4256
                             ────
                              509
```

FRACTIONS

Practices and expands fraction operations already learned

$$\frac{4}{9} - \frac{1}{9} = \frac{3}{9} = \boxed{\frac{1}{3}}$$

$$4\frac{1}{2} + 5\frac{2}{3} = 4\frac{3}{6} + 5\frac{4}{6} = 9\frac{7}{6} = \boxed{10\frac{1}{6}}$$

$$\frac{3}{8} \times \frac{1}{7} = \boxed{\frac{3}{56}}$$

$$\frac{4}{7} \div \frac{9}{3} = \frac{4}{7} \times \frac{3}{9} = \frac{12}{63} = \boxed{\frac{4}{21}}$$

Adds complex problems using fractions

$$\frac{1}{4} + \frac{2}{7} + \frac{3}{14} =$$

$$\frac{7}{28} + \frac{8}{28} + \frac{6}{28} = \frac{21}{28} = \boxed{\frac{3}{4}}$$

Divides fractions including mixed numbers

$$6\frac{3}{8} \div 7\frac{1}{2} =$$

$$\frac{51}{8} \div \frac{15}{2} = \frac{51}{8} \times \frac{2}{15} = \boxed{\frac{17}{20}}$$

185

DECIMALS

Reads and writes decimals to the 100,000th place
Thirteen and fifty-six hundred thousandths
13.00056

Multiplies a decimal times a decimal

$$
\begin{array}{r}
\overset{2}{\underset{1}{}}\ \overset{2}{\underset{1}{}} \\
2.607 \\
\times\ \ 4.2 \\
\hline
5214 \\
10428 \\
\hline
10.9494
\end{array}
\qquad
\begin{array}{r}
\overset{34}{\underset{12}{}} \\
63.51 \\
\times\ \ 9.4 \\
\hline
25404 \\
57159 \\
\hline
596.994
\end{array}
$$

Divides a decimal into a decimal

$$
\begin{array}{r}
26. \\
2.4\,\overline{)62.9.} \\
48 \\
\hline
14\ 9 \\
14\ 4 \\
\hline
5
\end{array}
\qquad
\begin{array}{r}
1.9 \\
4.26\,\overline{)8.09.4} \\
4\ 26 \\
\hline
3\ 83\ 4 \\
3\ 83\ 4 \\
\hline
0
\end{array}
$$

Converts decimals to fractions

$$
.26 = \frac{26}{100} = \frac{13}{50}
\qquad
.482 = \frac{482}{1000} = \frac{241}{500}
$$

Converts fractions to decimals

$$
\frac{3}{5} = 5\overline{)3} = 5\,\overset{.6}{\overline{)3.0}} = .6
$$

$$
\frac{27}{50} = 50\overline{)27} = 50\,\overset{.54}{\overline{)27.00}} = .54
$$

$$
\begin{array}{r}
.54 \\
50\,\overline{)27.00} \\
25\ 0 \\
\hline
2\ 00 \\
2\ 00 \\
\hline
0
\end{array}
$$

LEVEL 2

Begins working with percent problems

$$6\% \ = \frac{6}{100} = .06 \quad \text{or} \quad \frac{6}{100} = .06 = 6\%$$

$$\frac{3}{4} = \quad 4\overline{)3} = \quad \begin{array}{r} .75 \\ 4\overline{)3.00} \\ 2\,8 \\ \hline 20 \\ 20 \\ \hline 0 \end{array} = 75\% \quad \text{or} \quad \frac{3}{4} = \frac{75}{100} = .75 = 75\%$$

LEVEL 3

Knows how to work percent problems

$$8\% = \frac{8}{100} = .08$$

$$\frac{1}{2} = \ .50 \ = 50\%$$

$$20\% \text{ of } 280 \text{ is } \boxed{?} \qquad \begin{array}{r} 280 \\ \times\ .20 \\ \hline 56.00 \end{array}$$

25 is what % of 150 =

$$\frac{25}{150} = 150\,\overline{)25} = \begin{array}{r} .16 \\ 150\overline{)25.00} \\ 15\,0 \\ \hline 10\,00 \\ 9\,00 \end{array} = 16\%$$

What Students Are Expected to Know Versus What They Actually Know

In the math charts you will find guidelines showing when arithmetic skills are expected to be taught and learned. It is important to remember, however, that many students do *not* learn math skills according to these guidelines. In fact, *many students learn arithmetic skills much later than they are supposed to, or never totally master them at all.*

WHAT DO STUDENTS KNOW?

The National Assessment of Educational Progress surveys school children across the United States to find out what academic skills students have. In 1973, and again in 1978, they tested the math abilities of students.

The results of these two surveys show that the average school child does not learn many arithmetic skills at the rate anticipated by the established guidelines. The surveys focused on three age groups: nine-year-olds, thirteen-year-olds, and seventeen-year-olds. Looking at a few scores for the nine- and thirteen-year-olds will demonstrate the difference between what students are "expected" to know in the way of math skills and what they "actually" know how to do.

Look at these results:

Nine-year-olds* should be able to work these kinds of problems:

$$\begin{array}{r} 34 \\ +10 \\ +25 \\ +89 \\ \hline \end{array} \qquad \begin{array}{r} 512 \\ -326 \\ \hline \end{array}$$

But only 50 percent could solve such problems correctly.

Thirteen-year-olds† should be able to work these kinds of problems:

$$28\overline{)3052} \qquad \frac{3}{4} + \frac{1}{2}$$

But less than 50 percent could solve such problems correctly.

WHAT CAN PARENTS DO?

The math guidelines we present are used in many classrooms. If you want to ensure that your child stays up with his class, make sure he learns the *baseline skills*. While you are doing this, keep in mind that it takes a great deal of time, practice, and concentration to learn and remember these skills and then use them accurately.

Analysis of the National Assessment information shows that parents can help their children correctly solve arithmetic problems and avoid mistakes by having their children

- frequently practice a learned skill
  Because: skills that are not used are forgotten.

- work each problem with concentration and accuracy
  Because: math is a precise skill and unless you are 100% right, you're wrong.
  (Too many errors are caused by carelessness.)

- try to understand what they are actually doing when they use an arithmetic skill
  Because: problem-solving skills built on memorization instead of understanding can't be transferred from one type of problem to another.

---

* About 75% of nine-year-olds are in the fourth grade; 25% are in the third grade.

† About 75% of thirteen-year-olds are in eighth grade; 25% are in seventh grade.

Learning Arithmetic

It is important to remember that your child must learn arithmetic skills *step-by-step*. It is not possible for her to become competent at new skills until she has learned the old ones. For example, a child who cannot accurately subtract and multiply will not be successful in division because she must use these previously taught skills to solve division problems.

It Takes Time to Learn and Master an Arithmetic Skill

1. First, your child must understand what he is actually doing when he begins working with an arithmetic operation (like addition, subtraction, etc.).

When he solves a problem like $14-6$ or $7\overline{)56}$, he must be able to make sense out of what he is doing—removing six objects from a group of fourteen objects, or splitting up a group of fifty-six objects into seven equal groups.

• Each new skill should be introduced by having the child perform simple arithmetic tasks using blocks or other objects. It is only by "seeing" what is actually happening that your child can really understand what takes place in the different arithmetic operations.

2. Next, he must memorize the basic facts of that operation.

• After your child understands what she is doing when she subtracts or multiplies, she must then learn the subtraction facts—from $\frac{1}{-0}$ to $\frac{18}{-9}$ —and multiplication facts—$\frac{1}{\times 0}$ to $\frac{9}{\times 9}$

• Children who do not memorize arithmetic facts are not successful in arithmetic. A child cannot concentrate on following the steps to complete a problem such as $59\overline{)4366}$ if he isn't sure what $5\overline{)45}$ is.

3. Then, he must apply these "facts" to learning the rules for solving more complicated problems.

• Each type of arithmetic operation has its own set of rules. After the facts are memorized, the rules are learned for solving problems like

$$\begin{array}{r} 4,782 \\ -2,936 \end{array} \qquad \begin{array}{r} 6549 \\ \times\ 87 \end{array}$$

4. Finally, and most important, your child must learn how to apply her ability to compute arithmetic to solving "real life" problems.

• Knowing how to compute $55\overline{)275}$ isn't of much use unless you can eventually figure out that it will take 5 hours for you to travel 275 miles, driving 55 m.p.h.

• Knowing how to solve $\frac{6}{100} = \frac{n}{450}$ or $\begin{array}{r} 450 \\ \times .06 \end{array}$ has no value if you cannot use these skills to determine what 6 percent sales tax will be on that $450 washing machine.

The most recent National Assessment of Educational Progress in Mathematics showed that children are declining in their ability to solve word problems.

In response to these findings, The National Council of Teachers of Mathematics recommends that "problem solving be the focus of school mathematics in the 1980's. . . . The ultimate goal in our teaching is the ability to use and apply the mathematics learned."

HELPING YOUR CHILD WITH ARITHMETIC

Next to physical education, math is the subject most elementary school children like best. Solving problems makes children feel good about themselves. Getting the right answer is fun. However, there will probably come a time when your child gets frustrated with math and will need your help. When this time comes, the feeling you communicate and the methods you use to help can make the difference between success or continued frustration.

Before Starting to Work, Set a Positive Tone:

Do tell your child that you are sure you can help and that you will be glad to.

Do be patient when assisting your child. No child likes to be slow at catching on, but sometimes it takes a little longer for a child to understand than parents expect.

Do look at the overall picture. Don't focus on just the problem at hand. Spend the time to find out if your child is making appropriate progress (see Math Charts pages 164–187) in learning all his arithmetic skills.

Do remember that arithmetic is learned step-by-step, and if your child has fallen behind, she will stay frustrated until you help her learn the skills she missed.

Don't tell your child that some people are just "no good" at math. Every child can learn the basic arithmetic skills unless convinced otherwise.

Don't tell your child that you weren't any good at math either (even if it's true!). Studies indicate that parents who show poor attitudes toward math negatively affect the math abilities of their children.

Don't make critical or sarcastic remarks. Comments like "Haven't you learned this stuff yet?" or "Isn't this the same thing I helped you with last night—what's wrong with you?" serve no good purpose.

Don't be surprised if you hear these kinds of comments when attempting to help your child with arithmetic: "That's not how my teacher said to do it!" or "The teacher doesn't write the problem that way, Mom!" Persist! Try to find out how the teacher *did* explain a particular kind of problem. Also, referring to your child's math book may help you get beyond this obstacle.

Helping with Computation

1. FIND OUT *WHY* YOUR CHILD IS MAKING A COMPUTATION ERROR; THEN HELP HIM TO CORRECT IT.

Check to see if he has learned the necessary skills that provide a foundation for solving the type of problem he is struggling with. It is pointless to concentrate on the immediate problem at hand if your child hasn't learned the steps that come before.

a. Ask your child to show you the kind of problem he is having difficulty with.

b. Use the Arithmetic Operations Guide, pages 198–216, to find a similar problem.

c. Drop back *two steps* to a less difficult problem.

d. Using large, neat print, write the easier problem on a piece of paper for your child to solve.

e. Check to see if your child can answer this less difficult problem. Try several examples.

f. Using this method, either move up or down through the learning steps until you find out what your child does know and at what point he begins making errors.

g. Start work on the first step at which your child cannot do the work accurately.

Check to see what specific types of mistakes your child is making. Help him to understand his errors; then correct them.

a. Write down a couple of examples.

b. Watch carefully as your child works through the problems. Try to see where he is making a mistake.

If your child says something like "I just don't know where to begin" or "What do I do now?" explain the entire problem to him step by step.

If your child completes the problem but makes an error, ask him to work the problem again. This time have him explain aloud what he is doing.

When your child describes what he is doing, he will probably catch his own error. If not, stop him where he makes his mistake and explain what needs to be done.

2. USE A HAND CALCULATOR.

The 1977–1978 National Assessment of Educational Progress reported that 75 percent of nine-year-olds and 80 percent of thirteen-year-olds have hand calculators available for their use. Present trends indicate that it won't be long before almost every school child has access to a calculator.

The widespread use of calculators allows children to accurately solve problems that many of them could not solve without a calculator. Still, the majority of time spent in elementary school math instruction today involves solving computation problems without the aid of a calculator. And, because it requires so much time to teach children to compute accurately, math skills such as estimating, measurement, and problem-solving get little time.

Despite all the time spent on learning to compute, many children cannot solve complex computation problems that involve multiplication, division, fractions, and decimals. However, with relatively little instruction, children *can* use calculators to accurately solve those problems.

Citing this evidence, an increasing number of university educators and researchers recommend that the use of calculators become a major part of every elementary school math program. Some experts even suggest that it is no longer appropriate to spend enormous amounts of time teaching complex arithmetic operations like long division (for example, $8962 \div 45$). These educators think that the time spent teaching these operations could be better used teaching children *when and why* to divide (or multiply, etc.), how to estimate an answer, how to use a calculator, how to solve difficult word problems, how to use geometry and measurement, and how to be accurate and competent using less difficult computation skills.

While these trends are discussed and curriculum recommendations debated, life in the elementary classroom continues in the old patterns. The chances are that your child will be asked to learn the same computation skills in elementary school as you were.

Meanwhile, there are some very simple ways that you can turn a calculator into a teaching tool for your child.

Have your child use a calculator to help him learn the multiplication tables, subtraction facts, etc. Follow these steps:

a. Have your child "log" in a problem such as 8×4.

b. Next, have your child tell you what he thinks the answer is.

c. Press the "equals" sign ($=$) to find out the correct answer.

d. If the answer is correct, go on. If the answer is wrong, write the problem down and try it again later.

IMPORTANT: the calculator is used not to replace memorization of the facts but rather to aid it.

Have your child use the calculator to increase computation accuracy.

For those times when we must compute a difficult problem without a calculator, the key is to be accurate. Your child needs to understand this need for accuracy. Instead of working for speed in solving lots of problems (something that just isn't done in the real world without a calculator), stress the importance of working a few problems correctly.

After solving each computation problem in a homework assignment, have your child use a calculator to check if his answer is correct. This type of immediate feedback is one of the best ways for a child to see a pattern to his errors and begin to correct them.

Teach your child to make sure the "calculator's answers" are reasonable and make sense.

Studies of children using calculators show that they often reverse the correct entry order for subtraction and division problems. In other words, they log in the wrong number first. Also, children sometimes press the wrong button by mistake.

FACT: Many children automatically accept whatever the calculator says as being correct. Children need to understand that calculators only give the "right" answer if given the "right" information in the proper order. They must learn to see if the calculator's answer makes sense.

3. HELP YOUR CHILD LEARN TO ESTIMATE

If a child can reasonably estimate the correct answer to a problem, it shows that he understands the problem and its solution. Unfortunately, learning how to estimate is a skill that is given relatively little time in most schools. Not surprisingly, most children have very poor estimating ability.

Children who cannot, or do not, estimate often give answers that make no sense. Most children merely go through the process of working out a problem. When they come up with an answer, they put it down and go on to the next problem. Few children take another look at the whole problem and see if their answer is reasonable and thus check to see if they might have made an error in computation.

Two steps to learning estimation

1. Round off the numbers in the problem to the nearest ones, tens, hundreds, thousands, etc.

> A child who estimates that $8\frac{7}{8} \div 2\frac{6}{7}$ is approximately 3 will catch a careless error that produces an answer like 27. A child who doesn't estimate won't catch it.

$$8\frac{7}{8} \div 2\frac{6}{7} = \text{ becomes } 9 \div 3 =$$

> A child who estimates that $18\overline{)3759}$ is approximately 200 will catch a computation error that produces an answer like 28. A child who doesn't estimate won't catch it.

$18\overline{)3759}$ becomes $20\overline{)4000}$

2. Find the solution to the simpler, rounded-off problem. Remember to cancel out the zeros on division.

$$20\overline{)4000} \text{ becomes } 2\overline{)400} \quad (200)$$

Helping with Word Problems

Mrs. Jones: "Let's work on some word problems."

Bob: "Ugh . . . I can never figure out those things."

Mrs. Jones: "But they're important—I mean, that's why you learn all these skills, so you can use them to figure out real life problems."

Bob: "These problems are stupid. I'd never want to figure out any of them. What kind are these, anyway—subtraction, division, multiplication, or what?"

Mrs. Jones: "They're division. C'mon, you can figure them out. Just divide the numbers."

Bob: "Well, okay, I'll see what I can do. . . ."

Solving word problems or story problems is referred to by educators as simply *problem solving.* Problem solving is supposed to be the application of a technical skill *to* a "real life" need. Let's face it, being able to solve 29)8607 is a worthless skill unless you will later need to, and can, use it to solve some real problem.

The fact is, most adults *will* need to use division, whether it's to establish a food budget or figure out what monthly payment you want to make to pay off that loan. It's also a reality that many of life's "real" problems involve two operations—adding and then dividing, multiplying and then subtracting—and also involve a lot more figures than are actually needed to solve the problem.

The Unfortunate Truth About Problem Solving Is:

• many children are still not convinced that it will be of any use to them in real life.

• most children approach story problems the same way they do computation exercises—mechanically, without thinking about what they are doing.

The result is that most children can do fairly well on simple word problems that include only the essential information and require the use of only one operation. *But most children do very poorly on problems that require picking out the important information from a variety of facts and/or require the use of more than one operation.*

Ask Yourself This Question:

With the widespread availability of hand calculators, who is better off:

• the student who *can* compute difficult arithmetic exercises but cannot figure out how to apply these skills to problem solving

OR

• the student who *can't* figure out how to solve difficult arithmetic exercises *but can* use a calculator and *can apply this skill* to problem solving?

The answer to this question is obvious. The first priority in teaching math should be problem solving! Yet, the majority of time spent learning arithmetic in school is still directed at computation. The back-to-basics movement has made many schools put even more emphasis on computation as opposed to problem solving. In fact, from 1973 to 1978, the National Assessment measured a significant decrease in the problem-solving abilities of students.

What Can Parents Do to Help?

Ask that problem solving be emphasized in school.

Since most of your child's arithmetic program *will* be devoted to learning computation skills, find out how much time *is* being spent on learning how to solve story problems. During your first parent conference, let the teacher know that you feel this skill is very important.

Stress to your child the importance of problem solving.

Your attitude toward math will affect your child's attitude. Many adults have never learned good problem-solving techniques and thus sympathize with their child's frustration. DON'T SYMPATHIZE TOO MUCH. If you do, it may become an excuse for your child not to learn this necessary skill.

Remember: the chances are that the more thought a problem requires, and the more frustrated your child becomes, the more important it is for him to spend time learning how to solve the problem.

SOLVING DIFFICULT WORD PROBLEMS

Difficult word problems usually contain one or both of the following ingredients:

1. There are more facts and information given in the problem than are needed to find the solution. This means students must look for the information that is essential to solving the problem.

This may not sound too difficult, but most students don't do very well on problems of this sort. Take this sample problem from the National Assessment survey that purposely includes unnecessary information:

One rabbit eats 2 pounds of food each week. There are 52 weeks in a year. How much food will 5 rabbits eat in one week?

To answer this problem, all you have to do is multiply 5 x 2 = 10. Yet *44% of all thirteen-year-olds got this problem wrong.* The most common mistake was that students saw three numbers in the problem, so without thinking they multiplied all three numbers.

2. The problem calls for the use of more than just one operation; that is, to find the answer you may have to add and then divide, or multiply and then subtract, etc.

Working with this kind of problem is much more difficult for students than the first kind. For example, a problem similar to this one was given by the National Assessment:

Soda pop costs 65¢ for a 36 oz. bottle. At the school picnic, Joyce's class sold cups holding 9 oz. for 25¢ each. How much profit did the class make on each bottle?"

To answer this problem, three simple operations are needed: 36 ÷ 9, 4 × 25, and 100 − 65. The difficulty, of course, is in deciding what exactly needs to be done. Thirteen-year-old students have so little ability to solve this type of problem that *89% answered it incorrectly.*

THE FOUR-STEP APPROACH TO PROBLEM SOLVING

You can assist your child in learning good problem-solving techniques. Use this four-step approach.

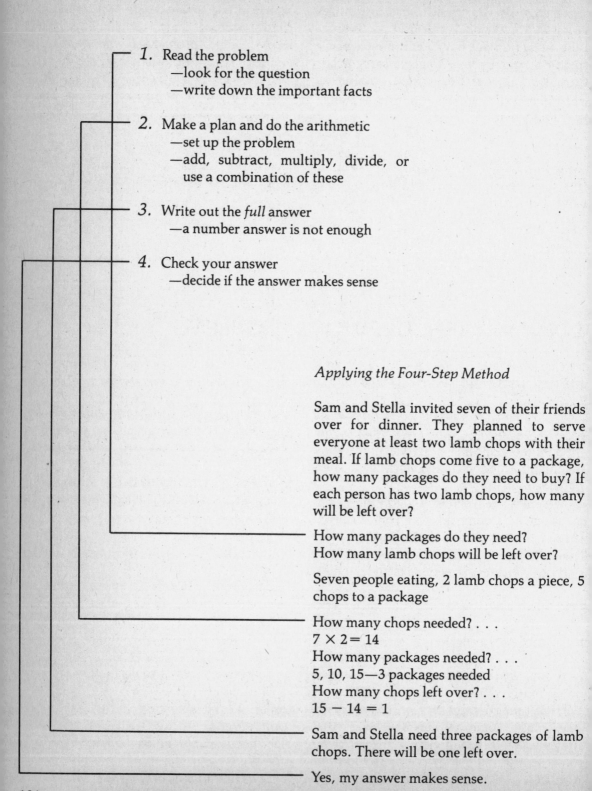

1. Read the problem
   —look for the question
   —write down the important facts

2. Make a plan and do the arithmetic
   —set up the problem
   —add, subtract, multiply, divide, or use a combination of these

3. Write out the *full* answer
   —a number answer is not enough

4. Check your answer
   —decide if the answer makes sense

Applying the Four-Step Method

Sam and Stella invited seven of their friends over for dinner. They planned to serve everyone at least two lamb chops with their meal. If lamb chops come five to a package, how many packages do they need to buy? If each person has two lamb chops, how many will be left over?

How many packages do they need?
How many lamb chops will be left over?

Seven people eating, 2 lamb chops a piece, 5 chops to a package

How many chops needed? . . .
7 × 2 = 14
How many packages needed? . . .
5, 10, 15—3 packages needed
How many chops left over? . . .
15 − 14 = 1

Sam and Stella need three packages of lamb chops. There will be one left over.

Yes, my answer makes sense.

SOLVING SIMPLE WORD PROBLEMS

Simple word problems require the use of just one operation (addition, subtraction, etc.) and include only the facts necessary to solve the problem. Most story problems in math textbooks fall into this category.

Learning how to *think* about these simple problems is important because it provides the backgound for working with more difficult problems. Most children can do simple word problems once they learn to look for the appropriate "cue" words. But many children solve these problems without ever understanding what they're doing. It's easy for children to use cue words and rely on them to the point where a story problem just becomes a computation problem and requires little thought. You can see this for yourself. You'll find you can solve the following problem just by reading the underlined words.

Susan and her four friends had 25 apples. They decided to share them 5 ways. How many apples should each girl get?

Answer: 5

In the Arithmetic Operations Guide (pages 198–216) we outline the type of simple word problems that usually go with each arithmetic operation. Included are sample word problems in which the cue words that are key to each type of operation are underlined.

Children need to learn how to solve these simple problems quickly and with few errors. You can help your child learn to *think* about these problems and what is being asked (instead of just relying on the cue words or the knowledge that "all the word problems on this page are multiplication problems").

One way to encourage this in your child is to help him approach simple word problems the same way he will eventually need to tackle more difficult problems, with the four-step method:

There are 30 children in Mr. Flint's class. If each child brings in 5 aluminum cans for the ecology drive, how many cans will they have in all?

STEPS:

1. Read the problem:
   Look for the question ⟶ how many cans does the class have?
   Write down the facts ⟶ 30 students . . . bring 5 cans each

2. Make a plan and do the arithmetic ⟶ $5 \times 30 = 150$

3. Write out the full answer ⟶ Mr. Flint's class collected 150 cans.

4. Check your answer ⟶ Yes, my answer makes sense.

Arithmetic Operations Guide

This section details how arithmetic skills are learned, step-by-step. Each arithmetic operation, or skill, will be presented in this manner:

1. A written explanation of what your child should understand about each operation

2. Tips on solving simple word problems. (A guide to solving more difficult word problems can be found on pages 195–196.)

3. A series of problems showing step-by-step what your child must learn to go from simple arithmetic facts to handling complicated problems

4. Helpful tips and suggestions that might make it easier for your child to learn the skill

ADDITION

UNDERSTANDING ADDITION

Addition is a way to combine numbers to find a total number of objects. To understand addition with numbers, a child needs to see that it is a fast way of combining objects

For example:

Bob has 3 balls		Pam has 2 balls		Sue has 4 balls		They have 9 balls in all
•••	+	••	+	••••	=	•••••••••
3	+	2	+	4	=	9

ADDITION WORD PROBLEMS

Simple word problems calling for the use of addition contain certain *cue words* and are written in a typical style. More difficult word problems can be figured out using the guide to problem solving (pp. 195–196).

—Maria bought a hamburger at 85¢, French fries at 50¢, and a soft drink for 45¢. <u>What was the price of the entire</u> meal?

—There are 15 boys and 17 girls in Mr. Gomez's second grade class. <u>How many</u> students are there <u>altogether</u>?

—Sam gave 8 comic books to his friend, Steve. He now has 12 left. <u>How many</u> comics did Sam have <u>before</u> he gave some to Steve?

—Eddie and his father went to the store to buy a few groceries. They spent 45¢ for lettuce, 89¢ for milk, $1.35 for some breakfast cereal, and $2.85 for some hamburger. <u>What was the total cost of all</u> the groceries?

—Suzanne wants to bake a cake. It will take 2 minutes to grease the pan, 5 minutes to mix the batter, 45 minutes to bake, and another 10 minutes to decorate with frosting. <u>How many</u> minutes will it take <u>in all</u> to make the entire cake?

198

STEPS TO LEARNING ADDITION

Before trying to help your child with addition, become familiar with the basic steps involved in learning to add. (See Helping with Computation, pages 191-193.)

---

1. Memorize the addition facts. (These are all the problems that combine the numbers 0 through 9.)

$$\begin{array}{r} 1 \\ +0 \\ \hline 1 \end{array} \quad \text{to} \quad \begin{array}{r} 9 \\ +9 \\ \hline 18 \end{array}$$

---

2. Add two numbers without carrying.*

$$\begin{array}{r} 342 \\ +615 \\ \hline 957 \end{array} \qquad \begin{array}{r} 60 \\ +22 \\ \hline 82 \end{array}$$

---

3. Add a one-digit and a two-digit number, carrying from the ones to tens place.

$$\begin{array}{r} {\scriptstyle 1} \\ 39 \\ +\ 8 \\ \hline 47 \end{array} \qquad \begin{array}{r} {\scriptstyle 1} \\ 38 \\ +\ 4 \\ \hline 42 \end{array}$$

---

4. Add two numbers, carrying over from the ones to the tens place.

$$\begin{array}{r} {\scriptstyle 1} \\ 35 \\ +28 \\ \hline 63 \end{array} \qquad \begin{array}{r} {\scriptstyle 1} \\ 239 \\ +416 \\ \hline 655 \end{array}$$

---

5. Add two numbers, carrying over into the hundreds and thousands place.

$$\begin{array}{r} {\scriptstyle 1\ 1} \\ 4652 \\ +1660 \\ \hline 6312 \end{array} \qquad \begin{array}{r} {\scriptstyle 1\ 1} \\ 8387 \\ +1299 \\ \hline 9686 \end{array}$$

---

6. Line up vertically numbers that have been written horizontally.

$$18+290+7+1004=$$

$$\begin{array}{r} 18 \\ 290 \\ 7 \\ +1004 \end{array}$$

---

7. Add up a column of numbers.

$$\begin{array}{r} {\scriptstyle 1} \\ 38 \\ 45 \\ 62 \\ +74 \\ \hline 219 \end{array} \qquad \begin{array}{r} {\scriptstyle 1\ 1} \\ 18 \\ 290 \\ 7 \\ +1004 \\ \hline 1319 \end{array}$$

---

*In many math textbooks today, *carrying* is called *regrouping* or *renaming*.

TIPS AND SUGGESTIONS
FOR HELPING YOUR CHILD WITH ADDITION

1. *Help your child learn what working with numbers is all about.* Addition is the first arithmetic skill learned. It is important that your child understand what he is doing when he adds numbers. You can help by having him work simple arithmetic problems using objects at home.

   —Ask your child to set the table. Ask him to count the number of knives, the number of forks, and the number of spoons. Now ask if he can figure out by "adding in his head" how many utensils there are all together. Have him check to see if he was right.

2. *Help your child learn the addition facts.*

   —Make addition flashcards or buy them at the store. Write the problem on one side and the problem and the answer on the other. When you practice with the flashcards, make sure you say the problem as you show it and have your child say the problem and the answer when she responds.

3. *Give your child assistance when he begins carrying.*

   —Check to see if your child is making one of these common errors:

CORRECT	WRONG	WRONG	WRONG
$\begin{array}{r} 1 \\ 34 \\ +\ 8 \\ \hline 42 \end{array}$	$\begin{array}{r} 34 \\ +\ 8 \\ \hline 32 \end{array}$	$\begin{array}{r} 2 \\ 34 \\ +\ 8 \\ \hline 51 \end{array}$	$\begin{array}{r} 34 \\ +\ 8 \\ \hline 312 \end{array}$
	Forgetting to carry over into the tens place	Reversing which number to put down and which number to carry	Putting the full "12" down instead of carrying over

4. *Teach your child to look for combinations of "10" when adding up a column of numbers.*

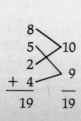

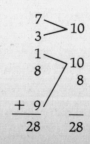

200

SUBTRACTION

UNDERSTANDING SUBTRACTION

Subtraction helps us in three major ways: (1) it is a way to find out "what's left" after taking something away; (2) it lets us compare and find out how much more or less one thing is to another; and (3) it tells us how much more we need to reach a certain total.

SUBTRACTION WORD PROBLEMS

Simple word problems calling for the use of subtraction are written in three main ways, each containing certain cue words. More difficult word problems can be figured out using the guide to problem solving (pages 195–196).

"Take away" problems

—Loretta had 30 marbles and gave 12 to her friend Will. How many did she have left?

—Mother gave John $10.00 to spend for his party. John wants to buy a cake and decorations. If he spends $5.75 on the cake, how much money will remain for decorations?

"Comparison" problems

—Lupe is 54" tall. Her sister, Eva, is 47" tall. How much taller is Lupe than Eva?

—Roger has $5.25. His brother Ron has $2.85. What's the difference?

"What's needed?" problems

—The Williamses want to drive from their home to Red Bluff. On their way they will pass through Sacramento. From their home, it is 250 miles to Sacramento and 380 miles to Red Bluff. When the Williamses reach Sacramento, how many miles will they still have left to drive to reach Red Bluff?

—Jackie wants a radio that costs $35.00. She has already saved $22.00. How much more money does she need?

STEPS TO LEARNING SUBTRACTION

Before helping your child with subtraction, you should be familiar with the basic steps involved in learning to subtract.

1. Memorize the subtraction facts.

$$\begin{array}{r} 1 \\ -0 \\ \hline 1 \end{array} \qquad \text{to} \qquad \begin{array}{r} 18 \\ -9 \\ \hline 9 \end{array}$$

2. Subtract two numbers without borrowing.*

$$\begin{array}{r} 8547 \\ -\ \ 302 \\ \hline 8245 \end{array} \qquad \begin{array}{r} 964 \\ -724 \\ \hline 240 \end{array}$$

3. Subtract a one-digit number from a two-digit number, borrowing from the tens to the ones place.

$$\begin{array}{r} 3\ \\ \cancel{4}7 \\ -\ \ 8 \\ \hline 39 \end{array} \qquad \begin{array}{r} 4\ \\ \cancel{5}2 \\ -\ \ 4 \\ \hline 48 \end{array}$$

4. Subtract any two numbers, borrowing from the tens to the ones place.

$$\begin{array}{r} 5\ \\ \cancel{6}3 \\ -28 \\ \hline 35 \end{array} \qquad \begin{array}{r} 4\ \\ 6\cancel{5}5 \\ -239 \\ \hline 416 \end{array}$$

5. Subtract two numbers, borrowing from the hundreds and thousands place.

$$\begin{array}{r} 5\ 2\ \\ \cancel{6}\cancel{8}12 \\ -1660 \\ \hline 4652 \end{array} \qquad \begin{array}{r} 5\ 7\ \\ 9\cancel{6}\cancel{8}6 \\ -8387 \\ \hline 1299 \end{array}$$

6. Practice subtracting from numbers containing zeros.

$$\begin{array}{r} 7\ 9\ \\ \cancel{8}\cancel{0}3 \\ -429 \\ \hline 374 \end{array} \qquad \begin{array}{r} 8\ 9\ \\ \cancel{9}\cancel{0}07 \\ -6247 \\ \hline 2760 \end{array}$$

*In many math textbooks today, *borrowing* is called *regrouping* or *renaming*.

202

TIPS AND SUGGESTIONS
FOR HELPING YOUR CHILD WITH SUBTRACTION

1. *Help your child learn the subtraction facts.*

—Remind your child that subtraction is the "inverse" of addition.

for example: if you know 5+6=11, you also know 11−5=6 and 11−6=5

—Make or buy subtraction flashcards. (See our advice on using addition flashcards on p. 200)

2. *Give your child assistance with borrowing.*

—It takes many children a lot of practice before they can borrow without making a mistake. Check to see if your child is making one of these common errors:

CORRECT

$$\begin{array}{r} {}^{7}\!8\llap{/}3 \\ -27 \\ \hline 56 \end{array}$$

WRONG

subtracts little number from big number instead of borrowing

WRONG

forgets to reduce the number borrowed from

3. *Give your child special assistance with borrowing involving zeros.*

CORRECT

$$\begin{array}{r} {}^{3}\,{}^{9}\!4\llap{/}0\llap{/}0 \\ -274 \\ \hline 126 \end{array}$$

WRONG

forgets to reduce *10* to *9* when borrowing with zeros

WRONG

subtracts any number from zero instead of borrowing

MULTIPLICATION

UNDERSTANDING MULTIPLICATION

Multiplication is a fast way of adding numbers that are the same.

For example:

$8 \times 5 = 5+5+5+5+5+5+5+5$ and $\begin{array}{r} 14 \\ \times\ 3 \end{array} = 14+14+14$

MULTIPLICATION WORD PROBLEMS

Simple word problems calling for the use of multiplication contain certain cue words and are written in a typical style. More difficult word problems can be figured out using the guide to problem solving (see pages 195–196).

—If stamps cost 20¢ apiece, <u>how</u> <u>much</u> does it cost for 15 stamps?

—If a car travels at 55 m.p.h., <u>how far</u> will it go <u>after</u> 6 hours?

—A car travels 30 miles on one gallon of gas. <u>How</u> <u>many</u> miles will it go on 10 gallons?

—<u>How</u> <u>much</u> do 5 shirts cost at $12.00 apiece?

—One inch equals 50 miles on a map. How many miles is 5 inches on the map?

—Jim earns $150 a week. <u>How</u> <u>much</u> will he earn in 6 weeks?

STEPS TO LEARNING MULTIPLICATION

Before helping your child with multiplication, you should be familiar with the basic steps involved in learning to multiply. (See Helping With Computation, pages 191–193.)

---

1. Memorize the multiplication tables

$\begin{array}{r} 1 \\ \times 0 \\ \hline 0 \end{array}$ to $\begin{array}{r} 9 \\ \times 9 \\ \hline 81 \end{array}$

---

2. Multiply a one-digit number times a two-, three-, or four-digit number without carrying.*

$\begin{array}{r} 21 \\ \times\ 3 \\ \hline 63 \end{array}$ $\begin{array}{r} 6431 \\ \times\ 2 \\ \hline 12862 \end{array}$

---

3. Multiply a one-digit number times a two-, three-, or four-digit number with carrying.

$\begin{array}{r} \overset{2}{4}5 \\ \times\ 5 \\ \hline 225 \end{array}$ $\begin{array}{r} \overset{621}{7832} \\ \times\ 8 \\ \hline 62656 \end{array}$

---

*In many math textbooks today, *carrying* is called *regrouping* or *renaming*.

4. Multiply a two-digit number by a two-digit number without carrying.	31 ×22 62 62 682	42 ×30 00 126 1260
5. Multiply a two-digit number by a two-digit number with carrying.	³ 64 ×28 512 128 1792	⁴ ⁱ 89 ×52 178 445 4628
6. Multiply a three-digit number by a three-digit number with carrying.	¹ ¹ ³ ¹ ⁵ ² 473 ×258 3784 2365 946 122034	⁵ ³ ⁵ ³ 985 ×706 5910 000 6895 695410

TIPS AND SUGGESTIONS FOR HELPING YOUR CHILD

1. *Help your child learn the multiplication tables.* Most children are expected to learn these facts in the third grade. You can help your child with this difficult task by offering a reward for learning each groups of facts—the 2's, 3's, 4's, 5's, 6's, etc.

In addition to flashcards (see our advice on addition flashcards page 200) these hints and reminders can make learning the multiplication tables easier for your child:

—Remember that 0 times any number is 0 and that any number times 0 is 0.

—The answers for the 3's all have digits that add up to 3, 6, or 9. For example, 3×6+18 (1+8=9); 3×7=21 (2+1=3); or 3×8=24 (2+4=6).

—The answers for all the 5's end in either 0 or 5. For example, 5×7=35 or 5×8=40.

—The answers for all the 9's have digits that add up to 9. For example, 7×9=63 (6+3=9) or 8×9=72 (7+2=9).

—Most important, you can reverse the order of the two numbers you are multiplying and the answer will be the same. For example, 4×9=36 and 9×4=36. Keeping this in mind, if your child learns his multiplication tables in order, by the time he reaches his 8's, he has only to learn 8×8 and 8×9. When he reaches his 9's, the only new problem will be 9×9.

2. *Teach your child to avoid careless mistakes by keeping numbers and columns clear, straight, and orderly.* If a child does messy work, it can lead to copying the problem wrong, multiplying the wrong numbers, adding the wrong numbers (in a two-digit problem), and other careless errors that can be avoided.

DIVISION

UNDERSTANDING DIVISION

Division is a way to distribute a given quantity or group of objects evenly. It tells us how many groups (of any size) we can pull out from a given number. It helps us measure the average speed, average length, average cost, etc. Division is also, by far, the most difficult arithmetic skill to learn.

DIVISION WORD PROBLEMS

Simple word problems calling for the use of division contain certain cue words and are written in a typical style. More difficult word problems can be figured out using the guide to problem solving, pages 195–196.

—Rick, Mike, and Fran earned $13.50 selling homemade greeting cards. How much will each one get if they split-up the money equally?

—A jet airliner flew 2,600 miles in 4 hours. What was its average speed per hour?

—We need to set up chairs in the auditorium for 225 people. If we set up the chairs in 15 rows, how many chairs will be in each row?

—Julie saves 75¢ each week. At this rate, how many weeks will it take to save $12.00?

—If a six-pack of soda costs $1.44, what is the price of one soda?

—Jan's father baked 100 cookies for the school party. If there are 30 children in Jan's class, how many cookies will each child get if they share equally? How many cookies will be left over?

STEPS TO LEARNING DIVISION

Before helping your child with division, you should be familiar with the basic steps involved in learning how to divide. (See Helping with Computation, pages 191–193.)

---

1. Memorize the division facts

$$\begin{array}{r} 0 \\ 1\overline{)0} \end{array} \qquad \begin{array}{r} 9 \\ 9\overline{)81} \end{array}$$

---

2. Divide a two-, three-, or four-digit number by a one-digit number with no regrouping and no remainders

$$\begin{array}{r} 621 \\ 4\overline{)2484} \end{array} \qquad \begin{array}{r} 3023 \\ 3\overline{)9069} \end{array}$$

3. Divide a four- or five-digit number by a one-digit number using 0 as a place holder in the answer (quotient)

```
    9030          4032
9)81270       4)16128
```

4. Divide a two-, three-, or four-digit number by a one-digit number with regrouping (with or without a remainder)

```
   91r6          1025
8)734         6)6150
  72            6
  14            01
   8             0
   6            15
                12
                30
                30
                 0
```

5. Divide a two-digit number by a two-digit number (with or without a remainder)

```
    4             5r3
23)92        13)68
   92            65
    0             3
```

6. Divide a three-digit number by a two-digit number (no regrouping, with or without remainders)

```
    8            2r58
54)432       63)184
   432          126
     0           58
```

7. Divide a three-digit number by a two-digit number

```
  12r51           34
62)795       28)952
   62            84
  175           112
  124           112
   51             0
```

8. Divide a four-digit number by a two-digit number

```
    43          205r19
39)1677      21)4324
   156          42
   117          12
   117           0
     0          124
                105
                 19
```

207

TIPS AND SUGGESTIONS
FOR HELPING YOUR CHILD WITH DIVISION

1. *Go slowly when explaining the process of division to your child.* Many parents have trouble explaining division (or any other arithmetic skill) to their child because they move too quickly and skip steps or take for granted that their child understands something that he doesn't.

    Study this explanation of a two-place division problem. Ask yourself if you would have covered all these steps.

— Find out where to begin work by asking these questions:

The problem: 58)286

Can 58 go into 2?   58)286   *No*

Can 58 go into 28?   58)286   *No*

Can 58 go into 286?   58)286   *Yes*
—Then the first digit of your answer goes over the "6."

2. *Estimate* how many times 58 goes into 286 by asking how many times does 5 go into 28 . . . The answer is 5, so try this number:

```
  58        5
× 5     58)286
 290     290 —this number is too large,
              try 4.
```

```
  58         4r54
× 4     58)286
 232     232 —this number is OK, so
          54  subtract and then put up
              the remainder of 54.
```

3. *Make sure your child knows how to check his answers in division by using multiplication.*

For example:

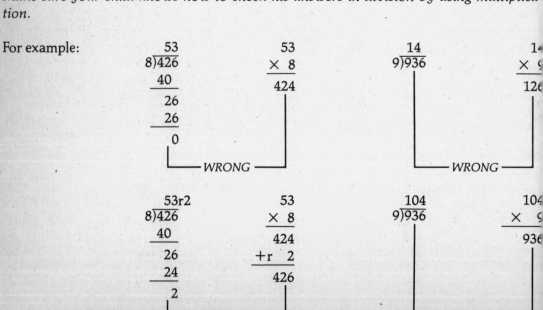

4. If your child is having trouble with division, don't just ask him to work the problem over. Figure out what type of error your child is making and then work on correcting that specific type of error.

Teach your child to aim for 100% accuracy every time he solves a division problem. Division is the most difficult arithmetic skill to learn because there are so many steps to solving one problem. Because there are so many steps, there are a number of places and ways in which errors can be made.

Look at the first problem on this page and then study the next *six* ways a child could err in solving it. *Is your child frequently making one or more of these mistakes?*

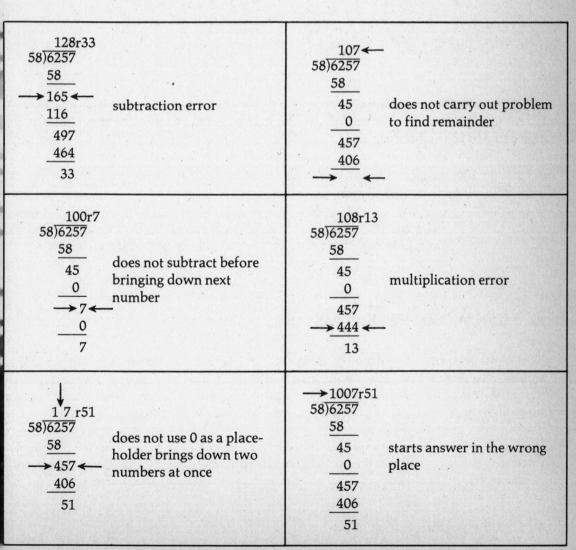

209

FRACTIONS

UNDERSTANDING FRACTIONS

A fraction is a number used to represent parts of a whole. A fraction has two parts: a numerator and a denominator. This is how they work:

$$\frac{3}{5}$$

= the numerator. The numerator tells how many parts of the denominator we're working with.

= the denominator. The denominator tells how many parts the whole object is divided into.

If a child understands what the numerator and denominator tell about the fraction, then he should understand that any fraction where the numerator is equal to the denominator is a fraction equal to "one whole" or "1."

For example: $\frac{100}{100}$ means something is divided into 100 parts *and* you have all 100 of them; that is, you have the whole thing, or 1.

$$\frac{100}{100} = \frac{50}{50} = \frac{2}{2} = \frac{1}{1} = 1$$

This is a difficult idea to get across to many children, but before working with fractions, a child should understand how and why.

FRACTION WORD PROBLEMS

Fraction word problems are solved by using addition, subtraction, multiplication, and division. Addition, subtraction, and division problems with fractions present no special difficulties, since they are worded the same way as problems with whole numbers. In the case of multiplication, however, special problems do arise because of wording.

Word problems that involve multiplication with fractions often use the word "of." When using fractions, either in computation or word problems, think of the multiplication symbol "×" as the word "of."

— What is ½ of ½?   Answer: $\frac{1}{2} \times \frac{1}{2} = \frac{1}{4}$

— Jackie went to the mountains to chop and gather wood. He brought back ½ a cord of wood. He kept ⅔ of it for himself and gave the rest to friends. What part of a full cord did he keep for himself?

To solve this problem, ask what is ⅔ of ½?

Answer: $\frac{2}{3} \times \frac{1}{2} =$

— Joan's recipe called for 2¾ cups of flour. She wanted to make only ⅓ of the amount that the recipe called for. How much flour should she use?

To solve this problem, ask what is ⅓ of 2¾?

Answer: $\frac{1}{3} \times 2\frac{3}{4} =$

A final note from the National Assessment of Educational Progress: *Fewer than 20 percent of thirteen-year-olds tested could solve a word problem that required multiplying fractions, while almost 70 percent could correctly multiply simple fractions.*

STEPS TO LEARNING FRACTIONS

Before trying to help your child with fractions, become familiar with the basic steps involved in learning fractions. (See Helping with Computation, pages 191–193.)

---

1. Identify fractional parts shown in the pictures

 $= \frac{5}{6}$ 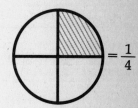 $= \frac{1}{4}$

---

2. Add and subtract fractions with the same denominator

$$\frac{3}{8} + \frac{4}{8} = \frac{7}{8} \qquad \frac{5}{7} - \frac{3}{7} = \frac{2}{7}$$

---

3. Find equivalent fractions

$$\frac{4}{8} = \frac{16}{32} \qquad \frac{4}{6} = \frac{8}{12}$$

---

4. Reduce fractions to lowest terms. *After reducing (or simplifying) fractions is learned, it is expected to be applied to all answers.*

$$\frac{8}{12} = \frac{4}{6} = \frac{2}{3} \qquad \frac{15}{40} = \frac{3}{8}$$

STEPS TO LEARNING FRACTIONS

5. Change improper fractions* to mixed numbers.† *After this skill is learned, it is expected to be applied to all answers*

$$\frac{6}{5}=1\frac{1}{5} \qquad \frac{19}{7}=2\frac{5}{7}$$

6. Change mixed numbers to improper fractions

$$3\frac{1}{5}=\frac{16}{5} \qquad 4\frac{1}{4}=\frac{17}{4}$$

7. Add and subtract with mixed numbers

$$\begin{array}{r} 4\frac{3}{5} \\ +2\frac{4}{5} \\ \hline 6\frac{7}{5}=7\frac{2}{5} \end{array} \qquad \begin{array}{r} 5\frac{3}{7}=4\frac{10}{7} \\ -2\frac{5}{7}=2\frac{5}{7} \\ \hline 2\frac{5}{7} \end{array}$$

8. Add and subtract fractions with unlike denominators**

$$\begin{array}{r} \frac{3}{5}=\frac{12}{20} \\ +\frac{3}{4}=\frac{15}{20} \\ \hline \frac{27}{20}=1\frac{7}{20} \end{array} \qquad \frac{3}{8}-\frac{1}{4}=\frac{3}{8}-\frac{2}{8}=\frac{1}{8}$$

9. Multiply fractions.

$$\frac{3}{4}\times\frac{2}{5}=\frac{6}{20}=\frac{3}{10}$$

$$3\frac{1}{2}\times2\frac{1}{5}=\frac{7}{2}\times\frac{11}{5}=\frac{77}{10}=7\frac{7}{10}$$

10. Divide fractions

$$\frac{4}{5}\div\frac{3}{7}=\frac{4}{5}\times\frac{7}{3}=\frac{28}{15}=1\frac{13}{15}$$

$$\frac{5}{8}\div3=\frac{5}{8}\times\frac{1}{3}=\frac{5}{24}$$

* Improper fractions are fractions that are greater than "1." Improper fractions have larger numerators than denominators.
† Mixed numbers are a combination of a whole number and a fraction
** Some math textbooks and teachers present multiplying and dividing fractions *before* adding and subtracting fractions with unlike denominators.

TIPS AND SUGGESTIONS FOR HELPING WITH FRACTIONS

Encourage your child to picture the fractions he is working with and then check his answers to see if they are reasonable.

The National Assessment tested thirteen-year-olds for their understanding of fractions (approximately two to three years after children this age were supposed to have learned operations with fractions.)

QUESTION: "Estimate the answer to

$\frac{12}{13} + \frac{7}{8}$

You will not have time to solve the problem using paper and pencil."

RESPONSES:	% of 13-year-olds responding this way
• 1	7%
• 2	24%
• 19	28%
• 21	27%
• I don't know	14%

Obviously, any child who understands and can visualize fractions cannot look at any other answer except 2 as being reasonable. What is clear from the National Assessment results is that *most children do not understand what fractions are all about.*

Visualizing fractions, and then estimating answers, is very difficult for most children to do.

— Work on visualizing and estimating skills by asking your child, "Is this fraction less than ½? equal to ½? more than ½?" Or more advanced, "Is ⅞ closer to ½ or 1? Is ⅙ closer to 0 or ½?"

— Remind your child what fractions stand for. For example: ⅛ of a pie is *less* than ⅕ of a pie. (Your child's first reaction may be just the opposite, since *8* is more than *5*.)

Help your child learn to reduce or simplify fractions to their lowest terms; that is, 50/100 becomes ½; 3/9 becomes ⅓, etc.

Many children just don't know how to go about simplifying fractions. They need assistance in choosing a starting point. These guidelines should help. (Remind your child that when simplifying fractions, both the numerator and the denominator must be divided by the same number.)

Your child needs to ask herself these questions:

Can the numerator divide evenly into the denominator?

$$\frac{8 \div 8}{32 \div 8} = \frac{1}{4}$$

Can the denominator divide into the numerator (improper fraction)?

$$\frac{27 \div 9}{9 \div 9} = \frac{3}{1} = 3$$

Can I think of a large (or the largest) number that will divide into both the numerator and denominator?

$$\frac{56 \div 8}{64 \div 8} = \frac{7}{8}$$

If the first three steps can't help you to reduce the fraction, then try these next three:

Check to see if both the numerator and denominator are even numbers and can be divided by 2.

$$\frac{10 \div 2}{16 \div 2} = \frac{5}{8}$$

Check to see if both the numerator and denominator can be divided by 3.

$$\frac{9 \div 3}{48 \div 3} = \frac{3}{16}$$

Check to see if the numerator and the denominator end in 0 or 5 and can thus be divided by 5.

$$\frac{15 \div 5}{35 \div 5} = \frac{3}{7}$$

DECIMALS

UNDERSTANDING DECIMALS

Decimals are another way of writing fractions. A decimal point is used to separate a number into two parts: a whole number and a fraction.

Before working with decimals, your child should understand the place value system as shown:

thousands	hundreds	tens	ones		tenths	hundredths	thousandths
9 ,	6	3	1	.	2	4	6

9,631.246

Using this place value system, your child should then learn the relationship between fractions and decimals. To see if he understands this relationship, try this: Write down a decimal such as .4 and show it to your child. Ask him to write the fraction that corresponds to this decimal. He should write 4/10. Try the examples that follow. If he can do this, then reverse the procedure by writing the fraction and having your child write the corresponding decimal.

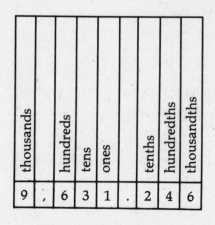

$$.4 = 4/10 \qquad .24 = 24/100 \qquad .006 = 6/1000$$

$$1.4 = 1\tfrac{4}{10} \qquad 31.246 = 31\tfrac{246}{1000} \qquad 1.046 = 1\tfrac{46}{1000}$$

$$.04 = 4/100 \qquad .046 = 46/1000 \qquad 631.24 = 631\tfrac{24}{100}$$

DECIMAL WORD PROBLEMS

Word problems that involve decimals are written in the same style as similar problems involving whole numbers and fractions.

214

STEPS TO LEARNING DECIMALS

Before trying to help children with decimals, become familiar with the basic steps involved in learning decimals. (See Helping with Computation, pages 191–193.)

---

1. Understand the place value of decimals and how decimals are related to fractions

$$1.06 = 1\frac{6}{100} \qquad .302 = \frac{302}{1000}$$

---

2. Line up numbers in a column with decimal points in a vertical line

$$16.83 + 2.9 + .006 = \begin{array}{r} \overset{1}{16.83} \\ 2.9 \\ +.006 \\ \hline 19.736 \end{array}$$

---

3. Subtract with decimals (includes extending out zeros to aid in borrowing)

$$6.9 - 1.238 = \begin{array}{r} \overset{8\;9}{6.\cancel{9}\cancel{0}0} \\ -1.238 \\ \hline 5.662 \end{array}$$

---

4. Multiply with decimals

$$\begin{array}{r} \overset{1}{\underset{2}{}} \\ 2.5 \\ \times 2.5 \\ \hline 12\;5 \\ 50 \\ \hline 6.2\;5 \end{array} \qquad \begin{array}{r} \overset{2\;\;1}{3.42} \\ \times\;.60 \\ \hline 000 \\ 2052 \\ \hline 2.0520 \end{array}$$

---

5. Divide with decimals

$$.5\overline{)348} \;=\; .5.\overline{)348.0.} \;=\; \begin{array}{r} 696 \\ 5\overline{)3480} \\ \underline{30} \\ 48 \\ \underline{45} \\ 30 \\ \underline{30} \\ 0 \end{array}$$

---

6. Change decimals into fractions

$$.8 = \frac{8}{10} = \frac{4}{5} \qquad .16 = \frac{16}{100} = \frac{4}{25}$$

---

7. Change fractions into decimals

$$\frac{3}{5} = 5\overline{)3} \;=\; 5\overline{)3.0}^{\;.6} = .6$$

$$\frac{1}{8} = 8\overline{)1} \;=\; 8\overline{)1.000}^{\;.125} = .125$$

215

TIPS AND SUGGESTIONS
FOR HELPING YOUR CHILD WITH DECIMALS

Help your child understand decimal place value. This skill becomes more important as the use of hand calculators increases. Unfortunately, many children do not really grasp what decimal numbers represent.

For example, the National Assessment asked students this question:

"Which number is the greatest?"

.19
.036
.195
.2

Less than 50 percent of the thirteen-year-olds answering this question knew that the correct answer was .2.

How can you help with this problem? —Remind your child that *0* can be added to the *right* side of a decimal without changing the value of the number. This will assist her in learning place value and comparison of decimals. Does your child understand this—

Does your child understand this— $.3 = .30 = .300$ because $\frac{300}{1000}$ reduces to $\frac{30}{100}$ and finally to $\frac{3}{10}$.

If he understands this, your child can take the same problem shown above and carry out all the numbers to the thousandths place. The answer becomes much more obvious.

"Which number is the greatest?"

.190
.036
.195
.200

CHAPTER 6

When I was a boy of fourteen, my father was so ignorant that I could hardly stand to have the old man around. But when I got to be twenty-one, I was astonished at how much he had learned in seven years.

—*Mark Twain*

Working Through the Rough Spots

"Margaret sure has been touchy lately. I just asked her to copy her paper over again and she started to cry."

"Gregg's teacher called me today and told me he has had six tardies in the last ten class meetings."

"Lamont, your counselor called today. He wants to have a conference with us. He said you are having trouble in three classes."

"Geoff's attendance is really becoming a problem. In the last three weeks he's had seven absences."

"Eric has been a real troublemaker since he enrolled at our school. He's been picking on the smaller children and writing on the walls."

"This note from your teacher says you are missing three assignments and have failed the last two tests."

"Carmen has looked so sad in class lately. She just sits and does not participate."

These children are all having trouble in school. The difficulties they are having are not because the work is too hard. It is because they are emotionally upset or concerned about something. They have a problem that is bothering them, and it is affecting their school work.

They need someone to *listen,* **to** *hear,* **and to** *understand.*

Understanding Rough Spots: Apparent Problems and Underlying Causes

We have talked with many parents who relate stories of their children having problems in school at one time or another. It's a rare child who goes through twelve years of school without experiencing some rough spots.

Some of the rough spots are normal and predictable:

• A seven-year-old girl thinks boys are "yucky" and can't work with any of them in class.

• An eight-year-old girl wants more attention.

• A fifteen-year-old boy wants more freedom.

• A thirteen-year-old boy is afraid to talk because his voice keeps changing.

Other rough spots may occur as your child goes through the day-to-day experiences of growing up:

• A twelve-year-old girl is embarrassed because she is just beginning to develop physically.

• A ten-year-old boy's best friend just moved.

• A twelve-year-old boy begins to assert his manliness by fighting.

• A nine-year-old girl feels she caused her parents' separation.

It is important to recognize that as your children grow they will go through many changes in their behavior, attitudes, and values. Try not to see every change as negative or as the final outcome of their personalities.

Some of the rough spots may be temporary and easy to handle—others may be *very serious and have long-lasting effects.* Your child's reaction to these problems can vary from being almost unnoticeable at school to the point where his school success is seriously threatened.

IMPORTANT: WHEN YOUR CHILD'S ATTITUDE OR BEHAVIOR CHANGES AND PROBLEMS BEGIN TO OCCUR AT SCHOOL, LISTEN CAREFULLY AND TRY TO UNDERSTAND THE CAUSE OF THE PROBLEM WHILE YOU LOOK FOR A SOLUTION.

Sometimes It's Important to Find the "Why" Behind Your Child's Behavior Before You Demand a Change

Nine-year-old Rudy has just been caught fighting on the playground for the second time this week. His teacher has also noted that Rudy is having difficulty concentrating on his work. Rudy's teacher decides to call home.

Consider these two parent responses:

Response A:

"I've told Rudy not to fight. He knows better than that. I just don't know what to do with him. There is no excuse. I guess he'll just have to learn the hard way."

In Rudy's situation Response A does not show an interest in *why* Rudy is fighting or in the difficulty he is having concentrating in class. While concerned, the response shows mainly frustration. This parent will probably be seen by Rudy as being angry and not really caring about him.

Response B:

"Thank you for calling. Rudy has been different around here too. It's all very new to me. Maybe Rudy is upset about his father and me. We had a big blow-up last weekend and his father has decided to move out."

In contrast, Response B shows interest in *why* Rudy is feeling so angry. The parent appreciates the teacher calling and is willing to explore what might be *causing* the problem. In this particular situation, the understanding and positive communication between parent and teacher led to Rudy receiving some special attention and an understanding ear from his teacher.

It Always Makes a Difference When Parents Listen, Try to Understand, and Effectively Communicate with Their Children

Traci, age sixteen, has previously been an excellent student. However, her parents have just received two progress notices from the school showing a big drop in her grades.

Consider these two conversations:
Conversation A:

Dad: "You've *never* done this poorly in school."
Traci: "Yes, I know, but . . ."
Dad: "No but's about it—you better get to work. You're never going to college this way, young lady."

In Traci's situation the response of Dad in Conversation A is similar to Response A in the first example. He is concerned about Traci but shows it by being critical. He cuts Traci off when she tries to explain and this is seen by Traci as being insensitive.

Conversation B:

Dad: "It looks like you're having a tough time in a couple of classes."
Traci: "Yeah."
Dad: "What seems to be the problem?"
Traci: "Well, John is in both of the classes and I can't seem to concentrate since we broke up."
Dad: "Well, I understand it's difficult for you to keep your mind on your work. Would you like for me to talk to your teachers?"
Traci: "No, Dad, thanks. I just need to talk to John and get things straightened out."
Dad: "OK, I'd like a note from your teachers in two weeks to show me you're back on track."

In contrast, the response of Dad in Conversation B is understanding and not threatening to Traci. It shows respect for Traci and quickly gets to the probable *cause* of the problem. Dad is sympathetic, helpful, and allows Traci the chance to assume responsibility for her own school work.

SCHOOL BEHAVIOR OR ATTITUDES CAN BE SIGNS OF TROUBLE

Much of the undesirable behavior children express at school can be lumped into four main areas. These categories do not represent all behavior and there is overlap. They are to be used as general signs of problems

Each child is unique. Children grow at different rates. They mature at different times. They repond to changes and problems differently. It is important that you apply these differences to YOUR CHILD.

Your child has a problem at school . . .

ATTITUDE/PERFORMANCE

Does your child

- have a sudden drop in grades?
- seem to be nervous while at school?
- not participate in class?
- have a don't-give-a-damn attitude in class or about school?
- not complete assignments?
- have problems with self-control while at school?

WHY ARE THESE THINGS HAPPENING?

INDIFFERENCE/INATTENTIVENESS

Does your child

- give up easily on her schoolwork?
- frequently visit or flirt instead of doing classwork?
- appear bored at school most of the time?
- not listen in class?
- not talk about school when at home?
- appear restless or jump from one activity to another without completing his work?
- put himself down when talking about school?

WHAT IS CAUSING THIS BEHAVIOR?

HOSTILITY

Is your child

- vandalizing school property?
- fighting with his classmates, yelling at his teacher, or just angry at school?
- swearing at her classmates or teachers?
- constantly picking on his classmates?
- always wanting to boss other classmates?
- walking around school with a chip on his shoulder?

WHAT IS YOUR CHILD ANGRY ABOUT?

ATTENDANCE

Is your child

- often truant from school?
- frequently absent without excuse?
- cutting specific classes?
- usually tardy?
- complaining of sickness just to stay home from school?

WHAT IS YOUR CHILD TELLING YOU ABOUT SCHOOL?

FROM THE "SIMPLE" TO THE "SERIOUS," ALL THESE PROBLEMS CAN AFFECT LEARNING.

The causes for undesirable behavior in school are numerous, often overlapping, and complex. Seldom can a parent or teacher place a finger on the exact moment a child's attitude or behavior changes. Through his behavior, the child is *signaling* his parents or teacher that something is bothering him.

You want to find out what's causing the problem.

These can cause serious problems in learning. Make sure you are in contact with school personnel and/or professional help outside of school.
- Death of a family member or a friend.
- Divorce or separation in the family.
- Recent move or a change in schools.
- Prolonged illness of a family member or close friend.
- Alcoholic parent(s).
- Use of drugs.
- Ongoing depression.
- (add your own here).

These are day-to-day living problems which require effective communication and follow-up between school and home.

- Competition between brothers or sisters.
- Conflict with a teacher.
- Peer pressure.
- In love.
- Arguments at home.
- Uninvolved in activities.
- No friends.
- Out of love. In love again.
- Poor hearing or vision.
- (add your own here).

These may not seem important to you, but to your child they may be of *major concern.* Approach these with understanding, respect, and TLC—tender loving care.

- Acne.
- Experimenting with a new fad.
- No prom date.
- Too short. Too tall.
- Too tired. Too "wired."
- Too thin. Too fat.
- No money. No car.
- She said. He said. Rumor.
- (add your own here).

Getting to the Bottom of Things—Talking with Your Child

The importance of effective communication cannot be stressed enough. When your child is experiencing a rough spot in school it becomes even more important. Something is going on inside of her that "doesn't feel right." She needs to talk about the problem. She wants to *talk* about it. She may not show that she wants to *talk* about it. You need to *help*. Be ready for that crucial time when you notice something "is not right."

Listening to feelings is the first step in communicating. It is important to know what you are thinking and/or feeling and how you are communicating this to your child.

HOW DO YOU FEEL? ____Guilty? ____Afraid? ____Loving? ____Annoyed?
____Happy? ____Sad? ____Excited? ____Open? ____Trapped? ____Hurt?
____Bored? ____Anxious? ____Put-Down? ____Left-Out? ____Free?
____Disappointed? ____Understanding? Add your own _____

BE AWARE OF YOURSELF. Your child is probably aware of what you are feeling.

These are just a few of the emotions parents and children feel. They are all part of living together and caring for each other. They are all *understandable*, *real*, and need to be *respected*.

Sit down with your child and circle the word that best describes what you and he are feeling. It will help break the ice and get things started on the right track.

HOW DO *YOU* FEEL?

When you are honest, direct, and communicate your feelings to your child, she will understand that both positive and negative feelings are OK to express. Your child will understand and respect you and will feel free to express her thoughts and feelings to you.

Ask yourself,
"How am I feeling about my child?"

Tell yourself,
"I need to be aware of what's going on inside of me and communicate it clearly and kindly to my child."

For example:

"I'm disappointed . . ."	versus	"You're dumb in school."
"I'm frustrated . . ."	versus	"You never get your work done on time."
"I'm embarrassed . . ."	versus	"Why don't you grow up?"
"I need some quiet . . ."	versus	"You make lots of noise."
"I want to be heard . . ."	versus	"You never listen."

The Main Ingredients in Communicating with Your Child:

HERE ARE SOME HELPFUL HINTS TO GET YOU STARTED.

When Your Child Starts Talking

Ask yourself,

"Can I see the world through her eyes?"
"Can I get 'inside' of him and feel what he feels?"
"Can I let her know I respect what she is saying?"

Be Aware of Body Language

Research shows that the majority of communication is nonverbal. This means you need to be aware of what you say without words.

Ask yourself:
'Is my *tone of voice* . . . ?
  —angry
  —happy
  —disappointed
  —afraid
'Are my *gestures* and body movements . . . ?
  —welcoming, encouraging (arms open)
  —intimidating (pointing my finger)
  —uncaring (slouched in the chair)
'Is my *face* . . . ?
  —frowning (wrinkled forehead)
  —angry, tense (biting my lower lip)
'Am I sitting/standing close to or far away from my child?"

When you respond

Ask yourself,

"Can I genuinely show concern, by inquiring about the problem?"
"Can I repeat back to him what he said and what he is feeling?"

Setting the Mood

It is very important to create a positive mood before discussing problems with your child.

Ask yourself:
"Do I feel comfortable talking with my child?"
"Do I encourage him to talk about his feelings?"
"Can I put the newspaper down, turn the TV off and listen to her?"
"Can I be patient with him?"
"Can I talk about *my* feelings with her?"

 If your answer is Yes to these questions, *you're on your way.*
 If your answer is No, then you'd better stop and ask yourself *Why*.

WHEN YOUR CHILD EXPRESSES HER FEELINGS, DON'T BE OFFENDED BY THEM. ACCEPT THEM AND WORK THROUGH THE "ROUGH SPOTS."

SOMETIMES YOU DON'T HAVE TO SAY ANYTHING TO YOUR CHILD. HE JUST NEEDS SOMEONE TO LISTEN AND TO CARE.

REMEMBER: CHILDREN LEARN TO
LISTEN BY BEING LISTENED TO.

GETTING YOUR CHILD TO TALK

Dad: "Hi, Bob."
Bob: "Hi, Dad."
Dad: "What did you do in school today?"
Bob: "Nothing."

End of conversation.

HERE ARE SOME DOS AND DON'TS FOR GETTING YOUR CHILD TO TALK:

Some Dos

Ask yourself, Can I say to my child . . .
"Tell me more about what you are thinking."
"Sounds like you're feeling _____."
"You have a right to say what you think."
"I want to get to know you better."
"Tell me more, I'll listen."
"This seems important to you."

When you can say these kinds of things you're on your way to a rewarding and effective conversation with your child. She will start to feel important and accepted. **THERE'S A BETTER CHANCE SHE WILL TALK AND LISTEN.**

Some Don'ts

Ask yourself, Do I . . .
—order him? "You must . . ."
—judge her? "You are bad."
—threaten him? "If you don't . . ."
—lecture her? "The facts are . . ."
—avoid talking? "Let's not talk about it."
—diagnose him? "What's wrong with you is . . ."

When you use these, your child will probably not want to talk with you. One thing is certain,
HE WILL NOT LISTEN.

Problems and Responses

HERE ARE SOME EXAMPLES OF EFFECTIVE COMMUNICATION BETWEEN PARENT AND CHILD

Kelly: "I hate my teacher. She's mean."

Dad: "What's going on with you and your teacher?"

Kelly: "She's always picking on me."

Dad: "Sounds like she's really on your case."

Kelly: "Yeah, she caught me passing a note in class and made me stay in during recess."

Dad: "You feel that's unfair."

Kelly: "Well, I don't think it's unfair, but John and Barbara were doing it too. They just didn't get caught."

Dad: "Well, what would you do if you were in Ms. Miller's place?"

Kelly calms down and begins to feel understood and respected, and at the same time begins to understand Ms. Miller's situation.

Carla: "Mom, I don't feel like going to school tomorrow."

Mom: "What's wrong, Carla?"

Carla: "I just don't feel very good."

Mom: "Carla, are you really sick?"

Carla: "No, I just don't feel like going to school."

Mom: "Are you nervous about something?"

Carla: "Yeah, I am. I have a speech tomorrow during third period. I'm really worried about it."

Mom: "I'd be a little nervous too. Would you like to practice with me?"

Carla: "OK, maybe that would help."

Carla nervously starts her speech. Mom, wanting the best for her, listens carefully and gives her support.

Craig: "I have a note from the vice principal. You have to sign it. It's for detention."

Mom: "What's this?"

Craig: "I was caught out of class second period."

Mom: "What's going on with second period?"

Craig: "I didn't do my homework and I didn't want a lower grade."

Mom: "Sounds like you're having a tough time doing your homework?"

Craig: "Yeah, I've had a lot of things on my mind."

Mom: "What seems to be the problem?"

Craig takes a deep breath and begins to explain his difficulty with his job and keeping his studies together.

When you genuinely show concern and paraphase what he is feeling and saying, he will know you are listening and understanding.

Get to Know Your Child a Little Better

TRY SOME OF THESE ACTIVITIES

GETTING TO KNOW YOU

This activity will help you get to know your child better.

Have your child complete these sentences. (If your child is not writing yet, read these to him and write his response.)

My teachers think _____.
My favorite class in school is _____.
I'm happy when _____.
If I could _____.
I like_____.
I'm unhappy at school when_____.
I believe _____.
The thing I want most from school is __
_____.
I wonder _____.
The thing I like best about myself is ____
_____.
_____.

(add your own here).

Ask yourself,

"Did I know this about my child?"
"Is there anything here that I can help her with?"

Fill this out yourself. Try to guess how your child will respond. Try to recall your feelings at his age.

SOME THINGS YOU CAN DO TO SHOW YOUR CHILD YOU'RE INTERESTED AND CARE ABOUT WHAT HE IS DOING

—Have your child show you around his school.
—Attend her athletic activities.
—Go to his school plays, concerts, or back-to-school night.
—Volunteer at school. (Even if only twice a year, do it!)
—Attend every scheduled parent conference.
—Share with him what your school experiences were like.
—Invite her teacher over for dinner.
— _____

(add your own here).

Getting Over the Rough Spots

Helping Your Child with a Contract

It has been our repeated experience that parents whose children are having problems in school are anxious, unhappy, and often confused about what to do to help.

When parents are clear about what they expect and clearly set limits with their child, they feel better about themselves and the child performs better in school.

Now that you have put together the main ingredients in communicating with your child, you may find it helpful to put some ideas down in writing.

A written contract is not always necessary. However, it does make expectations clearer and it helps avoid misunderstandings. It also communicates to your child that you are *serious* about helping him and making things better.

The Main Ingredients of a Successful Contract:

*1. MAKE YOUR CONTRACT
A POSITIVE ONE*

Ask yourself,
"How can I turn this undesirable behavior into positive behavior?"
For example:
"If you don't do your homework, you'll get all F's," versus
"When you do your homework, you can watch TV."
"If you cut classes . . . " versus
"When you go to class . . . "
"If you fight . . . " versus
"When you get along . . . "
"If you don't get a good grade . . . " versus
"When you get a B in . . . "

THE KEY: *Focus on the positive.* Sometimes it's difficult but stick with it. You're on the right track to helping your child be more successful.

2. IS IT REALISTIC?

Ask yourself,
"Is this a reasonable request?"
"Can he accomplish this goal?"
Keep in mind your child's age, maturity, and abilities.

For example,
Don't fall into these traps:

"When you finish all your homework tonight . . . "
Fact: He has a full week's work to do.

"When you get all A's . . . "
Fact: He has never received more than one A in an entire school year.

"When you start liking school . . . "
Fact: He doesn't like school and he may never like it, but he can be successful.

THE KEY: *Be aware of what your child can and cannot do.*

3. ARE YOU CLEAR ON WHAT YOU WANT?

Ask yourself,
"Have I told her what I want her to do as opposed to what I don't want her to do?"
You hope she will want the same thing. Sometimes this is not the case and you need to stand firm on what you want as her parent.
For example,
"If you cut your classes you can't use the car." The choice of going to school and using the car is up to her.
If, however, you say, "When you go to class you may use the car," it is clear that she has to go to class and there will be a reward for her behavior.

THE KEY: Be specific about what you want your child to do.

4. CAN IT BE DONE IN A SHORT AMOUNT OF TIME?

Ask yourself,
"Am I willing to wait two months to get my usual weekly paycheck?"
If your answer is NO, you're not much different than your child. He needs to be able to complete his contract in a short period of time.

For example,
"When you get along with your classmates today . . . " versus "When you stop fighting at school for the rest of the year . . . "
"When you complete your English homework this week . . . " versus "When you complete all your English homework this semester . . . "

THE KEY: Keep it short. What seems like a short period of time to you (an adult) may seem like forever to your child.

5. ARE YOU WILLING TO PAY THE PRICE?

Ask yourself,
"What does my child like?"
"What does my child want?"

Ask your child,
"What reward would you like to work for?"

THE KEY: Rewards need to be tailor-made with and for your child.

HERE ARE SOME IDEAS FOR REWARDS

Too much affection never hurt anyone.
—a hug
—a kiss
—"great job"
—"nice work"
—"looks great"
These need to be going on all the time.

—clothes
—money
—use of the car for Saturday night
—ice cream
—games
—phone privileges
—a friend spends the night
—a party
—TV time
—movies
—jewelry
—something special
— _____
(add your own here).

Ideally, positive behavior and success in school is self-rewarding. However, let's face it, sometimes this is not the case and you need to use other rewards to encourage positive behavior and successful school performance. Usually, once a child is set back on track, doing well in school and getting along with others will become rewards in themselves.

6. ARE YOU *READY TO FOLLOW THROUGH?*

Ask yourself,
"Am I willing to hold up my end of the contract?"
If your answer is *yes*, then go ahead.
If, however, your answer is *no*, then *stop*. It will not work. You must be ready to follow through with your part.

For example,
Steve is a sixteen-year-old boy who is cutting classes on a regular basis. His father is getting furious and very frustrated with his behavior. So, he decides the only way to let Steve know that he is serious about his attending school is to go to every class with him. This follow through took only two days until his son got the message. Steve did not miss another class unexcused for the rest of the semester.

THE KEY: Don't make a "deal" you won't enforce.

SOME FINAL THOUGHTS ON CONTRACTING

Parents need to support each other on the contract. Both of you need to agree and accept the contract. Don't have one of you playing the *"good guy"* and the other the *"bad guy."* This is confusing to your child and he will probably think, "This is important to Mom but not to Dad so 'the heck with it.' "

You can be understanding and caring and at the same time very clear about what you will accept and what you won't accept from your child.

You can give your child choices and the freedom to succeed and to make mistakes and yet hold onto those beliefs and values which are important to you.

Contracting can work when other methods fail. Here are a few samples:

Sample Contracts

Your third grader is having problems with her spelling. You want to help.

Try something like this:

> Let's get over the hump.
>
> When you and I finish working on your spelling words tonight from 6:30–7:00, we will play any card game you want.
>
> signed: _____(Mom)_____
>
> signed: _____(Child)_____

Your junior high student has received three progress notices for not completing his homework assignments.

Try something like this.

Have him take this homework assignment sheet to school with him. Have each teacher sign it and list his homework for the day.

HOMEWORK ASSIGNMENT SHEET

NAME: _____   DATE: _____

Period: Class	Homework assignment	Teacher signature
1. _____	_____	_____
2. _____	_____	_____
3. _____	_____	_____
4. _____	_____	_____
5. _____	_____	_____
6. _____	_____	_____
7. _____	_____	_____

When you complete your homework assignments tonight between 7:00–8:30 you can watch TV from 8:30–9:30.

Signed _____

Signed _____

While talking with your fifth grader's teacher you find out he has been picking on some of his classmates. *You want this to change.*

Try something like this:

When you have "gotten along" (not picked on or fought) with your classmates at school for one full week, you may invite one of your friends to sleep over on Friday night.

signed: ___(child)___   signed: ___(dad)___   signed: ___(teacher)___

You have just been notified by the attendance office that your high school student has cut four classes in the last week. *You want this to change.*

Try something like this:

When you have perfect attendance for the entire week, you may go to the dance on Friday night.

Weekly Progress Report

Name: _____ Date: From _____ To _____

Period	Subject	Teacher	Grade	Abs.	Tardies	Teacher comments:
1						
Home-room						
2						
3						
4						
5						
6						

Signed: _____

Signed: _____

Helping Your Child
Get That Homework Done

DO ANY OF THESE COMMENTS SOUND FAMILIAR?

"I just want to watch one more TV show before starting my homework."

"How can I do it? I don't even understand what the assignment is."

"I need seven sharp pencils before I start my math homework."

"I'm too far behind in social studies. I'll never catch up. So why even try?"

"This assignment isn't due until fifth period tomorrow. I have plenty of time to do it."

"This homework isn't important to my final grade. Why should I do it?"

"I did all my work at school and my teacher(s) didn't give me any homework."

"I want to talk to Jill about the dance tomorrow night. I'll start my homework later."

"WHERE IS YOUR HOMEWORK?"

—"I forgot it."
—"I left it on the bus."
—"My teacher lost it."

—"Yuck."
—"It's in my locker."
—"I can't find it."

—"You wrapped the fish in it."
—"I don't remember."
—"It's in the washer."

—_____
(add your own here)

Learning is not just limited to school. Working at home is a critical part of your child's educational progress. **When helping your child with a homework schedule be prepared for excuses, mistakes, bribes, and forgetfulness.**

You can help your child by planning a homework schedule with her.

> _What does a schedule do?_
> —It is an excellent way to help your child organize his time.
> —It usually enables her to have more free time and fewer hassles.
> —It usually limits nagging about his homework.
> —It may even keep her out of trouble.
> —It becomes habit forming.
> —It helps in establishing limits.

HERE ARE SOME HINTS ON GETTING HOMEWORK DONE:

HAVE YOUR CHILD . . .

make a weekly list of assignments that need to be done.
(If his teacher(s) only assign daily work, make a daily list.)

☐ For example:
   math—do three pages of fractions.
   English—study spelling words for test.
   social studies—work on map of Europe.
   art—do two drawings: one zucchini, one cherry.

work on one subject or project at a time.

☐ For example:
   complete all his math homework at once. Then move on to his spelling words. Have him complete the easier assignments first then move on to the more difficult ones.

check with you on her progress.

☐ For example:
   the math homework may be overwhelming and you can help her break it down into smaller units. This way she can complete it *step-by-step.*

share with you his completed assignment.

☐ For example:
   go over his work. See if it is complete. Ask him questions about it. *Be supportive.*

make a regular time schedule for homework.

☐ For example:
   7–8 PM Monday, Tuesday, and Thursday.
   6:30–8 PM Wednesday.
   day off Friday (when all is well).

do his homework in the same place.

☐ For example:
   set aside a *special place* for him to use every night. Be sure there are few distractions. Contrary to popular student belief, TV viewing or radio listening does not help while studying.

There's more . . .

What if your child says, *"I don't have any homework."*

Try this. It may help:

When your child does not have homework, he still needs to use the scheduled homework time productively. You'll be surprised at the homework that suddenly appears when you tell him, "I know you're done with your homework, but you still have a half hour of study time left."

Here are some productive ways to use that extra homework time:

☐ Have her—
   —Review her work.
   —Read the newspaper.
   —Pleasure read (whatever she's interested in).
   —Watch the news or a documentary on TV.
   —Do crossword puzzles.
   —Share her work or projects with you.
   —Write letters to friends or relatives.
   — _____
   (add your own here).

What's important here is that time has already been scheduled. A routine has been established. The expectation is set and it becomes habit forming. *Don't break the habit.*

...Television

SPECIAL NOTE ON TV WATCHING

Between the ages of six and eighteen, the average child spends roughly 15,000 to 16,000 hours in front of the TV set. He spends about the same amount of hours at school. *The tube needs to be limited.*

HERE ARE SOME IDEAS FOR REDUCING THE AMOUNT OF TV TIME

- Decide at the beginning of each week which programs she can watch.
- Allow only a certain number of hours for watching TV.
- Allow only certain times during the day for watching TV.
- Reduce your own TV watching.
- Allow watching TV only when his responsibilities are completed (homework, chores, etc.).
- Get a crummy TV.
- Keep the TV in the closet.
- _____

(add your own here).

The negative effects of watching too much TV are well known.

PROVIDE ANOTHER ALTERNATIVE AND LIMIT HER VIEWING

Getting Organized

Most children have trouble scheduling their time. They forget things they need or should remember. They get frustrated and so do you.

Sample Schedules

—a *daily schedule* for things happening now.

WHAT'S HAPPENING TODAY?

NAME: _____   DATE: _____

THINGS I NEED TO TAKE
TO SCHOOL TODAY:

new ruler
lunch
math homework

_____
_____
_____

(add your own)

CHORES I NEED TO DO TODAY:

take trash out
feed the dog
wash the dishes

_____
_____
_____

(add your own)

HOMEWORK I NEED TO DO
TODAY:

study spelling words
work on multiplication flash cards
finish Europe map

_____
_____
_____

(add your own)

MISCELLANEOUS TODAY:

soccer practice from 3–4 PM
fix the brake on my bike
go over to Steve's house

_____
_____
_____

(add your own)

Have your child make a bunch of these schedules. (If he wants to create his own schedule, by all means let him do it.)

Have him place it on the refrigerator or wherever it can be easily seen.

At the end of the week go through these with him. You may both be surprised by the results.

—a *weekly schedule* for some longer-range planning.

WHAT'S HAPPENING THIS WEEK?

NAME_____ WEEK FROM _____ TO _____

WEEKLY
School Schedule

AFTER SCHOOL
Monday

8 AM- _____
_____
_____
_____
_____
_____
_____
3 PM- _____

PM   3:00
4:00 _____
5:00 _____
6:00 _____
7:00 _____
8:00 _____
9:00 _____
10:00 _____
11:00 _____
12:00 _____

Tuesday

PM   3:00 _____
4:00 _____
5:00 _____
6:00 _____
7:00 _____
8:00 _____
9:00 _____
10:00 _____
11:00 _____
12:00 _____

Wednesday

PM   3:00 _____
4:00 _____
5:00 _____
6:00 _____
7:00 _____
8:00 _____
9:00 _____
10:00 _____
11:00 _____
12:00 _____

Thursday

PM   3:00 _____
4:00 _____
5:00 _____
6:00 _____
7:00 _____
8:00 _____
9:00 _____
10:00 _____
11:00 _____
12:00 _____

Friday

PM   3:00 _____
4:00 _____
5:00 _____
6:00 _____
7:00 _____
8:00 _____
9:00 _____
10:00 _____
11:00 _____
12:00 _____

WEEKEND SCHEDULE

Saturday

AM 9:00 _____
   10:00 _____
   11:00 _____
PM 12:00 _____
    1:00 _____
    2:00 _____
    3:00 _____
    4:00 _____
    5:00 _____
    6:00 _____
    7:00 _____
    8:00 _____
    9:00 _____
   10:00 _____
   11:00 _____
   12:00 _____

Sunday

AM 9:00 _____
   10:00 _____
   11:00 _____
PM 12:00 _____
    1:00 _____
    2:00 _____
    3:00 _____
    4:00 _____
    5:00 _____
    6:00 _____
    7:00 _____
    8:00 _____
    9:00 _____
   10:00 _____
   11:00 _____
   12:00 _____

When you and your child are planning his schedule, use the Helpful Hints section on pages 234–235 and the TV section on page 236 to help you get started.

Have your child answer these questions:

Yes No

__ __ Are the hours I spend after school used productively?

__ __ Is there makeup time for lost study time?

__ __ Is my time generally spent as planned?

__ __ Do I have adequate breaks?

__ __ How do I spend my time on weekends? Do I use my weekend time well?

__ __ Do I have too much or too little recreation time?

__ __ Would I like to change my schedule?

__ __ _____? (add your own).

Oftentimes parents are surprised to see how busy their child really is. *Maybe too busy?* Sometimes parents see large gaps of time not well spent. *Maybe not busy enough?*

CONTACTING SCHOOL PEOPLE

There may be times when you need to talk with someone other than your child's teacher. There may be a difficult problem your child is having at school that may require some special assistance.

In elementary school, the people who can provide special assistance will usually be the principal, the counselor, the vice-principal, or perhaps a school district psychologist.

At the junior high or high school level, you will probably meet with a counselor, a vice-principal, or maybe even the principal.

THESE PARENTS GET INVOLVED

"I'm Greg Brown's father. I have a note that says I have to come to the school to talk with the VP about my son's behavior. What time should I be there?"

"I would like to see my daughter's permanent record file. When should I come to see her counselor?"

"Hello, my name is Mrs. Swanson. I would like to schedule an appointment with my son's counselor."

"Derek, the principal called today. She wants to have a conference about your fighting."

"You're going to school with me tomorrow. I made an appointment with the VP. We're going to talk about your cutting classes."

"The school psychologist called and he wants to test Jimmy for some kind of special class. I'm pretty nervous about it."

THESE PARENTS LET PROBLEMS GO

—"I'm too busy to come to school."
—"You guys at the school know best."
—"When he gets to school, he's your problem."
—"I'm too tired to spend my time at school."

—"The school's so big, nobody even knows my child. So why should I come?"
—"School scares me."
—_____
(add your own).

We have talked with many parents who relate stories of their reluctance to get involved with the school. Their reasons for not being involved, as you can see, run the gamut from *"too busy"* to *"I'm afraid."*

THE FACT IS, THE SOONER YOU GET INVOLVED WITH SCHOOL PEOPLE, THE BETTER OFF YOUR CHILD WILL BE.

Talking with School People About a Major Problem:

Before you meet with a counselor or school administrator to discuss a problem your child is having, you need to be prepared.

THESE WILL HELP:

MAKE A LIST OF IDEAS THAT YOU FEEL COULD BE CAUSING THE PROBLEM

For example: She—
• Just broke up with her boyfriend.
• May be feeling upset about the separation of the family.
• Feels nobody likes her.
• Has been very concerned about her mom in the hospital.
• Has been very cocky since she made the volleyball team.
• Has always been a loner.
• Doesn't like her art teacher.
• _____
   (add your own).
Some of these are more serious than others. However, any one of them could be affecting her behavior and school performance. *Check them out. The more information out, the more help coming in.*

MAKE A LIST OF WHAT YOU THINK YOUR CHILD NEEDS AT SCHOOL

For example: He needs—
• To be separated from Johnny. They don't get along with each other.
• To learn to work together with his classmates.
• Help in organizing his time.
• A firm, no-fooling-around teacher.
• A relaxed, open classroom.
• To be constantly involved or he gets into trouble.
• To work with his hands.
• A friend.
• _____
   (add your own).

Work with your child. Determine his *strengths* and *weaknesses*. Then communicate these to his counselor.

THE MORE YOU CREATE A PARTNERSHIP WITH SCHOOL PEOPLE, THE GREATER THE CHANCE OF GETTING YOUR CHILD ON TRACK.

• *Relax.* School people are often just as nervous or anxious as you. Help them feel more comfortable.
• *Be prompt.* Schools are very busy places. If you're late, there is a good chance you'll have to return.
• *Involve your child.* When your child sees you talking with his counselor, he knows school is important to you and you are going to be in contact with people who can help.
• *Share your lists.* When you share your ideas on what your child needs and what might be causing the problem, it really helps in finding solutions.

• *Be realistic.* Teachers, counselors, and administrators *do not* have magic wands. It takes work to solve problems.
• *Approach the conference as a team.* This is a partnership. Everyone needs to work together for the quickest and best result.
• *End the conference on a positive note, with a plan of action.* (Maybe a contract would help?) *For example:* "I'm glad I found out John is having trouble with fighting. We'll talk with him at home and set up a contract for his behavior. Let's get back together in two weeks and see how he is doing."

School people are human too and sometimes you need to: *call back; make another appointment; be more assertive;* and by all means, *ask when you don't understand something.*

241

SPECIAL ALERT

There are some problems which are serious and require professional assistance. The following are examples:

A child who
- experiences intense fighting between brothers and/or sisters
- reacts with overwhelming anxiety to a fire, a car accident, the death or illness of a beloved person
- mentions suicide
- has a long history of stealing or lying
- is very angry or violent
- is suffering from drug or alcohol abuse
- has been abused by previous or present parents or other adults
- has a long-lasting depression

If one of these problems occurs, *seek professional help IMMEDIATELY.* Your school administrator, counselor, or district psychologist should be able to help or refer you to a person or agency that can. If you don't feel comfortable with these people or they are unable to help, refer to the list that follows to find the most appropriate agency.

WHERE TO TURN FOR HELP

There are times when you don't feel comfortable talking with school people about a serious problem. Or you may want more information about a certain problem.

The following is a list of resources to get you started in the right direction. You can usually find many of these agencies in your local telephone directory.

Alcoholics Anonymous, Inc., General Service Office, P.O. Box 459, Grand Central Station, New York, N.Y. 10017. There are over 25,000 local AA groups in more than 90 countries. You probably have a group in your area. The national office will send you literature on the disease of alcoholism and where you can find a group in your area.

Al-Anon Family Group Headquarters, P.O. Box 182, Madison Sq. Station, New York, N.Y. 10010. This is a support group of families with a specialized group for teenagers (Alateen). The emphasis is on the non-alcoholic. It is very difficult to live with an alcoholic. These people can help.

The American Association of Marriage and Family Counselors, 225 Yale Ave., Claremont, Calif. 91711. This association will refer you to three licensed marriage, family, and child counselors in your area.

Big Brothers/Big Sisters of America, 2220 Suburban Station Bldg., Philadelphia, Pa. 19103. Big Brothers/Big Sisters have roughly 400 agencies serving over 100,000 children throughout the United States. They will match with your child an adult volunteer. They will send you literature and make referrals to your local agency.

Do It Now Foundation, Institute for Chemical Survival, P.O. Box 5115, Phoenix, Ariz. 85010. This group will provide you with free pamphlets that are excellent regarding any alcohol- or drug-related problem. Their material is outstanding for your teenager.

Family Service Association of America (FSAA), 44 E. 23rd St., New York, N.Y. 10010. The FSAA has approximately 300 agencies across the U.S. The national office will provide for you the closest FSA in your area. They are staffed with psychologists, social workers, and trained volunteers.

National Center for the Prevention and Control of Rape, National Rape Information Clearinghouse, 5600 Fishers Lane, Parklawn Bldg., Rockville, Md. 20857. This center will provide you with information and educational materials that deal directly with rape prevention and treatment.

National Center on Child Abuse and Neglect, Department of Health P.O. Box 1182, Washington, D.C. 20013. This agency will provide you with publications and filmstrips on child abuse and neglect. If you have concerns regarding abuse, call your local Child Protective Services agency.

National Congress of Parents and Teachers (National PTA), 700 North Rush St., Chicago, Ill. 60611. The National PTA will send you a variety of materials dealing with health, education, and the general welfare of your child. They also have a very active TV Action Center that is zeroing in on television violence and its influence on your child.

Parents Without Partners, 7910 Woodmont Ave., Suite 1000, Washington, D.C. 20014. If you are a single parent, you may find a PWP group helpful. There are over 900 active groups in all fifty states. They offer educational, family, and social support for the single parent. There is probably a chapter in your area.

Resources for Youth, National Commission on Resources for Youth, 36 W. 44th St., New York, N.Y. 10036. This is a nonprofit educational organization. Its main goal is to find ways for young people to get involved in their school and community. Their newsletter is free and offers many suggestions for getting your child involved.

Runaway Switchboard, 2210 North Halsted, Chicago, Ill. 60614. Toll free 24-hour hotline: (800) 621-4000. If your child is a runaway, this is an excellent resource for trying to make contact with him. Their trained volunteers will provide you with information and referrals for around the country. They will also send you an informative fact sheet on runaways.

The Step Family Foundation, 333 West End Ave., New York, N.Y. 10023. There is help for the stepparent and stepchildren. When you send a self-addressed, stamped envelope to the foundation, you will receive a copy of their newsletter and a free descriptive brochure of their services.

Youth Liberation, 2007 Washtenaw Ave. Ann Arbor, Mich. 48104. This is a national information clearinghouse that will provide information for your child on the law and children's rights. They have a quarterly magazine along with several pamphlets on youth and the law.

Recommended Reading

ALBERTI, ROBERT, and EMMONS, MICHAEL. *Stand Up, Speak Out, Talk Back!* New York: Pocket Books, 1976. This is an expansion of their first book, *Your Perfect Right.* It offers revealing case histories and shows you how to gain more self-confidence and self-respect through resolving conflicts. It includes a 13-step self-training course in being more assertive.

DODSON, FITZHUGH. *How to Discipline—with Love.* New York: New American Library, 1978. This is an excellent book that provides practical, flexible, and timely methods for teaching your child desirable behavior. It's easy to understand and gives many examples.

GESELL, ARNOLD; ILG, FRANCES; and AMES, LOUISE. *Youth: Years from Ten to Sixteen.* New York: Harper and Row, 1956. This is an excellent reference for helping you to determine what is "normal" and what to expect at certain stages of your child's development. Use these as general guidelines and don't panic if your child is a few months ahead or behind the average.

GINOTT, HAIM. Edited by Robert Markel. *Teacher and Child.* New York: Macmillan, 1972. Parents and teachers will find the numerous examples in this book to be very practical for communicating with children. It will help you understand how teachers feel about teaching and how they cope.

GORDON, THOMAS. *Parent Effectiveness Training: The Tested New Way to Raise Responsible Children.* New York: McKay, 1970. This is becoming a classic on how to listen and communicate effectively with your child. It offers a "No-Lose" program for raising responsible children.

JAMES, MURIEL, and JONGEWARD, DOROTHY. *Born to Win: Transactional Analysis with Gestalt Experiments.* Reading, Mass.: Addison-Wesley Publ. Co., 1971. This book is filled with ideas and examples for increasing your self-awareness and helping you understand your relationship with your child.

WOOD, PAUL, and SCHWARTZ, BERNARD. *How to Get Your Children to Do What You Want Them to Do.* Englewood Cliffs, New Jersey: Prentice-Hall, Inc., 1979. This is a compact little book with a clear and concise method for changing your child's behavior. We don't recommend it for listening skills but for "Saying what you mean—Meaning what you say."

CHAPTER 7

If a little knowledge is dangerous, where is the man who has so much as to be out of danger?

—*Thomas Huxley*

"What's This I Hear About...?"

Dear Parent:

As you probably know, Jefferson Elementary School has been designated as a SIP school and will receive money from the state this year. This means, of course, that we will be forming a PAC to involve parents in making decisions about our school program.

All interested parents should plan to attend a meeting on October 6th, at 7:30 P.M. in the multi-purpose room next to the multi-media annex. Special topics for the evening include mainstreaming, competency testing, and IEPs.

I look forward to your attendance and input as a concerned parent.

Sincerely,
Paula Principal

Of course *YOU* are a concerned, interested parent, right? Should you attend this meeting at your child's school? Will you have anything to say about "mainstreaming" or "competency tests"? What's more, should you be happy or alarmed that your school has been chosen as a "SIP" school?

To help you clear up some of the confusion, what follows in this chapter is a catchall of terms, issues, and names of special programs you may come across while trying to keep tabs on your child's schooling.

YOU CAN BEST USE THIS CHAPTER IN TWO WAYS: as a quick overview to acquaint yourself with important school issues, or to look up a particular term or topic you have already run into in dealing with schools.

There will be terms, issues, and specific programs that are unique to *your* state, school district, or local school. It's up to you to ask when you need information.

True, schools should be in frequent contact with parents in an effort to keep everyone up-to-date. But DON'T LEAVE IT UP TO THE SCHOOL! You have one, or at most a few, schools to deal with. Each school has hundreds, sometimes thousands, of parents to keep happy.

You can't expect the school to anticipate all the questions or concerns you may have. You *can*, however, expect answers to your questions!

"What's This I Hear About...?"

- Accountability
- Alternative schools
- Bilingual/ESL programs
- Compulsory education
- Educational vouchers
- Gifted and Talented programs
- Grade inflation
- Home schooling
- Learning disabilities
- Mainstreaming
- Minimal competency standards (graduation proficiency tests)
- Parent groups
- Parents' legal rights
- School volunteers
- Standardized tests
- Student teachers
- Tuition tax credit

ACCOUNTABILITY

Accountability in education deals with holding teachers—and school districts—responsible for what they say they are going to teach or what they are legally bound to provide children and their parents. Parents who care about their child's education should become familiar with the school's program and what it aims to accomplish. Then stay on top of things throughout the school year, holding teachers and schools accountable.

What should you expect in elementary school?

In the lower grades, you should expect answers to these questions:
• What skills is your child expected to accomplish by the end of the year?
• What does he already know, at the beginning of the year, according to some kind of testing?
• How will the teacher check progress during the year and at the end of this grade? (And how will this progress be reported to you?)

What about junior high and high school?

As your child moves out of elementary school you will be dealing with a number of teachers each year. Here is what is reasonable to expect from each of them:
• A course outline or plan—some kind of description of what will be taught in the class (English, biology, etc.), what your child's grade will be based on, homework policy, class rules, and necessary supplies. Many districts require teachers to have a written plan. This should be made available to both students and parents.
• Some specific information about the skills and knowledge your child already has in a subject area (U.S. history, algebra, etc.). This should be based on some kind of test at the beginning of the course.
• Some plan for checking your child's progress during the year or semester.
• An explanation of *how* the teacher will determine if your child has learned the material at the end of the class (test scores, assignments, projects, etc.).

Remember: the key word in asking the school to be accountable is *results*. Has your child learned what the school says he should? Does he have the skills expected at his grade level? If not, why not and can something be done about it?

You should not hesitate to ask about your child's progress *before* the end of the year! The teacher should be able to point to reliable information such as test scores, the results of special assignments or projects, and daily observation of the student to show exactly what your child has accomplished.

Teachers also need *your* help:

Holding teachers accountable for what they should be doing *is* a parent's right and responsibility. However, we agree with many teachers who complain that some parents make unreasonable demands on the school, expecting them to teach children who have serious family problems or who simply don't try in school. *Parents must also be accountable* and should help their children understand school responsibilities such as completing assignments, asking for help, and cooperating in class.

ALTERNATIVE SCHOOLS

These are public schools, or school programs, that are different in some ways from the standard school in a particular school district. Alternative schools offer a *choice* or *option* to parents and students.

School districts and states differ in their definition of alternative schools. In fact, what may be considered an alternative in one district might describe a typical school program in another community. Supporters of alternative schools do agree that one kind of school, or one approach to learning, is not always enough to meet the individual needs of many different children.

According to the National School Public Relations Association, more than two-thirds of the nation's large school districts offer alternative programs and the trend appears to be popular among both parents and teachers. If alternative programs are offered in your school district, ask if a brochure is available describing alternative programs.

If you want to look into available school options for your child—

- Contact the schools directly
- Talk to the principal
- Visit the classroom
- Talk with parents whose children attend the school

Here are the most typical kinds of alternative schools found nationwide:

1. *Non-graded schools.* These are schools or programs in which children are grouped according to abilities rather than age or grade. For example, grades 1 and 2 or grades 1 through 3 may be combined. Sometimes called *family grouping*, non-graded programs are especially good for students who learn best at their own pace.

2. *Fundamental schools.* Also called *basic schools*, fundamental schools have gained popularity as the back-to-basics movement
250

has grown. Fundamental school programs as a rule are very structured. They put special emphasis on reading, math, and writing; expect students to follow strict rules of behavior (often including a dress code); and assign homework daily in all grades. Fundamental schools may be suitable for students who need a disciplined atmosphere where few decisions are left up to the child.

3. *Open schools.* These are schools or classrooms where an *open* approach is applied to learning. Students in these programs work at their own pace, often alone or in small groups, learning centers, labs, or "stations." Teachers in an open program work with students and jointly decide what the child will study and how he will be evaluated. Children who work well on their own (with little supervision) are more comfortable in an open class than are children who work best when told what to do and when to do it.

4. *Year-round schools.* These schools operate twelve months a year, although students attend for the same *total* number of days as in a traditional school. Most year-round programs use a staggered schedule, for example 9 weeks in school followed by a 3-week break (often called a "45-15" plan). Other schools divide the year into blocks of time and parents choose which part of the year they wish their children to take vacation. Parent and teacher supporters of the year-round idea feel that shorter breaks away from school contribute to greater academic success. Many year-round programs are set up to make the most efficient use of school buildings as well.

5. *School-within-a-school.* Many alternative programs are offered within the same school building where a traditional program is operating. Such a program is generally referred to as a *school-within-a-school*. The program will usually be specifically defined as a fundamental program, career focus program, or whatever, depending on the alternative program offered within the school.

6. *Magnet schools.* "Magnet school" is

another general term used to describe an alternative school. Magnet schools are found in large cities throughout the country, so-named because they *attract* students who share a particular interest, or have similar needs or abilities. Magnet schools were developed in some communities as one way to bring about voluntary desegregation, drawing children from a variety of neighborhoods. A wide range of programs is offered by magnet schools—everything from fundamental schools to programs which emphasize computer science, the performing arts, or concern for the environment.

7. *Continuation schools.* Continuation schools are alternative high schools usually set up to serve students who have dropped out of the regular school program or who have been expelled from school because of unacceptable behavior. Because the daily schedule is usually quite flexible, students who work part-time can also attend continuation schools. Such programs, sometimes called extended day schools, usually have small classes which allow for more personal attention to each student.

8. *Vocational schools and work experience programs.* These are alternative high schools, or options within a regular high school, which combine on-the-job experience with an on-campus required program. In such schools, students receive credit for the time they spend working on a job in the community.

> Remember: alternative programs differ a great deal, and the name of a program may be misleading. For the most accurate picture of what a particular alternative program offers, direct contact with the school is a must!

BILINGUAL AND ESL PROGRAMS

Bilingual programs provide instruction in two languages—English and the native language of the student. The primary goal is to help each child learn English while at the same time helping him learn the basic skills and knowledge he needs to keep up in school. Bilingual programs are usually designed for kindergarten through twelfth grade students, with the greatest emphasis on the early grades.

*ESL—English as a second language—*is a special program found in both elementary and secondary schools. In these classes students are taught to speak, read, and write English in much the same way foreign languages are taught to English-speaking students. In ESL programs students are not encouraged to use their native language in the classroom.

Who are these programs for?

Over 3½ million school age children in the U.S. have a limited understanding of English or do not speak the language at all.

Students who need special instruction are located throughout the country, with large numbers living in Texas, New York, Florida, and California. In Los Angeles alone 20 percent of the district's students are limited English-speaking.

The Bilingual Education Act provides that "an equal opportunity for learning" be given to all students, including those whose language might be a barrier to learning. It is up to each state to decide what kind of special attention is given to children needing English language instruction: eighteen states require funding for bilingual programs; twelve states permit funding for bilingual classes; five states do not allow bilingual education in their schools; and the remaining states have no laws currently affecting these programs. States may apply to the federal government for grants to help support bilingual education programs.

Supporters of bilingual programs point to research that shows that students who receive instruction in two languages while in elementary school do significantly better in school than those who go through ESL programs or no programs at all. They indicate that children learn best if they can gain basic skills in their own language at the same time they learn English. When they are ready to handle subjects like science and math in English, they then can be enrolled in a full day of English instructed classes. They will not be as far behind if they have kept up with basic skills.

Those who favor the ESL approach believe special attention can be given to each student learning English in one or two periods a day. They feel the student will profit from spending most of the school day in a regular, English-speaking classroom.

Yet another viewpoint is that "total immersion" is the best way to learn English.

Those who favor this approach say the fastest, most effective way for children to learn English is to start right out in the regular classroom. The faster that English can be learned, the better, even if it means sacrificing learning in other subjects.

Whether a child is enrolled in a bilingual program or an ESL class, actively involved parents can make a big difference in their child's progress in learning English.

For the most up-to-date information on bilingual or ESL programs contact The National Clearinghouse for Bilingual Education. A toll-free hotline is available to answer your questions: (800) 336-4560.

COMPULSORY EDUCATION

All children in the United States are required to attend school, but the number of years a child must attend is determined by each state.

In the majority of states, children are required to start school by the time they are *seven years old.* Fourteen states require that children be in school if they are *six years old,* and in the states of Arizona, Pennsylvania, and Washington, children must be enrolled in school by the time they are *eight years old.*

Most states require children to stay in school until they have completed high school or have reached the age of sixteen. The following states have different age requirements:

• *School required until eighteen:* California, Hawaii, New Mexico, Ohio, Oklahoma, Oregon, Utah, Wisconsin

• *School required until seventeen:* Maine, Nevada, Pennsylvania, Tennessee, Texas, Virginia, Washington
• *School required until fifteen:* Arkansas, Louisiana
• *School required until thirteen:* Mississippi

Some states are flexible concerning both the age requirement for starting kindergarten and the older student who may want to stay in school or reenter school beyond the required age.

Although this is the most up-to-date information from the National Center for Educational Statistics and a number of state departments of education, state requirements *do* change. *Check with your local school district or state department of education if you are not sure about the current law in your state.*

EDUCATIONAL VOUCHERS

In an educational voucher system, parents would receive a voucher or certificate for a specified amount of money to be used in paying for the school they wish their child to attend—public, private, or parochial school.

Such a voucher plan is actually a procedure for giving public tax money directly to parents to spend for education.

Proposals for educational vouchers have gone to the voters in a few states, such as

252

Michigan and New Hampshire, and a several year experiment using a voucher system was tried in Alum Rock, California. As yet, however, no states have passed laws permitting the use of school vouchers. If increasing numbers of parents decide to send their children to private schools, the idea of vouchers will continue to be discussed throughout the country.

Proposed plans vary, but basically a voucher system would work like this: The Stein family, living in Ohio, receives a voucher from the state to be exchanged for a year of education for their fourth-grade son. The voucher is worth $2,433.00, the current cost for educating an elementary school student in Ohio. If the Stein family selects a school that requires a fee beyond this amount, they must pay the remaining school costs themselves.

Supporters of educational vouchers believe parents should be able to select the school that will best suit the needs of their children, and vouchers would allow this choice. Many feel that schools, both private and public, would improve if parents and children were choosing among schools. Parents, they feel, would be more involved and responsible for their children's education if they chose a school whose goals and program they agree with. Also they say that vouchers would give children of all economic backgrounds a wider choice of school opportunities.

Those against the voucher plan believe that the quality of public school programs would quickly drop as limited state money is re-channeled to include private schools. They express concern that a voucher system could result in economic and racial segregation for school children. It is possible, they believe, that state money could end up supporting schools that encourage values directly opposed to many of this country's democratic principles. Those against vouchers also feel that managing such a system— deciding who gets to go to which school, waiting lists versus empty schools—would be a costly nightmare. It is possible, they also contend, that the public schools would become overloaded with disadvantaged students who often have learning problems.

As a parent, your personal philosophy plus the kind of education you want for your children, will determine *your* view on the voucher debate. If you wish to find out if a voucher plan is under consideration in your state, the best source is the office of your state representative or the state department of education.

GIFTED AND TALENTED PROGRAMS

"Gifted and talented" is the term used by schools to refer to children who have been identified as capable of outstanding performance. A gifted/talented child may be exceptionally capable in one, a few, or perhaps all of the following areas, according to the U.S. Office of Education:

• General intellectual ability—the child who is highly capable in almost everything he does
• Specific academic ability—the student who is particularly outstanding in certain areas—math, languages, etc.
• Creative or productive thinking—the child who comes up with new and unique ways to solve problems

• Leadership ability—the child who shows natural ability to lead, organize, manage "the big picture"
• Visual or performing arts—the student with exceptional talent in music, painting, drama, etc.

How is a child identified by the schools as gifted or talented?

It must be said that *all* children are "special" and certainly have gifts and talents that parents and teachers can point to. However, the child who is identified as gifted or talented by the schools, or other experts, is considered unusually highly capable. It is generally agreed among educators and parents of the gifted that special programs and classes geared to the specific needs and abilities of these children *do* help gifted and talented youngsters realize their potential. For this reason, all states have some kind of guidelines for educating the gifted, and in seventeen states special programs for the gifted are required by law.

A variety of sources and evaluation methods are used to spot gifted and talented children. Typical are the following:

1. standardized tests (included are aptitude tests, achievement tests, tests which measure IQ, tests which identify creativity, and tests designed to identify gifted ESL— English as a Second Language—students and culturally different gifted children.
2. reports and recommendations from teachers
3. observations by parents

Special programs

Some schools have programs for the gifted and talented. Whether a particular program is appropriate for *your* child must be the parents' decision in cooperation with the school. While it is not required, developing *an individual education plan* for a gifted child is usually the best way to plan his education. Such a plan provides an excellent opportunity for bringing together parents and teachers. Ask your school to work with you in setting up goals for your child that match his exceptional abilities or talents. Special help can be provided in a number of ways:

• participation in special classes for the gifted offered at your child's school
• specialized instruction and independent study under the direction of his teacher
• enrollment in special classes in the community, at local colleges, etc. (In many parts of the country, parents of gifted children have organized enrichment classes for their children. Some helpful resources in this area are listed in the next column.)
• involvement in a *mentor program* (experts in education for the gifted recommend

254

that gifted and talented children develop a relationship with a gifted/talented successful adult—other than a parent—who can serve as a role model in a field that interests the child.)

Some important information

Without experiences in school, and at home, that tap the interests and abilities of gifted children, these children *often* develop problems in school. Some gifted children try to hide their talents in an effort not to appear "different." Some are labeled "behavior problems" simply because their energies and curiosity are misunderstood. Actively working with the school, as you should for any child, is the best way to give support to a gifted student.

Some Helpful Resources

There are many organizations and support groups dedicated to helping the gifted and talented child. Parents and community leaders have developed outstanding programs for children to attend after school and on weekends. They are ready to recommend helpful learning materials in a variety of subjects and willing to share ideas on how to cope with the special needs, and problems, facing some gifted children. Most groups can also advise parents on how to recognize signs that indicate the possibility that a child is especially talented or gifted before he begins school.

The Council for Exceptional Children
1920 Association Drive
Reston, Va. 22091

National Association for Gifted Children (NAGC)
2070 County Road H.
St. Paul, Minn. 55112

National/State Leadership Training Institute on the Gifted and Talented
316 W. Second St., Suite PH-C
Los Angeles, Calif. 90012

These organizations can also put you in touch with local groups in your area. And in each state's department of education there is a consultant for the gifted and talented.

Some helpful publications

Chronicle of Academic and Artistic Precocity. Timely information published six times a year. Department of Special Education, Arizona State University, Tempe, Arizona 85287.

G/C/T., P.O. Box 66654, Mobile, Ala. 36660. A helpful magazine for parents and educators of gifted, creative and talented students.

Gifted Child Quarterly. Available from NAGC at the address given above.

Gifted Children Newsletter. For subscription information, and a sample copy, write:
Gifted and Talented Publications, P.O. Box 115, Sewell, N.J. 08080.

GRADE INFLATION

Grade inflation describes grades—*A, B, C, D*—that in many instances do not carry the same meaning they did ten or fifteen years ago. It has always been true that an *A* from one math teacher was harder to come by than from another, or that an *A* English student at one high school might be much less competent or prepared than an *A* student from a neighboring school. Now added to this grade dilemma is "inflation."

Colleges across the country complain that freshmen are arriving less prepared every year. College admissions test scores declined during the 1970's and growing numbers of college students must take remedial classes in math, writing, and reading. Yet at the same time, students are entering college with higher grades than ever before.

We won't enter the debate as to why this has occurred. The important point here for parents is not to look at grades as the single indicator of how much your child has learned or what skills he has developed. You should be looking at what your child can actually do in terms of reading, writing, math, and so on. Is he making the kind of progress that should be expected? Is he being challenged and working to his capacity? See the chapters on reading, writing, and math for information on how to evaluate your child's skills.

HOME TEACHING

Home teaching, or home schooling, is practiced on a small scale throughout the country by parents who choose to keep their children out of school and educate them at home.

Thiry-two states, plus the District of Columbia, permit parents to teach their children at home as long as they agree to meet certain requirements. Some states require that parents be qualified teachers with approved training and credentials.

In many states the home teaching plan or program must be approved. In some states such as Vermont and Wisconsin the proposed home study plan must be sent to the state department of education for approval. In other states the local school district is responsible for approving the plan. Approval is usually given for one school year. The instruction at home must be "equivalent" to what the child would receive at a public school. In some states specific subjects must be included in the home teaching program, and sometimes certain materials and textbooks are required.

Why home teaching?

Parents express various reasons for choosing to remove their children from school. Some point to bad experiences in schools. Others simply believe they can give their children better individual attention and encouragement, and want to be directly involved in their education. Most indicate that learning is not necessarily better because it takes place in a school building.

Those who disagree with the idea of parents teaching their own children believe that parents will provide a narrow and very limited education. They feel that attending school gives children many experiences, including important social contacts, not possible in the home. There is a sincere concern that children will not have opportunities to know a variety of people and hear differing viewpoints. Many feel that parents are not as capable as professionally trained and experienced teachers.

But the fact remains that it is the parents' choice, within certain states, to teach their children at home.

In 1981 there were an estimated 10,000 to 15,000 children being taught at home. While this is not a large portion of the 45 million school-age children, there are a growing number of parent support groups for parents interested in home learning for their children.

Some tips to interested parents

1. Carefully check the laws of *your* state. Call your state Department of Education (sometimes called Public Instruction) and ask for a copy of the state's home instruction or home study guidelines. If not available, ask for a copy of the law governing teaching children at home.

2. Find out how these laws have been interpreted. (Several home teaching cases have gone to court with results both in favor of and against parents.)

3. Get in touch with the local school district office and ask for their policy or guidelines on home study.

4. Prepare a written home study plan that describes what the child will study for the school year ahead. Include a clearly written explanation of *why* you have chosen to teach your child at home. (In some states this should be submitted to the local superintendent of schools. In other states the plan must be approved by the state department of education.)

5. Get in touch with home teaching organizations to share ideas. Some helpful resources:

• Center for Independent Education, 747 Front St., San Francisco, Calif. 94111.

• Home Education Resource Center, 337 Downs St., Ridgewood, N.J. 07450.

• National Association of Home Educators, Star Route, Smithton, Mo. 65350.

• *Growing Without Schooling* is a bimonthly magazine devoted to all aspects of home schooling. For a sample copy and subscription information, write *Growing Without Schooling*, 729 Boylston St., Boston, Mass. 02116.

LEARNING DISABILITIES

Estimates from experts vary, but as many as 10 million school age children are considered by some to have learning disabilities. For this reason alone, all parents should be familiar with the term and have a basic understanding of what it means.

• A child with a learning disability, or learning handicap, *has average, or above average, intelligence*, but has problems learning because the *way* he learns differs from the way most children learn.

• A child with learning disabilities has trouble with one or more of the basic processes necessary for understanding language. Sometimes the difficulty is in processing what he hears or sees. Problems in processing information show up in one or more of these areas: listening, thinking, reading, writing, speaking, and computing. (Many technical terms are used in discussing these problems, among them perceptual problems, neurological handicaps, dyslexia, and minimal brain dysfunction.)

• Children who have physical handicaps (vision, hearing, motor), or are mentally retarded, or emotionally disturbed are *not* described as having learning disabilities. Their problems are of a different nature.

• Learning disabled children, if not identified and taught in an appropriate manner, are often failures in school.

• Children, and eventually adults, who have learning disabilities do *not* grow out of their learning problem. They must learn to cope and adjust, and given the right kind of support and education they will.

• Often parents are the first ones to spot a learning disability. If you suspect your child may be having problems of this nature, follow through on your hunch.

• Parents of children with learning disabilities must be particularly alert in following the child's school progress. There are people in the community and in many schools who are trained to help these children, but *it is likely that the parent will have to seek out the needed assistance.*

• The law provides that learning disabled children receive education that meets their particular needs.

Your Legal Right as a Parent to a Special Program for a Learning Disabled Child...

Public Law 94-142: The Education for All Handicapped Act. This law defines the way that each child's program must be planned and states that parents *must be involved* in this process. As soon as a child has been identified as possibly having some kind of learning handicap, parents must give permission before any testing can take place.

Testing includes observation of your child; a physical exam if needed; review of your child's physical, mental, and emotional history; and tests to determine the possible learning handicap.

At this point you are looking for your child's capabilities, his level of achievement, and his current needs both in school and at home. If you consent to testing, give your full cooperation in providing personal records, information, opinions—anything that might help.

After testing, a conference is held with parents, teachers, and child, if appropriate. Next, an Individualized Education Plan (IEP) is designed.

The Individualized Education Plan (IEP)

The parent must give consent before a child can be enrolled in a special program. Before giving permission, be sure you have clear answers to these questions:

• What is the level of your child's achievement and how does the learning plan relate to improving his skills?

• What exactly will be provided for your child in terms of special classes, counseling, etc.?

• Exactly who will be responsible for working with your child and overseeing his program (particularly important when several teachers are involved, so that you have a regular contact at the school who is on top of the situation)?

• When will each service be provided (how much of the school day—morning, afternoon, etc.)?

• What is the plan for evaluating your child's progress? How will you be informed and involved?

Individual learning plans may be drawn up in a variety of ways. Each works if it meets the child's special needs:

- special help in a regular classroom all day
- attendance in a special class full time
- part-time instruction in regular class, part in a special program or learning center
- full-time instruction in a special school if public school cannot do the best job (public school funds must pay for private instruction if the school receives any federal funds)

Least Restrictive Environment

You will hear the term *least restrictive environment* applied to educating children with learning disabilities and other handicaps. The law requires that every child be enrolled in a school program that is as close to "normal" as possible. This approach to helping learning disabled children is very important in that it does not completely separate the child from the very situations he must learn to deal with. When teachers and parents agree that a child can make satisfactory progress by being taught in a regular classroom (full-time or part-time), that is usually the best place for the learning disabled child to be.

Staying on Top of Your Child's Program

If a parent wants to review the Individual Education Plan once it has gotten under way, he may ask for another evaluation. In some states, the evaluation must take place within a specified time (30 days, 50 days, etc.). Check your own state regarding this.

As with all children in school, you are entitled to written notices, access to records, and any other information that might be helpful in checking your child's progress.

If your child must change schools, be sure that the new school is tuned in to the special learning problem. Decide whether you think

258

a new evaluation should take place or whether your child can easily be placed into a program similar to the one that has been working successfully. *You should not count on the new school being aware of your child's learning problem, but you should expect them to cooperate in setting up a learning plan for the year.* *

*Recent surveys indicate that in almost all states there are schools not in compliance with laws governing students having learning handicaps. Once again, the responsibility must be the parents' if a child is to receive the education legally due him.

Some Helpful Resources

Parents of childen with learning disabilities are extremely active and have organized quite a network of support groups. Here are some that can provide a variety of information, including how to spot early signs of a learning disability, how to deal with special problems that face the learning disabled, and how to get materials to use in working with your child.

Academic Therapy Publications
20 Commercial Blvd., Novato, Calif. 94947. Publishes materials for the learning disabled, including a free directory listing schools, summer camps, and other facilities across the country (biennial).

Association for Children with Learning Disabilities
4156 Library Road, Pittsburgh, Pa. 15234. Publishes a helpful, free booklet, *Taking the First Step.*

Closer Look
A Project of the Parents' Campaign for Handicapped Children and Youth, P.O. Box 1492, Washington, D.C. 20013

Council for Exceptional Children
1920 Association Drive, Reston, Va. 22091. Provides information and services on behalf of handicapped and gifted children.

Foundation for Children with Learning Disabilities
99 Park Ave., New York, N.Y. 10016. Concerned with making educators and the public aware of the special needs of learning disabled children and services that are available nationwide.

MAINSTREAMING

When children with special needs (such as children with physical handicaps or learning disabilities) are placed in a regular classroom, this procedure is known as *mainstreaming*. The current trend is against separate classrooms for children with special needs since, as a rule, handicapped students make the greatest progress when attending school with non-handicapped children.

At some time in your child's school experience it is likely he will have classmates who are physically handicapped or who have certain learning disabilities. Mainstreaming offers the opportunity for non-handicapped children to learn about and accept people who are different in some ways from them and to discover their many similarities.

MINIMAL COMPETENCY STANDARDS

Minimal competency standards have been established in many states so that educators and parents can better define the minimum skills and knowledge a child should be learning in school.

For years, parents have been asking "What does an eighth-grade education mean?" "What does a high school diploma stand for?" In response to such questions (and a few lawsuits), many states and school districts have set minimum guidelines for skills. Establishing minimal competency standards serves several major purposes:

• It tells teachers that they must concentrate on helping all students to learn certain basic skills (minimal competencies or proficiencies).
• It tells parents what minimal skills their children need to have (sometimes called *survival skills*).
• It tells students what they must learn in order not to fail.
• It demands active and constant communication between all parts of the educational system—from the state level to the local school teacher, and then to the parent and child.
• It requires that all students be tested on certain skills and that some evaluation of the test scores take place.

Thirty-nine states have passed laws or set policies requiring every school to concentrate on teaching *every* child certain skills by the time he reaches particular grade levels. Most of these states, however, have not yet put real teeth into their laws by actually saying, "If a child cannot prove he knows these minimum skills he cannot move from one grade level to the next," or more crucial, "cannot graduate from high school." In these states, minimal competency standards are used primarily to evaluate and make improvements in school programs. As of 1981, however, seventeen states had laws requiring students to show proficiency in certain skills in order to graduate from high school.

Graduation Proficiency Tests

Proficiency tests, also called minimal competency tests, are given to determine whether a student possesses skills considered necessary to get along as an adult in the real world—as an employee, citizen, family member, etc.

Requirements in your state

The following states require students to pass a graduation proficiency (competency) test before receiving a diploma: Alabama, Arizona, California, Delaware, Florida, Georgia, Maryland, Nevada, New York, North Carolina, Oregon, Tennessee, Utah, Vermont, Virginia.

In many other states the option to require minimal competency tests is given to each school district. Because of this, several individual districts require students to pass such tests. Check with your school district office for the most up-to-date information.

Some information that might be helpful

1. No two states are exactly alike in their approach to setting minimum competencies or testing students.

2. In most states, minimum competencies include basic reading, writing, and math skills. A typical test requires the student to perform at a level no higher than eighth grade. Some states include practical "life skills" as part of their competency requirements—such things as knowing how to complete a job application, reading and understanding a warning on a medicine label, etc.

3. In some states, minimal competencies are set by the state legislature; in other states, by the state department of education; and in the remaining states the local school district is responsible for deciding which skills are considered minimum.

4. Proficiency tests are usually multiple-choice tests with a predetermined passing score for *each* proficiency. Often a student can pass one section of the test—math, for example—and still need to pass parts of the reading test. In some districts, students might be asked to apply their learning by actually performing a task—such as reading a label and then following the directions given. *Students taking these tests are not competing with each other. These are pass/fail exams testing specific skills.*

5. States differ with regard to the number of times a student is tested and at what grade level the testing takes place. In most states, at least *four* chances are given for students to pass, and in many districts unlimited opportunities are given to pass the exam. Sometimes testing begins in the upper elementary grades, and in some districts not until junior high or early high school.

Public sentiment supports competency testing. The fact that close to forty states have passed laws requiring competency testing, or given the option to local school districts, speaks for itself. Supporters believe competency testing is a good way to hold schools accountable for providing at least a basic education to as many students as are capable of learning. They believe schools will improve their programs as a result of test scores being made known to the parents and the public at large.

Those who question minimum competency testing insist that such testing alone cannot ensure that children will learn. The instruction must do that job and there is no guarantee that instruction will improve as a result of testing programs. Other critics are concerned that teachers will focus on the "minimum" level, and students who are capable of going far beyond minimum skills will be short-changed. Another concern is that students may be tested on skills that the school, in fact, has not helped them learn.

As yet, there is no hard-core evidence that because of minimum competency testing schools have improved or more learning has taken place. Many districts can, however, point to specific areas of concern that have been pinpointed as a result of test scores—large percentages of students in high school who need remedial writing instruction, for example. And in some districts, parents indicate they have a better feel for just what is being taught in their schools (or at least what their children have or have not learned).

Even if your child is in elementary school, you should *start now* to inquire about minimal competency requirements and testing programs. Here are some key questions:

___ Does this school district require high school students to pass a minimum competency test before they can graduate?

___ Does this school district require children to pass competency tests in order to move from junior high to high school, or be promoted to the next grade in elementary school?

___ When are competency tests given? (In which grades? How often? Can students or parents request to have the test given?)

___ Can the school district provide you with a copy of the required proficiencies, along with any other written graduation policies?

___ How are proficiencies tested? (What kind of test?)

___ Is the school teaching the same skills/proficiencies that are being tested? (For example, if students are expected to know how to fill out a job application, when is this skill taught—in a particular grade, class, over a period of years?)

___ What happens if your child does not pass a test or a portion of the test? (What classes or special instruction are available? How can a parent help? Are teaching materials available?)

___ Is your child going beyond the minimal skills required in the district? (This is very important if you feel your child is capable of achieving at a higher level than is being expected of him. The math, reading, and writing chapters will be of help to you here.)

PARENT GROUPS

In a typical school district there is usually one, and often several, school support or advisory groups in which parents can play a role. Such parent organizations, committees, and councils go by a variety of names, serve different purposes, and range from small-town PTAs to nationally organized citizen groups.

Parents, working with a shared goal, can make a significant difference in the quality of education their children receive. The following is a quick look at what parent groups are currently doing *with* and *for* schools across the nation.

PTA

The local PTA (Parent-Teacher Association), usually a branch of the National PTA, has traditionally been the main support group for the local school. (Some communities have PTOs—Parent-Teacher Organizations, not affiliated with the National PTA.) PTAs vary in activities and purpose throughout the country, but for the most part, the typical PTA has been a fund-raising group helping to buy band uniforms or football equipment and providing other kinds of support services requested by the school.

Not until recently have PTA groups become involved in controversial school issues or participated in major decisions affecting the school. Currently, the PTA, according to its national officials, is placing more emphasis on parent participation in the educational process itself. Their activities also include helping parents understand important school- and child-related issues such as testing, school financing, educational programs for the handicapped, and tuition tax credits. The PTA has developed a nation-wide campaign that promotes quality TV programming for children and combats TV violence. You may wish to check with your local PTA or PTO to see if the organization's aims and activities fit with your idea of effective parent involvement in education.

Parent Groups Required by Law

Parent participation, in the form of an advisory council or committee, is sometimes required in order for a school to receive federal money for a particular school program such as bilingual education or programs for the gifted and talented. These councils and committees vary in exactly how they work with the school. Some are strictly advisory groups and school officials use such councils as they see fit. Other parent participation groups get directly involved in program planning and help decide how money will be spent.

A growing number of states and school districts also have laws or policies requiring parent involvement in public schools. For example, in Salt Lake City, school community councils operate in *every* school, and teachers, principals, and parents join in school decision making. In Maryland, citizen advisory committees are required in every county and serve as advisors to school boards. And in California, any school receiving state money for a "School Improvement Program" (SIP) must have a council— half of which must be parents—which participates in setting up and evaluating the school program.

All of these parent participation groups work on the assumption that there must be cooperation between the home and school in order for the school to be most effective in helping children learn.

262

Voluntary Parent Advisory Groups

In many communities, particularly small school districts, the link between the school and the community is a "parent council" or "parent committee" that works with the principal. This kind of group is often effective in voicing parents' views concerning school decisions that will affect their children. While the school principal often organizes such a parent group, it is sometimes appropriate for parents to organize themselves and ask that the principal meet with them on a regular basis.

Special Purpose Parent Groups

Parents sometimes organize for a special purpose or to achieve an important school-related goal. Such a committee or council meets for a period of weeks or months, devoting its time and talents to such things as solving a school vandalism problem, supporting a candidate for the school board, or taking a stand on the issue of closing down a local school due to declining enrollment. Parent involvement is extremely valuable in dealing with such issues.

Parents-Only Groups

In recent years, a number of parent groups have organized to represent the special interests and rights of parents concerned with their children's education. Such groups are active in major cities like Detroit, Washington, D.C., Chicago, and Philadelphia, and are sometimes referred to as *parent unions*. The Philadelphia Parent Union is a particularly active group, participating in school district issues such as budget decisions, teacher contracts, helping local schools in providing appropriate education to handicapped children, and providing information and assistance by maintaining a telephone hotline.

Participants feel that parents need a forum for exchanging views and discussing school-related problems and concerns, just as school administrators and teachers do.

Another kind of parents only group operating in some schools is the *parent caucus*. Such a group is usually formed to take a particular stand on an issue like school vouchers or disagreeing with a school board decision to cut a particular program from the school. A parent caucus can operate within a PTA or PTO and take stands on issues that the larger organization may not wish to get involved in or support.

School Foundations

School foundations have been formed in small suburban communities as well as large city school districts, particularly in parts of the country hardest hit by decreasing public funds for schools. Since some school districts are facing the possibility of going bankrupt, parents and other community members have organized private foundations which raise money to help support public schools. Money is usually handed over to the school board for general use in the school district and is not tagged for specific programs.

Successful school foundations operating in Salt Lake City, New York, Tulsa, and several southern California school districts have helped their local schools maintain important academic programs and services such as bus transportation which otherwise would have been eliminated. Most school foundations have at least one full-time staff member and are willing to talk with parents in other communities interested in starting a fund-raising support group. Another example of parent power in action!

Some Resources

Center for the Study of Parent Involvement
5237 College Ave., Oakland, Calif. 94609 (415–652–4968).

Council for Basic Education
725 15th St. N.W., Washington, D.C. 20005. Publishes a monthly newsletter helpful to parents. This group is dedicated to providing quality education in the academic subjects.

National Committee for Citizens in Education
410 Wilde Lake Village Green, Columbia, Md. 21044. Publishes a very informative monthly newsletter, *Parents Network*, and maintains a toll free information hot-line (800-NETWORK).

National PTA
700 N. Rush St., Chicago, Ill. 60611. Publishes many useful booklets on a variety of school-related issues (publication list available on request).

PARENTS' RIGHTS

As you take on the important responsibility of your child's education, you should realize that parents have certain *legal rights*. What follows is a general summary of parent rights that you should be aware of:

Choosing the Best Education for Your Child:
You have the right to—

• Choose whether your child goes to public, parochial, or private school.
• Choose among alternative schools available in your district (although in some districts students are required to attend school within a designated attendance area).
• Educate your child at home as long as you comply with your state laws (see Home Teaching, pages 255–256).

Classroom Instruction:
You have the right to—

• Receive information about what is being taught, what methods and materials are being used, and how achievement is evaluated at your child's school.
• Visit your child's classroom with advance notice to the teacher or principal. (Classroom visitation policies vary a great deal from state to state. Be sure to investigate your own state's laws.)
• Request conferences with the teacher or principal.
• Look at materials used in the classroom and review any materials purchased with federal money for special programs.
• Receive information concerning minimal competencies, proficiencies, or skills your child is supposed to accomplish. In states where minimal competency laws are in effect, the school must inform you of your child's test results. (See Minimal Competency Standards, pages 259–261).

Parent Involvement:
You have the right to—

• Voice your opinion on *what* is taught in your child's classroom. You do *not* have the final say and should work with the school and/or school board in making your views known.
• Participate as member of a parent committee or council—such groups may be required by law, or voluntary.
• Attend school board meetings to learn what is going on in your school district. (Only personnel matters may be conducted "behind closed doors." All other business, by law, is open to the public.)
• Have your voice heard in the evaluation of teachers or other school personnel. You should find out the proper procedure, for example, for giving support to a good teacher or voicing a complaint if you feel a teacher is not competent.
• Be heard when school policies are set or changed, such as establishing a school dress code, or changing high school graduation requirements. (Again, you are *not* the decision maker, but have the right to give your views as a parent.)

Personal Privacy and Safety:
You have the right to—

• Expect that your child will be physically and emotionally safe while at school.
• Expect adequate supervision of your child during the school day.
• Demand, in many states, that your child be excused from certain classes or activities

or the reading of certain books that you object to because of your moral or religious beliefs.

Student Behavior at School:
You have the right to—

• Be informed in advance about school rules, attendance policies, dress codes, procedures for visiting the school, etc.
• Appeal a school decision that affects your child's rights.
• Challenge a school decision to place your child in a special class for students considered to have behavior problems.
• Appeal a decision made by the school to suspend or expel your child from school.
• Challenge the school if you believe "unreasonable force" has been used on your child resulting in physical or emotional harm.

Testing Information:
You have the right to—

• Information about which tests your child is given and what the purpose is for testing.
• Information about any psychological testing the school does involving your child. Your permission *must* be given *before* such testing can take place.
• Information concerning test scores, what they mean and how they are used (see Standardized Tests, page 267).

School Records:
You have the right to—

• Look at the records the school keeps on your child.
• Challenge anything in the child's record which you feel is inaccurate, misleading, or an invasion of privacy, and get a satisfactory response from the school. (If the problem is not cleared up, you have the right to insert written information into your child's school file.)

• Insist school records are kept confidential. (They may not be shown to anyone other than school personnel, unless you give permission.)

> *The Family Educational Rights and Privacy Act* was established to bring about these rights involving student records. For further information, or answers to how to file a complaint, contact:
>
> Fair Information Practices
> Dept. of Education
> 200 Indiana Ave., S.W.
> Washington, D.C. 20201

Student "Tracking" or Grouping:
You have the right to—

• Know if your child has been placed in a particular ability group, and how this placement was decided, and by whom.
• Request that your child be removed from a particular "track" if such grouping is not contributing to his success in school or seems to be harmful to the child in any way.

Programs for Children with Special Needs:
You have the right to—

- Expect an appropriate education in the least restrictive environment available for any child with a special learning need or handicap. *This includes children who are physically, mentally, or emotionally handicapped, as well as those with learning disabilities that may interfere with their progress in school.* (See section on learning disabilities, page 256.)
- Insist that your child be tested for any suspected disability.
- Receive notice and an opportunity to be heard at each stage of the testing and diagnosis procedure in determining appropriate placement for your child.

Public Law 94-142: Education for All Handicapped Act provides that *all* children must be given an education that matches their needs and abilities. States receiving federal money to help educate handicapped children must provide free education to these children, and educate them within the public school program if at all possible (see Mainstreaming, page 259).

If Your Rights as a Parent Are Being Ignored—

You have the right to appeal any decision or to question a school policy that does not respect your rights.

1. If a teacher disregards your rights, a simple reminder of your legal guarantees should be enough to set things straight.

2. If the problem cannot be settled with the teacher, express your concern to the principal and ask that your rights be recognized.

3. If contact with the principal does not produce acceptable results, you should contact the district superintendent of schools.

4. If you are not satisfied at this point, contact your local school board.

5. If the problem is still not solved, write your state department of education. They should be able to clear up any legal issues and assist you in handling the problem.

6. The final resort is legal action. Usually this is not necessary, although an issue concerning your child's education may certainly be important enough to carry to court. (And, in fact, some major parent rights have come about as a result of court decisions.)

Parent Rights in Your States

For the most accurate information about legal rights that apply to parents in your state, check with your state department of education.

For a breakdown of basic parent rights, state by state, we recommend the *parent rights card* available from:

National Committee for Citizens in Education
410 Wilde Lake Village Green
Columbia, Md. 21044

NCCE also runs a toll-free number. For answers to questions concerning parent rights or other school matters call 800-NETWORK.

SCHOOL VOLUNTEERS

The need for volunteers assisting in public schools has increased as school funding for many programs has been cut and the number of children in each classroom has increased. Volunteers free teachers from certain tasks so they can devote more time to *teaching*. Schools in every state utilize parents, as well as retired people and college students, as volunteers. Participation as a school volunteer is often the first step for parents who wish to become actively involved and informed about school programs.

How can volunteers help? Here are a few ways school volunteers can contribute:

• Tutoring—giving special help in basic skills, under the direction of the classroom teacher
• Helping in the library
• Assisting handicapped students
• Conducting field trips
• Providing career information in special interest areas
• Grading papers
• Giving clerical assistance
• Organizing "homework centers" and assisting students
• Lending special skills and knowledge to an enrichment class for gifted children
• Supervising activity on the playground or in the cafeteria

And the list goes on and on. If there is not an active volunteer program in your school district, you may want to contact one of the major volunteer organizations. The National School Volunteer Program conducts training workshops and provides information about school volunteer programs throughout the country.

(National School Volunteer Program,
300 N. Washington St.
Alexandria, Va. 22314)

STANDARDIZED TESTS

Standardized tests differ from the weekly spelling test, math quiz, or history exam the teacher gives your child. A standardized test, prepared by test publishers, is given to children all over the country and the scores are based on a "norm"—the average performance of all the children taking the test. These tests are given with specific time limits, standard instructions, and machine-scored answer sheets.

Your child will undoubtedly take a number of standardized tests from the time she enters elementary school until she completes high school. Standardized tests are used for a variety of reasons and always *measure the school performance of students in comparsion with other students.* Typical uses of standardized test scores include:

• Evaluating how well the school program is working (both school district and state tests are given in many schools).

• Evaluating teachers and teaching methods (in some districts the performance of students on these tests is used as part of the teacher's evaluation).
• Making decisions about individual students (identifying children who may have learning disabilities, singling out gifted children, determining who will take the "advanced" math class, etc.).
• Evaluating what students have learned or their learning potential.

Too often both teachers and parents place far too much emphasis on standardized test scores. Remember, these tests are simply *one* way to look at a child's achievement or potential. A *test* score should *never* be the single piece of information used for making decisions about a child's education. There is too much room for error in both test taking and test "making." (A child who is confused about test instructions, is too tired or hungry, distracted or nervous, can come up with a test score that is *not* an accurate measure of his ability or potential.)

The two main types of standardized tests your child will take are *achievement tests* and *aptitude tests*. You should be familiar with what they are intended to test and how the scores are used at your child's school.

Achievement Tests

These are used to determine what, or how much, students have learned in a particular school subject such as reading, spelling, science, and so on. A math achievement test, for example, is designed to measure how much a student has learned in math compared to other students in his class, in his school, in the school district, in the state, or even in the entire country. The following achievement tests are widely used in schools across the nation:

- California Achievement Tests
- California Assessment Program (CAP) Achievement Series
- Comprehensive Tests of Basic Skills (CTBS)
- Iowa Tests of Basic Skills
- Iowa Tests of Educational Development
- Metropolitan Achievement Tests
- Science Research Associates (SRA) Achievement Series
- Stanford Achievement Tests

Aptitude Tests

These standardized tests are supposed to test a child's *ability to learn*. Results of these tests are sometimes used to plan programs that will match student abilities. Aptitude tests are not intended to test school subjects like math and reading directly, but are designed to test a wide range of abilities— verbal ability, mechanical ability, creativity, reasoning, etc.

Many types of aptitude tests are referred to as IQ (intelligence quotient) tests. These tests are being used less and less by schools; and, as research continues to show their weaknesses and biases in measuring learning

potential, many educators are placing less emphasis on IQ scores in judging a child's capabilities.

In some school districts IQ scores may never be used for making educational decisions about children. Many schools, however, still give these tests, and the scores are considered *one way* to place children in certain classes or programs. Remember: test scores are *not* a total description of your child and can vary significantly from year to year or from one week to the next depending upon your child's frame of mind, his health or energy level, or the general testing conditions.

The most frequently used aptitude tests include:

- California Test of Mental Maturity
- Henman-Nelson Tests of Mental Ability
- Lorge-Thorndike Intelligence Tests
- Short Form Test of Academic Aptitude
- Stanford Binet I.Q. Test
- Wechsler Preschool & Primary Scale of Intelligence
- Wechsler Intelligence Scale for Children

Interpreting Test Scores

Test scores will be presented to you in a variety of forms, many of which will be meaningless if the scoring system isn't explained, and often it isn't. Here is a quick guide to understanding test scores:

Raw Scores. The number of questions your child answers correctly on the test. This number alone doesn't mean much. (*Example:* 38 pts.)

Percentiles. Score ranging from 1 to 99— 76th percentile, 87th percentile, and so on.

Example: Brian receives a test score showing him to be in the *78th percentile*. On this test he did as well, or better, than 78% of the students who took the test. (Don't interpret this score to mean he got 78% of the test questions correct.)

Stanines. Scores ranging from 1 to 9 which provide a broader, more general score than percentiles. Many counselors prefer this kind of score as a more realistic, *general idea* of student ability or achievement. A stanine of 4, 5, or 6 on a test is considered to be in the average range.

Grade Equivalents. These scores appear like 4.9, 5.6, etc. This kind of score tells where a child is achieving in relation to other children in his own and other grades. This takes a little explaining:

Examples: Susan takes a standardized reading vocabulary test during the fifth month of the fifth grade. She scores 5.5. This means she scored as well as the average fifth grader taking this test at the same time.

Jeff takes the same test. He scores 7.2. This means he scored as well as the average student in the seventh grade taking the test during the second month of the school year. It does not necessarily mean Jeff could handle all seventh grade work, nor does it mean he should be in the seventh grade.

Camille takes the same test during the fifth month of her fifth grade year. Her score is 3.8. She scored as well as the average student in the eighth month of the third grade. The score does not mean she belongs in a lower grade or should be doing third-grade work. (She probably does need extra help in vocabulary.)

Remember—these scores show comparisons. A higher than average score *could* mean a child is exceptionally bright, or the high score *could* mean that the children in the higher grades are not scoring very well. Just as important, grade equivalent scores can change over a period of time as the average scores for a certain grade level get higher or lower.

College Entrance Exams

If your child plans to attend college, he may be required to take a college entrance test, sometimes called a preadmission exam, during his junior or senior year of high school. There is a continuing debate about whether or not such tests are the most reliable means for telling whether or not a student will be successful in college. The fact remains, however, that about 1,000 colleges and universities require applicants to take these tests, and the scores are used to help determine who will be accepted into these schools. (Recent research shows that neither test scores nor high school records alone are as good as using both pieces of information to predict how well a high school student will fare the first term in college.) Some information about college entrance tests may help you in assisting your college bound student.

1. SAT (Scholastic Aptitude Test). The SAT is taken by a million and a half high school students each year and is designed to test verbal and mathematical aptitude. However, test experts and college officials agree that the kinds of high school courses and training a student has had will definitely affect his score on these tests. For example, the student who has taken algebra and geometry will do better on the math "aptitude" test than the student who has not had this preparation.

The SAT is divided into two main sections with a third section recently added:

Verbal section—tests skills in reading, word knowledge and vocabulary. Emphasis is placed on analyzing what is read, seeing word relationships (analogies), understanding words with opposite meanings (antonyms).

Math section—covers math that is usually taught in grades 1 through 10. Emphasis is on reasoning and problem solving, including algebra and geometry.

Test of standard written English—a shorter section of the test with emphasis on recognizing correctly written sentences and word usage. A sample of the student's own writing is not required on this test.

2. ACT (American College Testing Program). Some colleges ask applicants to take this test. The ACT exam tests the student's general knowledge and skills in English, math, social studies, and natural science.

3. Achievement Tests. These are usually given in conjunction with SATs. Some colleges require high school students to take one or more of these one-hour exams that are given in English composition, math, biology, chemistry, social science, and several foreign languages. Scores from these tests are often used to help place freshman students in particular courses that match their abilities. The writing exam—English composition—is required by some colleges to determine the applicant's ability to communicate in writing.

4. PSAT (Preliminary Scholastic Aptitude Test). Many eleventh graders take this test as a warm-up or practice for the SAT. It is usually given during the first three months of the junior year. PSAT scores are used to determine eligibility for the National Merit Scholarships and other forms of college financial aid.

You and your high school student should plan ahead for college entrance tests. By the end of the tenth grade you or your child should talk with the school counselor to find out when college entrance exams will be given in your area and which ones your child should plan to take.

Some test tips for your high school child

A solid high school background is the best training a child can have for taking the tests, but the student *can* prepare for the tests. The following recommendations—from students who have taken college entrance tests—should help your child in preparing for such tests.

• Brush up on math skills, especially if you have not taken any math classes recently.
• If a choice is given regarding which achievement test you may take, choose a subject in which you have recently had a class.
• If possible, take the PSAT to become familiar with the kinds of questions you will face on later tests, the time limits, etc.
• If you are not satisfied with your first exam score, you may take the test again and hope for a higher one. Students taking the test a second time frequently score higher. (Be sure to leave enough time to submit your scores to colleges in the fall of your senior year.)
• Keep in mind that test scores are not the end of the world! Just do your best and don't worry about it. (That goes for parents, too.)
• Take a look at some of the many study guides on the market designed to help students prepare for admissions exams. These books, large paperback editions, offer review programs for all sections of the test, give sample practice questions, and explain answers and give typical time limits found on tests. Study guides will not make up for a serious lack of preparation in school, but many college-bound students have found them helpful. Two bestsellers: *Barron's How to Prepare for College Entrance Examinations—SAT* by Brownstein and Weiner and *How to Prepare for American College Testing (ACT)*, rev. ed., by Murray Shapiro et al.

STUDENT TEACHERS

Student teachers, sometimes called practice teachers, are college and university students who are completing their teacher training with on-the-job practice in the classroom. Like all teachers, they vary in ability, but many do have that added spark of enthusiasm at the start of a new career.

Normally, the student teacher works along side and under the supervision of the regular classroom teacher. Gradually the student teacher takes on the handling of subject matter, classroom behavior, and grading. While it may appear that the student teacher is directly in charge of the classroom, as a parent you should know that everything that happens in class is the ultimate responsibility of the regular, experienced teacher.

The chances are your child will be taught by a competent student teacher. However, if there are problems you feel cannot be resolved with the student teacher, by all means contact the regular classroom teacher for assistance.

TUITION TAX CREDIT

A tuition tax credit plan would give an income tax "break" to parents whose children attend private schools. There are currently several bills before Congress proposing such tax credit. (Parents of those attending private colleges already receive some tax credit.)

In 1981 between 4 and 5 million children were enrolled in private schools. In a *Newsweek* poll (April 1981) 16 percent of those surveyed had children in private schools. Of those polled, 13 percent said they would move their children from public to private schools if a tax break of $250 to $500 were in effect. Another 12 percent said it was "fairly likely" they would do the same.

Supporters of tuition tax credit proposals believe families should be able to choose a school for their children that matches their own standards and values. They also point out that parents of private school children pay for the public schools through taxes and then must pay again for private school. Supporters argue that tax credits will also open up private school opportunities to more children, not just those who can already afford to go to private schools.

Those against tax credit feel it is *not* the public's responsibility to help parents who choose private education for their children. They say tax dollars should *not* support schools over which the public has no control. It is possible, they point out, that government money could end up supporting schools that may teach values directly opposed to our democratic way of life. Some argue that tuition tax credit would increase attendance at private schools, thereby taking tax money *away* from public schools. It could also encourage economic and racial segregation which would be a step backwards in education. To date the Supreme Court has ruled against *state* decisions to provide tax credits for tuition.

You will probably hear more about tuition tax credit as various proposals are voted on in Congress. You may wish to express your viewpoint to your representative or senator.

Remember—As in any profession or line of work, teachers use terms and abbreviations that have instant meaning for them but may be unclear to you. By all means never hesitate to ask what a term means, what a program is, or what an abbreviation stands for. Politely inform Mrs. Jones that you don't know what a SIP school is or does. She may even use the full term (School Improvement Program) the next time she talks with a parent. Progress!

Bibliography

The
Preschool
Years

AGRAN, PHYLLIS. "Motor Vehicle Occupant Injuries." *Pediatrics*, November 1981, 67-78.

AMES, LOUISE BATES. *Child Behavior*. Gesell Institute. New York: Harper & Row, 1955.

———*Don't Push Your Preschooler*. New York: Harper & Row, 1980.

BASS, CAROL. Child Care Center, University of Southern California, Los Angeles, Calif. Interview, October 1981.

BECK, HELEN. *Don't Push Me, I'm No Computer*. New York: McGraw-Hill Book Co., 1973.

BELL, T.H. *Your Child's Intellect*. Salt Lake City, Utah: Olympus Publishing Co., 1973.

BLOOM, BENJAMIN. *All Our Children Learning*. New York: McGraw-Hill Book Co., 1981

BRIGGS, DOROTHY. *Your Child's Self-Esteem*. Garden City, N.Y.: Doubleday & Co., 1970.

BUTLER, MICHAEL. Farm School, University of California at Irvine, Irvine, Calif. Interview, October 1981.

CHESS, STELLA, and WHITBRED, JAN. *How to Help Your Child Get the Most Out of School*. Garden City, N.Y.: Doubleday & Co., 1974.

COLLIER, LIZETTE. Kindergarten Teacher, Placentia, Calif. Interview, November 1981.

CORVALLIS EDUCATION ASSOCIATION. *Enjoy and Teach Your Preschooler*. Corvallis, Ore., 1974.

COSTELLO, JOAN. *A Parent's Guide to Nursery Schools*. New York: Random House, 1971.

———"The 'Bad Apple' Teacher." *Parents*, March 1981, 106.

DAVIES, DON. *Citizen Participation in Education*. New Haven, Conn.: Yale University Press, 1973.

DELMAN, JUDITH. American Montessori Society, New York. Interview, September 1981.

DODSON, FITZHUGH. *How to Parent*. New York: Signet Books, 1970.

FINE, BENJAMIN. *Modern Family Guide to Education*. Garden City, N.Y.: Doubleday & Co., 1962.

GAINER, WILLIAM. *Santa Clara Inventory of Developmental Tasks*. Santa Clara, Calif.: Santa Clara Unified School District, 1974.

GELATINER, BARBARA. "All Day Kindergarten." *Working Mother*, September 1981, 162-166.

GALINDO, BERNICE. Child Care Licensing, County of Orange, Santa Ana, Calif. Interview, November 1981.

GIBBS, BETSY. Child Care Center, University of California, Los Angeles, Calif. Interview, September 1981.

GRANT, W. VANCE. National Center for Educational Statistics, Arlington, Va. Interview, October 1981.

GRASSBAUGH, STEVE. Roston-Montessori Schools, Orange, Calif. Interview, November 1981.

HEFFERMAN, HELEN. *Elementary Teachers' Guide to Working with Parents*. West Nyack, N.Y.: Parker Publishing Co., 1969.

HOOVER, ALMA. Past President, California Council for Participation Nursery Schools. Buena Park, Calif. Interview, September 1981.

HUDSON, NANCY NOBLE. Saddleback College, Irvine, Calif. Interview, November 1981.

ISAACS, SUSAN. *Intellectual Growth in Young Children*. New York: Schocken Books, 1971.

KATZ, LILIAN G. "Tips on Selecting a Preschool." *Parents*, March 1981, 102.

KING, DOROTHY. Verano Preschool, University of California at Irvine, Irvine, Calif. Interview, October 1981.

KINSEY, HELEN. Placentia Unified School District. Plancentia, Calif. Interview, June 1981.

LEATHERMAN, ANN. Department of Human Resources (Child Care Licensing). Austin, Tex. Interview, September 1981.

LILLARD, PAULA POLK. *Montessori: A Modern Approach*. New York: Schocken Books, 1973.

MACHADO, JEANNE. *Early Childhood Experiences in Language Arts*. Albany, N.Y.: Delmar Publishers, 1975.

MACK, JEANNE. *Early Childhood Development and Education*. Albany, N.Y.: Delmar Publishers, 1975.

McDARGH, EILEEN. "How to Help Your Child Succeed in School." *Dawn*, August 1981, 9-12.

McDIARMID, NORMA. *Loving and Learning*. New York: Harcourt Brace Jovanovich, 1975.

McDONAHAY, MARY JO. "Day-Care Headache Is a Nightmare." *Los Angeles Times*, December 2, 1981.

McGRATH, NANCY. "Should You Teach Your Baby to Read?" *Parents*, October 1980, 66.

McLINTOCK, JACK. "The Edith Project." *Harpers*, March 1977, 21.

MUSSEN, PAUL; CONGER, JOHN; and KAGEN, JEROME. *Child Development and Personality*. New York: Harper & Row, 1974.

NEISSER, EDITH. *Primer for Parents of Preschoolers*. New York: Parents Magazine Press, 1972.

ORANGE COUNTY HEAD START. *General Information and Directory*. Santa Ana, Calif.: Orange County Head Start, 1980.

PASCOE, JOHN. "The Association Between Mothers' Social Support and Provision of Stimulation to Their Children." *Developmental and Behavioral Pediatrics*, March 1981, 15-19.

PETERSON, RENITA. Head Start, Orange County, Santa Ana, Calif. Interview, May 1981.

PINES, MAYA. *Revolution in Learning*. New York: Harper & Row, 1966.

PITCHER, EVELYN GOODENOUGH. *The Guidance Nursery School.* New York: Harper & Row, 1964.

RADLER, DAN. *Success Through Play.* New York, Harper & Row, 1960.

ROBERTS, MARY. The Children's Foundation, Washington, D.C. Interview, June 1981.

SCHWEBEL, MILTON, and RAPH, JANE. *Piaget in the Classroom.* New York: Basic Books, 1973.

SPOCK, BENJAMIN. *Baby and Child Care.* New York: Pocket Books, 1977.

TINKER, MILES. *Preparing Your Child for Reading.* New York: Holt, Rinehart & Winston, 1971.

TOLAND, CONNALLY. "Clues for Choosing the Best Day-Care Center." *Christian Science Monitor.* December 8, 1980.

WARREN, BILL. Former Head of Day Care Licensing, State of Massachusetts. Washington, D.C. Interview, June 1981.

WESTMINSTER SCHOOL DISTRICT. *Your Child's Potential to Learn.* Greenfield, Ma.: Channing Bete Co., 1980.

———*Your Child Entering School.* Greenfield, Ma.: Channing Bete Co., 1980.

WILE, ELIZABETH. *What to Teach Your Child.* Elizabethtown, Pa.: Continental Press, 1978.

ZACCARIA, MICHAEL. Alliance for Children, U.S.A. San Antonio, Tex. Interview, 1981.

ZEIGLER, RAYMOND. *Better Late Than Early.* New York: R.D. Associates, 1975.

The Reading Chapter

AUSTIN, MARY C.; BUCH, CLIFFORD L.; and HUEBNER, MILDRED H. *Reading Evaluation: Appraisal Techniques for School and Classroom.* New York: The Ronald Press Co., 1961.

BARBE, WALTER B., and ABBOTT, JERRY L. *Personalized Reading Instruction: New Techniques That Increase Reading Skill and Comprehension.* West Nyack, N.Y.: Parker Publishing Co., 1975.

CHALL, JEANNE S. *Learning to Read: The Great Debate.* New York: McGraw-Hill Book Co., 1967.

———"Reading 1967-1977: A Decade of Change and Promise." *Phi Delta Kappa Education Foundation.* Bloomington, Ind., 1977.

THE CHILDREN'S BOOK COUNCIL. "Children's Choices for 1981." Reprinted from *The Reading Teacher,* October 1981.

COHEN, DOROTHY H. *The Learning Child.* New York: Vintage Books, 1973.

COOPERMAN, PAUL. *The Literacy Hoax.* New York: William Morrow & Co., 1978.

CORVALLIS EDUCATION ASSOCIATION and CORVALLIS SCHOOL DISTRICT. *Enjoy and Teach Your Preschooler.* Corvallis, Ore.

CRAMER, J. WARD. *The Reading Teacher's Handbook.* Portland, Ma.: Weston Walch Publisher, 1970.

DALE, EDGAR, and CHALL, JEANNE. "A Formula for Predicting Readabililty." *Educational Research Bulletin,* 27 (January 21, 1948): 11-20.

DECHANT, EMERALD. *Reading Improvement in the Secondary School.* Englewood Cliffs, N.J.: Prentice-Hall, 1973.

———*Children's Books—A Bibliography with Grade Level Readability.* San Diego, Calif.: Department of Education, San Diego County, 1980.

———*High Interest Low Vocabulary Books—A Bibliography.* San Diego, Calif.: Department of Education, San Diego County, 1980.

DURR, WILLIAM K. *Reading Instruction, Dimensions and Issues.* Boston: Houghton Mifflin Co., 1967.

EKWALL, ELDON E. *Diagnosis and Remediation of the Disabled Reader.* Boston: Allyn & Bacon, 1976.

FADAR, DANIEL. *The New Hooked on Books.* New York: Berkeley Publishing Co., 1976.

FRY, EDWARD. "Fry's Readability Graph: Clarification Validity and Extension to Level Seventeen." *Journal of Reading,* Vol 21 (1977): 242-252.

HARRIS, ALBERT JOSIAH, and SIPAY, EDWARD R. *How to Increase Reading Ability: A Guide to Developmental and Remedial Methods.* 6th ed., rev. and enlarged. New York: D. McKay Co., 1975, 658–675 (The Harris-Jacobson Readability Formulas).

HARRIS, THEODORE L. "Reading." *Encyclopedia of Educational Research.* New York: Macmillan, 1969.

HARRIS, A.J., and JACOBSON, M.D. "Comparison of Fry, Spache and Harris-Jacobson Formulas." *Reading Teacher* 33 (May 1980): 920-926.

JACOB, GALE SYPHER. *Independent Reading, Grades One Through Three: An Annotated Bibliography with Reading Levels.* Williamsport, Penn.: Bro-Dart Publishing Co., 1975.

JENSEN, M.A. "Helping Young Children Learn to Read: What Research Says to Teachers." *Young Child,* 36 (November 1980): 61-71.

LARRICK, NANCY. *A Parent's Guide to Children's Reading.* Garden City, N.Y.: Doubleday & Co., 1975.

LOVE, HAROLD D. *Parents Diagnose and Correct Reading Problems.* Springfield, Ill.: Charles C. Thomas, 1970.

MILLER, WILMA H. *The First R: Elementary Reading Today.* New York: Holt, Rinehart & Winston, 1972.

———*Reading Diagnosis Kit.* New York: Center for Applied Research in Education, 1974.

NATIONAL ASSESSMENT OF EDUCATIONAL PROGRESS. "Elementary Reading Skills Improve." *N.A.E.P. Newsletter,* 14 (Spring 1981): 1-4.

———Three National Assessments of Reading: Changes in Performance, 1970-1980. Denver, Colo.: The National Institute of Education, 1981.

OWEN. R. "50 Questions Parents Ask About Reading." *Instructor*, 90 (February 1981): 66-68.

PERCY, BERNARD. *Help Your Child in School.* Englewood Cliffs, N.J.: Prentice-Hall, 1980.

PRYOR, FRANCES. "Poor Reading—Lack of Self-Esteem?" *The Reading Teacher*, 28 (January 1975): 358-359.

ROBINSON, ALAN H., and RAUCH, SIDNEY J. *Corrective Reading in the High School Classroom.* Newark, Del.: International Reading Association, 1966.

SCHIAVONE, JAMES. *Help Your Child to Read Better.* Chicago: Nelson-Hall, 1977.

SCHOLASTIC BOOK SERVICES. *The Complete Paperback Catalog,* Volume II (Fall 1981). N.J.: Scholastic Books.

SMITH, CARL B. *Treating Reading Difficulties.* Washington, D.C.: U.S. Dept. of H.E.W., Office of Education, U.S. Government Printing Office, 1970.

SPACHE, GEORGE D. *Diagnosing and Correcting Reading Disabilities.* Boston: Allyn & Bacon, 1981.

———*Good Reading for Poor Readers.* Champaign, Ill.: Garrard Publishing Co., 1978.

———"A New Readability Formula for Primary-Grade Reading Materials." *Elementary School Journal* 53 (March 1953): 410-413.

———*Toward Better Reading.* Champaign, Ill.: Garrard Publishing Co., 1963.

STRANG, RUTH. *Diagnostic Teaching of Reading.* New York: McGraw-Hill Book Co., 1964.

SUCHER, FLOYD, and ALLRED, RUEL A. *Sucher-Allred Reading Test.* Atlanta: The Economy Co., 1973.

TAYLOR, STANFORD E., et al. *EDL Core Vocabularies.* New York: EDL/McGraw-Hill Book Co., 1979.

UNITED STATES COMMISSION ON CIVIL RIGHTS. *Racial Isolation in the Public Schools.* Washington, D.C., 1967.

WILE, ELIZABETH M. *What to Teach Your Child: A Handbook for Parents of 4-6 Year Olds.* Elizabethtown, Pa.: The Continental Press, 1978.

WISEMAN, DOUGLAS E., and HARTWELL, KAY L. "The Poor Reader in Secondary Schools." *The Education Digest* (October 1980), 56-59.

The Writing Chapter

AHMAN, J. STANLEY. "A Report on National Assessment in Seven Learning Areas." *Today's Education,* January 1975, 14-16.

ARMSTRONG, WILLIAM. Bay Area Writing Project (pamphlet), University of California, Berkeley, 1981.

———*87 Ways to Help Your Child in School.* Woodbury, N.Y.: Barrons Educational Series, 1961.

BEADLE, MURIEL. *A Child's Mind.* Garden City, N.Y.: Doubleday & Co., 1970.

BETTELHEIM, BRUNO. "Why Children Don't Like to Read." *Atlantic Monthly,* November 1981, 25-31.

BETTER, JENNIFER. *How to Identify a Quality Language Arts Program.* Cupertino, Calif.: Cupertino School District, September 1981.

BRADLEY, YETIVE. *Parents: A Part of the Team.* Urbana, Ill.: California Association of Teachers of English, 1979.

BRANDT, ANTHONY. "Why Kids Can't Write." *Family Circle,* January 13, 1981, 18-20.

BURNS, PAUL; BROMAN, BETSY; and LOWE, ALBERTA. *The Language Arts in Childhood Education.* Skokie, Ill.: Rand McNally, 1971.

BURROWS, ALVINE TREUT, et al. *They All Want to Write.* New York: Holt, Rinehart & Winston, 1964.

BYER, FRED. *Language Arts—Writing K-3.* Patterson, Calif.: Stanislaus County Schools, Calif., 1975.

CALIFORNIA STATE DEPARTMENT OF EDUCATION. *6th Draft of Handbook for Planning an Effective Writing Program.* Sacramento, Calif.: State Department of Education, 1981.

CARLSON, RUTH. *Writing Aids Through the Grades.* New York: Teachers College Press, 1970.

COLEMAN, MARY E. "Written Teacher Comments on Student Compositions." *Educational Digest,* September 1980, 40-42.

DAWSON, MILDRED; ZOLINGER, MARIAN; and ELWELL, ARDELL. *Guiding Language Learning.* New York: Harcourt, Brace & World, 1962.

DIAZ, RALPH. *Language Arts, Kindergarten and First Grade.* Bartow, Fla.: Polk County Public Schools, 1980.

DRUM, KEVIN. "Tough Writing Requirements Could Backfire." *Los Angeles Times,* March 9, 1981.

EMIG, JANET. *The Composing Processes of Twelfth Graders.* Urbana, Ill.: National Council of Teachers of English, 1971.

ENDSLEY, PAT TANABE. *Project Write.* Berkeley, Calif.: Tanabe-Endsley, 1981.

FADIMAN, CLIFTON, and HOWARD, JAMES. *Empty Pages.* Fearon Pitman Publishers, 1979.

GALLO, DONALD, ed. *Teaching Writing: Advice from the Professionals.* Hartford, Conn.: Connecticut Council of Teachers of English, 1977.

Language Arts Learning Continuum. Santa Clara, Calif.: Santa Clara Unified School District, June 1978.

Language Arts Mastery at Specified Grade Levels. Santa Clara, Calif.: Santa Clara Unified School District, June 1978.

Language Arts 7th and 8th Grade Priority List. Santa Clara, Calif.: Santa Clara Unified School District, May 1978.

MILNER, JOSEPH. "English in the Eighties: A Global Projection." *Phi Delta Kappan,* February 1981.

MOFFETT, JAMES. *Student Centered Language Arts and Reading.* Boston: Houghton Mifflin, 1978.

MULLIS, INA. *Highlights and Trends from National Assessment: Writing and Change in Writing Skills.* Denver, Colo.: NAEP, 1976.

OLIVER, KENNETH. *A Sound Curriculum in English Grammar: Guidelines for Teachers and Parents.* Washington, D.C.: Council for Basic Education, 1977.

PROVOST, GARY. *Make Every Word Count.* Cincinnati, O.: Writers Digest Books, 1980.

RIEMER, GEORGE. *How They Murdered the Second R.* New York: W.W. Norton & Co., 1969.

ROBINSON, H. ALLEN. *Reading and Writing Instruction in the United States: Historical Trends.* Newark, Del.: International Reading Association, 1977.

RODERICK, KEVIN. "U.S. Students Make Some Gains in Writing Skills, Study Finds." *Los Angeles Times,* January 16, 1981.

SEALEY, NANCY, and SEALEY, LEONARD. *Children's Writing.* Newark, Del.: International Reading Association, 1979.

———"Schools Must Break Down the Black English Barrier." *Phi Delta Kappan,* October 1979, 425.

SCRIVIN, MICHAEL. *Evaluation of the Bay Area Writing Project.* San Francisco: University of San Francisco, 1980.

SHAUGHNESSY, MINA. *Errors and Expectations.* New York: Oxford University Press, 1977.

SHERWIN, STEPHEN. *Four Problems in Teaching English.* Urbana, Ill.: National Council of Teachers of English, 1969.

SMITH, JAMES. *Creative Teaching of the Language Arts in Elementary Schools.* Boston: Allyn & Bacon, 1973.

SQUIRE, JAMES. *A Study of English Programs in Selected High Schools Which Consistently Educate Outstanding Students in English.* Urbana, Ill.: University of Illinois Press, 1966.

STEWIG, JOHN. *Read to Write.* New York: Hawthorn Books, 1975.

STONE, GEORGE. *Issues, Problems, and Approaches in the Teaching of English.* New York: Holt, Rinehart & Winston, 1961.

STRICKLAND, RUTH. *The Language Arts in the Elementary School.* Lexington, Mass.: D.C. Heath & Co., 1957.

Students Can Write. Santa Clara, Calif.: Santa Clara County Commission on Writing, Santa Clara County Schools, 1977.

TIBBETTS, ARN, and TIBBETTS, CHARLENE. *What's Happening to American English?* New York: Charles Scribner's Sons, 1978.

VAN ALLEN, R. *Beginning Writing Experiences.* La Habra, Calif.: La Habra City Schools, 1962.

VENABLE, T.C. "Declining SAT Scores." *Phi Delta Kappan,* February 1981.

WARRINER, JOHN E. *English Grammar and Composition.* New York: Harcourt, Brace & World, 1957.

WHITBREAD, J., and CHESS, S. *How to Help Your Child Get the Most Out of School.* Garden City, N.Y.: Doubleday & Co., 1974.

———"Why Johnny Can't Write." *Newsweek,* December 8, 1975, 59.

WIENER, HARVEY. *Any Child Can Write.* New York: McGraw-Hill Book Co., 1978.

WILSON, SLOAN. "Why Jessie Hates English." *Saturday Review,* September 18, 1976, 11-13.

———*Writing Achievement 1969-79: Results from the Third National Writing Assessment.* Denver, Colo.: NAEP, 1979.

———*Written Communication in the Elementary Schools.* Arundel Village, Md.: Arundel County Schools, 1963.

ZINSSER, WILLIAM. *On Writing Well.* New York: Harper & Row, 1976.

The Math Chapter

ADDISON-WESLEY MATH SERIES. *Mathematics in Our World.* Menlo Park, Calif.: Addison-Wesley Publishing Co., 1981.

BARATTA-LORTON, MARY. *Mathematics Their Way.* Menlo Park, Calif.: Addison-Wesley Publishing Co., 1976.

BEHRMANN, POLLY, and MILLMAN, JOAN. *How Many Spoons Make a Family: A Book of Primary Math Experiences for Children.* San Rafael, Calif.: Academic Therapy Publications, 1971.

BRUECKNER, LEO J.; GROSSNICKLE, FOSTER E.; and RECKSEH, JOHN. *Developing Mathematical Understanding in the Upper Grades.* Philadelphia: The John Winston Co., 1957.

CARPENTER, THOMAS P. et al. "Calculators in Testing Situations: Results and Implications from National Assessment." *Arithmetic Teacher,* Vol 28, Number 5 (1981): 34-37.

———"Decimals: Results and Implications from National Assessment." *Arithmetic Teacher,* Vol 28, Number 8 (1981): 34-37.

———"Solving Verbal Problemns: Results and Implications from National Assessment." *Arithmetic Teacher*, Vol 28, Number 1 (1980): 8-13.

———"Students' Affective Response to Mathematics: Results and Implications from National Assessment." *Arithmetic Teacher*, Vol 28, Number 2 (1980): 34-37.

COLLIER, HERBERT L. *How to Help Your Child Get Better Grades.* New York: Pinnacle Books, 1981.

EARP, WESLEY N., and TANNER, FRED W. "Mathematics and Language." *Arithmetic Teacher*, Vol 28, Number 4 (1980): 32-35.

FOX, LYNN. "Mathematically Able Girls: A Special Challenge." *Arithmetic Teacher*, Vol 28, Number 6 (1981): 22-23.

GINSBERG, HERBERT, and OPPER, SYLVIA. *Piaget's Theory of Intellectual Development.* Englewood Cliffs, N.J.: Prentice-Hall, 1979.

HARCOURT BRACE JOVANOVICH MATH SERIES. *HBJ Mathematics Program.* New York: Harcourt Brace Jovanovich, 1981.

HEATH MATH SERIES. *Heath Mathematics Program.* Lexington, Mass.: D.C. Heath & Co., 1981.

HOLT MATH SERIES. *Holt Mathematics.* New York: Holt, Rinehart & Winston, 1981.

HOUGHTON MIFFLIN MATH SERIES. *Mathematics for Individual Achievement.* Boston: Houghton Mifflin Co., 1977.

LEAKE, LOWELL. "Some Reflections on Teaching Mathematics for Elementary School Teachers." *Arithmetic Teacher*, Vol 28, Number 3 (1980): 42-44.

MACMILLAN MATH SERIES. *Macmillan Mathematics.* New York: Macmillan, 1982.

McGRAW-HILL MATH SERIES. *McGraw-Hill Mathematics.* New York: Webster Division, McGraw-Hill Book Co., 1981.

McKILLIP, WILLIAM D. "Computational Skill in Division: Results and Implications from National Assessment." *Arithmetic Teacher*, Vol 28, Number 7 (1981): 34-37.

MORRIS, JANET. "Math Anxiety: Teaching to Avoid It." *The Mathematics Teacher*, Vol 74, Number 6 (1981): 413-417.

NATIONAL COUNCIL OF TEACHERS OF MATHEMATICS. *An Agenda for Action: Recommendations for School Mathematics for the 1980's.* Reston, Va.: National Council of Teachers of Mathematics, 1980.

———*Mathematics Learning in Early Childhood.* Reston, Va.: National Council of Teachers of Mathematics, 1975.

OVERMAN, ROBERT JAMES. *The Teaching of Arithmetic.* Chicago: Lyons & Carnahan, 1961.

POST, THOMAS R. "Fractions: Results and Implications from National Assessment." *Arithmetic Teacher*, Vol 28, Number 9 (1981): 26-30.

RATHMELL, EDWARD C. "Concepts of Fundamental Operations: Results and Implications from National Assessment." *Arithmetic Teacher*, Vol 28, Number 3 (1980): 34-37.

REISMAN, FREDRICKA K. *Teaching Mathematics—Methods and Content.* Boston: Houghton Mifflin Co., 1981.

REYS, ROBERT C. "Calculators in the Elementary Classroom: How Can We Go Wrong!" *Arithmetic Teacher*, Vol 28, Number 3 (1980): 34-40.

RUDNITSLY, ALAN N.; DRICKAMER, PRISCILLA; and HANDY, ROBERTA. "Talking Mathematics with Children," *Arithmetic Teacher*, Vol 28, Number 3 (1980): 14-17.

SCOTT FORESMAN MATH SERIES. *Scott Foresman Mathematics.* Glenview, Ill.: Scott, Foresman & Co., 1980.

SILVER BURDETT MATH SERIES. *Mathematics for Mastery.* Palo Alto, Calif.: Silver Burdett Co., 1981.

SWENSON, ESTHER J. *Teaching Arithmetic to Children.* New York: Macmillan, 1968.

WESCOTT, ALVIN M., and SMITH, JAMES A. *Creative Teaching of Mathematics in the Elementary School.* Boston: Allyn & Bacon, 1967.

WHEATLEY, GRAYSON H. "Calculators in the Classroom: A Proposal for Curricular Change." *Arithmetic Teacher*, Vol 28, Number 4 (1980): 37-39.

WILHELM, SHARON, and BROOKS, DOUGLASS M. "The Relationship Between Pupil Attitudes Toward Mathematics and Parental Attitude Toward Mathematics." *Educational Research Quarterly*, Vol 5, Number 2 (1980): 8-16.

WILLOUGHBY, STEPHEN S. *Teaching Mathematics: What Is Basic.* Washington, D.C.: Council for Basic Education, 1981.

Curriculum Guides to Mathematics were obtained from the following school districts:

Ann Arbor, Michigan
Bellevue, Washington
Buffalo, New York
Cypress, California
Des Moines, Iowa
Jackson, Mississippi
Little Rock, Arkansas
Newark, New Jersey
Santa Ana, California
Vernon Public Schools, Rockville, Connecticut
Watertown, Massachusetts

Working Through the Rough Spots

BANDURA, ALBERT. *Principles of Behavior Modification.* New York: Holt, Rinehart & Winston, 1969.

BARKAS, J.L. *The Help Book.* New York: Charles Scribner's Sons, 1979.

BERNE, ERIC. *What Do You Say After You Say Hello?* New York: Grove Press, 1972.

BRANDEN, NATHANIEL. *The Psychology of Self-Esteem.* New York: Bantam Books, Inc., with Nash Publishing, 1971.

CHARKHUFF, R.R. *Helping and Human Relations: A Primer for Lay and Professional Helpers, Vol 1: Selection and Training.* New York: Holt, Rinehart & Winston, 1969.

———*Helping and Human Relations: A Primer for Lay and Professional Helpers, Vol II: Practice and Research.* New York: Holt, Rinehart & Winston, 1969.

COHEN, SIDNEY. *The Drug Dilemma.* New York: McGraw-Hill Book Co., 1969.

DRIEKURS, RUDOLF. *Psychology in the Classroom.* New York: Harper & Row, 1957.

ERICKSON, ERIK H. *Youth: Change and Challenge.* New York: Basic Books, 1963.

FAWCETT, JAN. *Before It's Too Late: What to Do When Someone You Know Attempts Suicide.* American Association of Suicidology; Health Information Services. Merck, Sharp & Dohme, 1976.

GLASSER, WILLIAM. *Schools without Failure.* New York: Harper & Row, 1969.

HARRIS, THOMAS A., M.D. *I'm OK—You're OK.* New York: Harper & Row, 1967.

JOURARD, SIDNEY. *The Transparent Self.* New York: D. Van Nostrand Co., 1964.

LEONARD, GEORGE B. *Education and Ecstasy.* New York: Delta Books, 1968.

LERNER, JANET W. *Children with Learning Disabilities.* Houghton Mifflin Co., 1971.

LeSHAN, EDA J. *The Conspiracy Against Childhood.* New York: Atheneum Publishers, 1974.

MASLOW, ABRAHAM. *Toward a Psychology of Being.* New York: D. Van Nostrand Co., 1962.

MITCHELL, ANITA, and JOHNSON, C.D. *Therapeutic Techniques: Working Models for the Helping Professional.* Sacramento, Calif.: California Personnel & Guidance Association, 1973.

NEILL, A.S. *Summerhill: A Radical Approach to Child Rearing.* New York: Simon & Schuster, 1977.

POWELL, JOHN. *Why Am I Afraid to Tell You Who I Am?* Chicago: Argus Communications, 1967.

ROGERS, CARL. *Freedom to Learn.* Columbus, Ohio: Charles E. Merrill Publishing Co., 1969.

———*On Becoming a Person.* Boston: Houghton Mifflin Co., 1961.

ROOSEVELT, RUTH, and LOFAS, JEANETTE. *Living in Step.* New York: McGraw-Hill Book Co., 1977.

SILBERMAN, C.E. *Crisis in the Classroom.* New York: Random House, 1970.

SHEEHY, GAIL. *Passages.* New York: E.P. Dutton, 1976.

SCHIMMEL, DAVID, and FISCHER, LOUIS. *The Rights of Parents in the Education of Their Children.* Columbia, Md.: The National Committee for Citizens in Education, 1977.

WINN, MARIE. *The Plug in Drug.* New York: The Viking Press, 1974.

"What's This I Hear About . . . ?"

ASSOCIATION FOR CHILDREN WITH LEARNING DISABILITIES, Pittsburgh, Pa.

BARAN, ALAN. "Tuition Tax Credit Plan." *Los Angeles Times*, May 3, 1981.

BROWNSTEIN, SAMUEL C., and WEINER, MITCHEL. *Barron's How to Prepare for College Entrance Examinations—SAT.* New York: Barron's Educational Series, Inc., 1980.

BATHGATE, DONALD G. "U.C. Scoreboard Needs a New Fuse." *Los Angeles Times*, September 28, 1981.

BEYER, KEN. "School Power." Laguna Beach Education Foundation, Laguna Beach, Calif. Interview, October 1981.

BEYETTE, BEVERLY. "The Unschooling of Our Children." *Los Angeles Times*, September 23, 1981.

BOSWORTH, JANE A. "What Every Parent Should Know . . . The Other Side of the Desk." *Dawn*, August 1981, 16-18, 61-64.

BRANDT, RONALD S. *Partners: Parents and Schools.* Association for Supervision and Curriculum Development. Alexandria, Va.

"The Bright Flight." *Newsweek*, April 20, 1981, 66-73.

BROWN, DALE. "Steps to Independence for People with Learning Disabilities." *Closer Look*, Washington, D.C.

BRUTTEN, MILTON; MANGEL, CHARLES; and RICHARDSON, SYLVIA O. *Something's Wrong with My Child.* New York: Harcourt Brace Jovanovich, 1973.

BARUM, BELINDA BUSTEED. "Extracurricular, Low-Budget, Parent-Powered." *Christian Science Monitor*, September 8, 1981.

BRYANT, ALICE. Los Angeles Unified School District. Interview, September 1981.

BUSKIN, MARTIN. *Parent Power—A Candid Hand-*

book for Dealing with Your Child's School. New York: Walker & Co., 1975.

CALIFORNIA STATE DEPARTMENT OF EDUCATION. "A Handbook Regarding the Privacy and Disclosure of Pupil Records." Sacramento, Calif.

———"California High School Proficiency Examination." Sacramento, Calif., 1979.

———"California Master Plan for Special Education." Sacramento, Calif.

———"Parents Can Be Partners." Sacramento, Calif.

———"School-Community Participation in Determining School Effectiveness." Sacramento, Calif.

———"Student Rights and Responsibilities Handbook." Sacramento, Calif.

"Can Public Learn from Private?" Time, April 20, 1981, 50.

"A Chat with Harold Lyon." G/C/T, September-October, 1980, 3-9.

COOMBS, JERROLD R. "Can Minimum Competency Be Justified?" Education Digest, April 1979, 2-5.

COUNCIL FOR BASIC EDUCATION. "Where Can I Go for Help?" Washington, D.C.

———"Alternative Fundamental Schools." Washington, D.C., July 1979.

COUNCIL FOR EXCEPTIONAL CHILDREN. "Your Gifted Child and You." Reston, Va.

CRISCUOLO, NICHOLAS P. "Only Two Parents Showed Up." Teacher, September 1978, 94-95.

CTB/McGRAW HILL "Parents Guide to Understanding Tests." Monterey, Calif.: CTB/McGraw-Hill, 1976.

D.C. CITIZENS FOR BETTER PUBLIC EDUCATION. "A Handbook on Standardized School Testing." Washington, D.C.

DAVIS, THOMAS. Principal, Alhambra High School, Martinez, Calif. Interview, October 1981.

DeGROOT, JANE, ed. Education for All People: A Grassroots Primer. Boston, Mass.: Institute for Responsive Education, 1979.

"Directory of Facilities and Services for Learning Disabled, Ninth Edition." Academic Therapy Publications. Navato, California, 1981-1982.

EARLY, TRACY. "Wanted: Money, Power, Status, and a Degree." Christian Science Monitor, August 17, 1981.

EDUCATION SECTION, Christian Science Monitor, October 26, 1981, B1-B12.

EDUCATIONAL RESEARCH SERVICE. "Evaluations of Year Round School Programs." Arlington, Va.

EXCEPTIONAL CHILDREN MAGAZINE, Vol 48 Number 2, October 1981.

FALLOWS, JAMES. "The Tests and the 'Brightest': How Fair Are the College Boards?" Atlantic Monthly, February 1980, 37-48.

FERNANDEZ, HAPPY. Parent Union of Philadelphia Public Schools. Philadelphia, Pennsylvania. Interview, October 1981.

FEINBERG, LAWRENCE. "Number of High Scores on College Board Exams Drops Dramatically." Washington Post, March 2, 1981.

FISHER, LOUIS, and SCHIMMEL, DAVID. The Rights of Parents in the Education of Their Children. Columbia, Md.: The National Committee for Citizens in Education, 1977.

FORTUNE, THOMAS, "Test Blocking 500 Seniors," Los Angeles Times, May 25, 1981.

FREEDMAN, GABRIEL P., et. al., ed. Scholastic Aptitude Test. New York: ARCO Publishing, Inc., 1980.

GALLAGHER, JAMES, and WEISS, PATRICIA. "The Education of Gifted and Talented Students: A History and Prospectus." Council for Basic Education, Washington, D.C.

"Getting Testy." Time, November 26, 1979, 110.

Gifted Children Newsletter. Boulder, Colorado, October 1981.

GINSBERG, GINA, and HARRISON, CHARLES H. How to Help Your Gifted Child—A Handbook for Parents and Teachers. New York: Simon and Schuster, 1977.

GRANT, W. VANCE. Digest of Education Statistics. Washington, D.C.: U.S. Gov't. Printing Office, 1980.

GRAY, DENNIS. "Guidelines on Minimum Competency Testing." Education Digest, October 1980, 2-6.

———"Minimum Competency Testing: Guidelines for Policymakers and Citizens." Council for Basic Education, Washington, D.C.

HARRIS, JAMES. "Parents Inc." Teacher, September 1978, 85-87.

HENDERSON, ANNE. "P.L. 94-142: How Does Your State Measure Up and What You Can Do About It." Network National Committee for Citizens in Education, Columbia, Md.

HOWARD, JAMES. "About Alternative Schools." Columbia, Md.: Council for Basic Education Bulletin, Vol 23, Number 10, June 1979.

———"About Fundamental Schools." Columbia, Md.: Council for Basic Education Bulletin, Vol. 23, Number 10, June 1979.

———"Fundamental School Roundup." Columbia, Md.: Council for Basic Education Bulletin, Vol 25, Number 9, May 1981.

HOLT, JOHN. Teach Your Own. New York: Delacorte Press/Seymour Lawrence, 1981.

HOWLETT, PAT. Public Information Director, Association of California School Administrators, San Francisco, Calif. Interview, October 1981.

JONES, PHILLIP, and JONES, SUSAN. Parents Unite. Ridgefield, Conn.: Wynden Books, 1976.

KADONAGA, CYNTHIA. "Proficiency Testing: Can 38,000 Seniors Be Wrong?" Los Angeles Times, May 6, 1981.

KAERCHER, DAN. "A Report to Parents on Minimum Competency Tests." Better Homes and Gardens, May 1980, 27-28, 32, 37.

KARMEL, LOUIS J. "Testing in Our Schools—A

Macmillan Guidebook for Parents." New York: Macmillan Publishing, 1966.

KIMMEL, CAROL. "Parent Power: A Plus for Education." *Educational Leadership*, October 1976, 24–25.

KLEIN, STANLEY D. "Psychological Testing of Children—A Consumer's Guide." Boston, Mass.: The Exceptional Parent Press, 1977.

"Legal Implications of Minimal Competency Testing." *Phi Delta Kappan* Fastback #138. Bloomington, Ind.: Phi Delta Kappa Education Foundation, 1981.

LESSINGER, LEON. *Every Kid a Winner— Accountability in Education.* New York: Simon & Schuster, 1970.

LILLIE, DAVID. *Teaching Parents to Teach.* New York: Walker & Co., 1976.

LOCKWOOD, LAUMA. "Telling It Like It Is—Practical Guidance for Parents in Getting Through School the Second Time Around." Grand Rapids, Mich.: Citizens for Responsive Education.

LYON, HAROLD C., JR. "Our Most Neglected Natural Resource." *Today's Education,* February–March 1981, 15GE–20GE.

———"The Federal Perspective on G & T." *Journal for the Education of the Gifted,* Vol IV, No. 1.

MALONE, JULIA. "Drive Begins for Tuition Tax Credit." *Christian Science Monitor,* June 8, 1981.

MARTINSON, RUTH A. "The Identification of the Gifted and Talented." National State Leadership Training Institute on the Gifted and Talented, Los Angeles, Calif.

MASTERS, CHARLOTTE. "School Volunteers: Who Needs Them?" *Phi Delta Kappan* Fastback #55, Phi Delta Kappa Foundation, Bloomington, Ind., 1981.

McDERMOTT, EDWIN, J. "Family Choice in Education." *America,* November 1979, 250–253.

MITGANG, LEE. "College Program Gives Gifted Youngsters a Challenge." *Los Angeles Times,* August 26, 1981.

MORGAN, STANLEY R. "Shared Governance in the Salt Lake City Schools." Salt Lake City School District, Salt Lake City, Utah, 1981.

MOUAT, LUCIA. "Reagan and Tax Credits— Changes Ahead for Schools." *Christian Science Monitor,* December 29, 1980.

NARIN, ALLAN. "The Reign of ETS." *Today's Education,* April–May 1980, 58–64.

NATIONAL ASSOCIATION FOR GIFTED CHILDREN, St. Paul, Minn.

NATIONAL ASSOCIATION OF SECONDARY SCHOOL PRINCIPALS BULLETIN, Reston, Va., January 1980.

NATIONAL CENTER FOR EDUCATIONAL STATISTICS. W. Vance Grant, Director, Washington, D.C.

NATIONAL CLEARINGHOUSE FOR BILINGUAL EDUCATION. *Forum,* Rosslyn, Va., September 1981.

———"Helping to Educate the Children of a Multilingual Nation." Rosslyn, Va., 1981.

———"Parent & Community Involvement in Bilingual Education." Rosslyn, Va., 1981.

———"What Is Bilingual Education?" Rosslyn, Va., 1981.

NATIONAL COMMITTEE FOR CITIZENS IN EDUCATION. Columbia, Md. "Tuition Tax Credits Surface in the House." *Network,* March 1981.

———"Parents Organizing to Improve Schools." Columbia, Md., 1980.

———"Parents' Rights Card." Columbia, Md., 1980.

NATIONAL INSTITUTE OF EDUCATION. "Your Child and Testing." Washington, D.C., 1980.

NATIONAL SCHOOL PUBLIC RELATIONS ASSOCIATION. "Alternative Schools: Why, What, Where and How Much." Arlington, Va.

———"A Parent's Guide to Public Education for the Handicapped." Arlington, Va.

———"A Parent's Guide to Standardized Aptitude and Achievement Testing." Arlington, Va, 1978.

NATIONAL SCHOOL VOLUNTEER PROGRAM, Alexandria, Va.

NATIONAL/STATE LEADERSHIP TRAINING PROGRAM FOR THE GIFTED AND TALENTED, Los Angeles, Calif.

NEW HAMPSHIRE STATE DEPARTMENT OF EDUCATION. "New Hampshire Voucher Experiment." Concord, N.H., October 1976.

NEW MEXICO STATE DEPARTMENT OF EDUCATION. "New Mexico High School Proficiency Exam." Albuquerque, N.M.

NEW ORLEANS PUBLIC SCHOOLS, Division of Instruction and Child Advocacy. "Elementary Program." New Orleans, La.

OFFICE OF GIFTED & TALENTED, U.S. Office of Education, Washington, D.C.

OSMON, BETTY B. *Learning Disabilities: A Family Affair.* New York: Warner Books, 1979.

PARSONS, CYNTHIA. "52 Ways to Improve Schools." *Christian Science Monitor,* weekly articles, January–December 1981.

———"More, Not Less, Public Support for Public Schools." *Christian Science Monitor,* December 29, 1980.

PASADENA UNIFIED SCHOOL DISTRICT. "Fundamental School Program." Pasadena, California.

PIERCE, KENNETH M. "Trying the Old Fashioned Way." *Time,* March 9, 1981, 65.

PIPHO, CHRIS. Associate Director, Department of Research and Information, Education Commission of the States. Denver, Colorado. Interview, November 1981.

POSTMAN, NEIL, and WEINGARTNER, CHARLES. *The School Book.* New York: Delacorte Press, 1973.

RAMIREZ, BEN. Assistant Principal, John Marshal Jr./Sr. High School, Pasadena, California. Interview, September 1981.

"A Really Final Exam." *Newsweek*, May 28, 1979, 97.

REILLY, WAYNE. "No Problem Appears to Be Too Severe for This School." *Christian Science Monitor*, October 4, 1980.

REMSBERG, BONNIE. "I Wisk I Culd Read An Writ." *Family Circle*, September 22, 1981, 52, 54, 61-62, 142.

RENZULLI, JOSEPH. *A Re-examination of the Definition of the Gifted and Talented*. Ventura, Calif.: Ventura County Superintendent of Schools Office, 1979.

RIEGEL, RODNEY. "Minimum Competency Testing." *Phi Delta Kappan* Fastback #137. Bloomington, Ind.: Phi Delta Kappa Education Foundation, 1981.

RIOUX, WILLIAM. *You Can Improve Your Child's School*. New York: Simon & Schuster, 1980.

ROBERTS, CAROL. Assistant Principal, Greenville Fundamental School, Santa Ana, California. Interview, November 1981.

RODERICK, KEVIN. "More Families Turning to Home School." *Los Angeles Times*, September 28, 1981.

———"Test Stymies 1st Class of Seniors—but Not for Long?" *Los Angeles Times*, June 21, 1981.

ROSENFELD, ANNE. National Association of Independent Schools, Boston, Massachusetts. Interview, August 1981.

ROSE, CAROL. "Why Gifted Children Need Your Help." *Parade*, January 25, 1981, 14-17.

ROSNER, JEROME. *Helping Children to Overcome Learning Difficulties*. New York: Walker & Co., 1975

ROSS, VIRGINIA. National School Public Relations Association. Arlington, Va., Interview, October 1981.

ROWELL, J. CY. "The 5 Rights of Parents." *Phi Delta Kappan*, Bloomington, Ind., February 1981.

RYAN, CHARLOTTE. "The Testing Maze—An Evaluation of Standardized Testing in America." *National PTA*, Chicago, Illinois, 1979.

SALT LAKE CITY SCHOOLS. "The School Community Council." Salt Lake City, Utah,

"S.A.T. Scores: Are Students Improving?" *Christian Science Monitor*, November 9, 1981.

SHEPHERD, EVE. National School Board Association, Washington, D.C. Interview, September 1981.

SINCLAIR, ROBERT, ed. *A Two-Way Street*. Institute for Responsive Education, Boston, Mass., 1980.

SOMERS, STEVE. Director, National Coalition for Parent Involvement in Education, Alexandria, Va. Interview, August 1981.

STAFFORD, LINLEY. National Education Association, Washington, D.C. Interview, August 1981.

STRENIO, ANDREW J., JR. *The Testing Trap*. New York: The Dial Press/James Wade, 1981.

TASK TEAM OF ADVOCATES FOR SPECIAL KIDS, Garden Grove, Calif.

"Tests on Trial in Florida . . . And in New York." *Time*, July 30, 1979, 66-69.

TROMBLEY, WILLIAM. "Bilingual Educators Fear Reagan Ax Will Fall." *Los Angeles Times*, June 30, 1981.

TUCKER, CARL. "English Spoken Here." *Saturday Review*, May 12, 1979, 56.

"Tuition Tax Credits Surface in House." *Network*, March 1981.

UNIVERSITY OF MASSACHUSETTS. National Directory of Public School Alternatives. Amherst, Mass., 1977-1978.

WAGGONER, DOROTHY. Education Program Officer, U.S. Department of Education, Office of Bilingual Education, Washington, D.C. Interview, January 1982.

WALKER, CHARLES W., JR. "What's Happening in New Jersey." *Today's Education*, April–May 1980, 49g.

WEBER, GEORGE. "Uses and Abuses of Standardized Testing in the Schools." Council for Basic Education (Occasional Paper #22), Washington, D.C.

WELLBORN, STANLEY. "Signs of Hope for Our Schools." *U.S. News & World Report*, September 7, 1981, 50-52.

"Why Public Schools Fail." *Newsweek*, April 20, 1981, 62-65.

WILLIAMS, DENNIS A. et al. "Education." *Newsweek*, April 20, 1981, 73.

WISE, ARTHUR. "A Critique of Minimal Competency Testing." Rand Corporation, Washington D.C., September 1977.

"Your Child's School and the Back to Basics Movement." *Better Homes and Gardens*, April 1979, 15-16, 18, 20, 22, 26, 30.

Keep A Healthy Kitchen!

DC SUPER HEROES SUPER HEALTHY COOKBOOK   (L51-227, $8.95)
by Mark Salzman, Judy Garlan and Michelle Grodner
Foreword *by Dr. Joan Gussow*
Everyone's favorite Super Heroes present twenty-eight delightful, original recipes designed to show children that healthy snacks and foods need not be dull or bland but can be colorful, fun, and very tasty. Recipes include: a complete list of foods and utensils needed, step-by-step illustrated instructions, and an action cartoon of the Super Hero sponsoring the recipe.

THE ALLERGY COOKBOOK AND FOOD-BUYING GUIDE   (L37-901, $7.95, U.S.A.)
by Pamela Nonken and S. Roger Hirsch, M.D.   (L37-902, $9.95, Canada)
Anyone with allergies to one or more kinds of food knows how difficult it is to shop for or cook food without hidden allergens. This is a guidebook designed to help end the worry. Featured are: lists of safe foods by category and brand name, identifications of specific allergens, recipes for over three hundred allergen-free dishes, and hints for substituting allergen-free ingredients in conventional recipes.

For Every Parent's Library

ANYONE CAN HAVE A HAPPY CHILD   (J90-795, $2.95)
by Jacob Azerrad, Ph.D.
The author, a clinical psychologist, bases his program for successful parenting on the premise that a happy child is one who has a positive outlook on life, self-esteem and the esteem of others, and has the ability to express warmth and understanding.

COUPLES WITH CHILDREN   (J30-269, $3.50)
by Randy Meyers Wolfson and Virginia DeLuca
The inevitable changes that occur in a husband-wife relationship when there's a new baby in the house deal a great shock to a marriage. This book is the first to address these dramatic, stressful changes and to offer support and advice for the first few months of parenthood. The authors include a detailed bibliography of books of interest to new parents and an excellent extensive list of places to contact for support (clinics, counseling, etc.).

SON-RISE   (J30-645, $3.50)
by Barry Neil Kaufman
The extraordinary journal of two people who defy all professional advice concerning their autistic son—and change him from a lifeless, totally withdrawn child into an affectionate, loving, and highly verbal human being.

THE COSMIC MIND-BOGGLING BOOK

by Neil McAleer

(037-932, $8.95, U.S.A.)
(037-933, $11.50, Canada)

The author brings the wonders of the cosmos down to earth in terms and analogies to which our limited senses can relate.

• Hop in your car to understand the meaning of cosmic distance:

If you could drive to the Sun at 55 miles an hour, it would take 193 years to get there.

• Turn on a light switch to understand the meaning of cosmic energy:

One second of our Sun's total energy equals 13 million times the total energy used in the United States each year.

• Play ball to understand how the Universe has expanded:

When the Universe was less than a trillionth of a second old, its radius was just over 3 feet, the size of a big beach ball you could hold in your arms.

• Take a walk to appreciate the variety of shapes of masses in the Universe:

On the surface of the cigar-shaped asteroid called Eros, lovers walking hand-in-hand would see no horizon, but they might lean over its edges to view the starry sky below.

Take a few hours to read **THE COSMIC MIND-BOGGLING BOOK** and understand and appreciate the facts that boggle your mind.